*Jess and Norma*

# JESS and NORMA

*A lifetime of laughter and our unbreakable bond*

JESSICA ASQUITH AND
NORMA BURTON

EBURY SPOTLIGHT

UK | USA | Canada | Ireland | Australia
India | New Zealand | South Africa

Ebury Spotlight is part of the Penguin Random House group of companies whose addresses can be found at global.penguinrandomhouse.com

Penguin Random House UK
One Embassy Gardens, 8 Viaduct Gardens,
London SW11 7BW

penguin.co.uk
global.penguinrandomhouse.com

Penguin Random House UK

First published by Ebury Spotlight in 2025

1

Copyright © Jessica Asquith and Norma Burton 2025

The moral right of the author has been asserted.

Penguin Random House values and supports copyright. Copyright fuels creativity, encourages diverse voices, promotes freedom of expression and supports a vibrant culture. Thank you for purchasing an authorised edition of this book and for respecting intellectual property laws by not reproducing, scanning or distributing any part of it by any means without permission. You are supporting authors and enabling Penguin Random House to continue to publish books for everyone. No part of this book may be used or reproduced in any manner for the purpose of training artificial intelligence technologies or systems. In accordance with Article 4(3) of the DSM Directive 2019/790, Penguin Random House expressly reserves this work from the text and data mining exception.

Typeset by Francisca Monteiro

Printed and bound in Great Britain by Clays Ltd, Elcograf S.p.A.

The authorised representative in the EEA is
Penguin Random House Ireland, Morrison Chambers,
32 Nassau Street, Dublin D02 YH68.

A CIP catalogue record for this book is available from the British Library

Hardback ISBN 9781529957266

Trade Paperback ISBN 9781529957297

Penguin Random House is committed to a sustainable future for our business, our readers and our planet. This book is made from Forest Stewardship Council® certified paper.

MIX
Paper | Supporting responsible forestry
FSC® C018179

*For our beloved Michael. The kindest, hardest working and most creative, caring and loving husband, Dad and Grandad.*

*You gave us the most beautiful life. We hope we've made you proud x*

# Contents

*Dear friends … — 9*

1. Childhood — 13
*Norma's famous slow cooker chicken casserole — 45*

2. School — 47
*Our favourites — 67*

3. Love — 69
*A word from Jake … — 89*

4. Family and Friends — 95
*Norma's secrets to a long life — 117*

5. Work — 119
*Getting to know you … — 139*

6. Grief — 143
*It's good to talk … — 157*

7. Fame and Social Media — 161
*Going viral — 187*

8. Technology — 191
*Norma's best one-liners — 203*

9. Holidays — 205
*Lingo Bingo — 213*

10. Past Versus Present — 217
*Let's play … Mrs and Miss — 231*

## CONTENTS

11. Fashion and Beauty — 233
*Our favourite days out together* — 249

12. Ageing and Caring — 253
*Just how Norma likes it ...* — 275

13. Life Lessons — 279
*A word from Kate* — 287


A Final Word — 289
Dear Jess, dear Nan ... — 293


Afterword — 299
Acknowledgements — 301

# Dear friends ...

**Jess**  First of all, thank you for being here. This is such a special moment for me and Nan and we can't tell you how excited we are to share it with all of you. Reading books was always a big part of our relationship when I was growing up and if we'd been told back then that we'd eventually be writing one ourselves – together – we wouldn't have believed it.

**Norma**  It's another adventure in this rather peculiar journey we've found ourselves on. The last couple of years have been nothing short of extraordinary. Like a dream.

**Jess**  When we posted our first Jess and Norma video in March 2022, we had no idea that it would become what it has. We get requests for selfies in the street, we've had television appearances, meetings with celebrities and we've grown a community of more than four and a half million friends and followers!

**Norma**  And now, of course, we've been given the opportunity to write this book.

**Jess**  Who would have thought you could become a celeb at this grand old age, eh?

**Norma**  I'll be asking you to fan my face and peel grapes for me soon, Jess.

**Jess**  All right, Your Majesty! It's true that we've got followers from all around the globe and still can't get over the fact that people recognise us wherever we go. Nan says it's like having a huge extended family.

| | |
|---|---|
| Norma | We have to leave the house half an hour earlier to account for the number of times we get stopped when we're out and about. |
| Jess | And we don't move quickly at the best of times, do we? I'm going to have to get you a balaclava, Nan, so people don't recognise you. |
| Norma | Oh no, Jessica, I'll never get bored of stopping for a chat. Everyone has been so lovely. We've met some fantastic people. |
| Jess | Writing this book has been a dream of ours for quite a while now. We know how lucky we are to have each other and we're so proud that the world gets to see how special our bond is. But there's a story behind our relationship that most people don't know and it's one we feel ready to tell. |
| Norma | We've been through an awful lot together – good and bad – haven't we? |
| Jess | We have. But those more personal details have never felt quite right for the internet or social media. In this book we want to open up about the bigger picture – from our childhoods to falling in love; from coping with grief to family ties. And, obviously, social media fame, which has been the plot twist neither of us saw coming. |
| Norma | You're telling me. |
| Jess | As many of you will know, I've been Nan's full-time carer for a while now and we're going to discuss a bit more about that arrangement as well as sharing our different perspectives on life in general. |
| Norma | And I believe we're going to reveal the secret recipe for my famous chicken casserole … |
| Jess | Hold onto your hats for that, everyone. You're going to hear |

## DEAR FRIENDS ...

|  | from both of us throughout the book – we've written every page of it together, so it's more like an extended conversation than anything else. |
|---|---|
| Norma | Which brings us to the other reason we wanted to write it ... |
| Jess | ... To encourage more communication and stronger connections between the generations. Finding that common ground through conversations that go beyond surface-level chit-chat about the weather. |
| Norma | Although admittedly, we do love a natter about that as well! |
| Jess | But we'd also like to inspire people to have more meaningful heart-to-hearts which delve a little deeper and ask thoughtful questions. |
| Norma | We can all learn so much from each other, can't we? Family stories, social history, lived experiences, different points of view ... and finding the time to sit down and talk is so important because life is precious and short. |
| Jess | You can see how we've all lost a bit of that. It used to be quite normal for extended families to live close by and for kids to have their grandparents just around the corner. |
| Norma | Yes, but as the world has opened up and more people have gone off to university, settling in different parts of the country or even further afield, families have become somewhat fragmented. Those connections can be distant. |
| Jess | And, let's face it, people are either rushing about trying to manage a million things at once or they're buried in their phones, which means we've even less time to nurture our relationships. |
| Norma | I think that mobile phone is surgically attached to your hand, Jess. |
| Jess | I'm as guilty of that as anyone. But a good chat can work |

wonders – and so to that end, more than anything, we hope to spur people on to pick up the phone, get in the car or hop on the bus and speak to their older relatives. Don't put it off and leave those questions unanswered and tales untold.

**Norma** One day, sadly, it will be too late. There are questions I wish I'd asked loved ones when they were still alive. Things I'll now never know the answers to.

**Jess** We are so grateful to every single person who has taken the time to watch our videos and send us the kindest messages. We know a lot of you guys find comfort from watching our videos because our relationship reminds you of a loved one. We're always so touched to hear your stories. Hopefully you'll find this book just as heartwarming and we promise to give you plenty of Jess and Norma giggles along the way.

**Norma** Without further ado, I think we ought to get going, Jessica.

**Jess** Are you telling me to shut up?

**Norma** I am, love.

**Jess** OK, boss. Here we go.

*With love,*
*Jess and Norma*
*xxx*

CHAPTER ONE

# Childhood

**Norma**  When I think of my childhood, I remember an open fire in the living room. I think of fish and chip suppers on holidays in Scarborough, my mother's home-baked bread and the scent of her Cuticura talcum powder.

**Jess**  When I think of mine, it's Nan. It's this house – the one everyone will recognise from our videos, with the well-cushioned armchair she sits in, the brown leather sofa and the archway to the dining room. It's her home-made chicken casserole, the Royal Jelly soap in the bathroom and afternoons snuggled up together watching *Tracy Beaker*. Always surrounded by love.

**Norma**  That's what every child deserves, to be loved and to feel loved, isn't it? Don't get me wrong, when I was growing up we did have some difficult times, but I was so very loved and I was happy.

**Jess**  Um, 'difficult times' is a bit of an understatement, Nan. You lived through a world war, for goodness' sake.

**Norma**  Yes, that's true. But we didn't think of it like that; we were all just trying to get on with life as best we could. I'll always be thankful to my parents for everything they gave me and taught me. I needed that security blanket of a happy home because I was quite shy and reserved as a little girl. I tended to hang back and certainly never liked being in the spotlight.

Which is funny to think now, considering everything that's happened in the last few years.

## CHAPTER ONE

**Jess**  You're certainly not shy these days! You and Alfie Boe are practically best mates and I'm surprised you've not been given a leading role on *Corrie* the number of times you've been on that set.

**Norma**  We have friends in high places now, don't we? There's no way young Norma would have had the confidence or pluck for all this. I always felt a bit inadequate as a youngster.

**Jess**  And now you're a TikTok sensation.

**Norma**  So they tell me.

**Jess**  What do you think you'd tell baby Norma, if you could go back in time, to give her a bit of a confidence boost?

**Norma**  Ah, I'd love to tell her that everything would be OK and that it will all work itself out. There was nothing to fear because life would turn out to be a very happy one indeed.

**Jess**  That's so sweet. If only it were possible for us to do that for our younger selves. We'd be able to save ourselves so much heartache and worry.

At first glance, our childhoods are worlds apart, but I've always thought there are some interesting similarities that have given me and Nan a real understanding of each other. For a start, her father passed away when she was just seven years old and I didn't see my own dad as much as I'd have liked. However, the biggest similarity is the enormous love both of us were cocooned in. Me from Nan and Nan from her mum.

**Norma**  My mother and her own wonderful family, whom I still think about often, laid such strong foundations for us all, Jess. That love and grounding has lived on.

Mum was one of ten – she had three brothers and six sisters – and they were all such lovely people. They were very tight

## CHILDHOOD

knit so I had lots of aunties and uncles around me. We were always together. Most of them settled in Headon, the village where they grew up – a couple lived in Upton, which was walking distance – and the whole lot of us would congregate after church on a Sunday. Happy times. The village of Headon wasn't too far away from Retford, a market town in Nottinghamshire that my mum moved to when she married my dad in 1916.

Number 46 Nelson Street. That was our family home, a rented three-bed end terrace I shared with my parents and two older sisters, Joan and Betty. I can still remember the rent man coming up the front path to collect the money every month. Even now, all these years later, I live only a few miles from that house. I've never been one to stray too far from home.

**Jess** Number 46 is still there, standing strong! Me and my partner Jake went to view a house on that same street when we were looking to buy our own place in 2022 – it would have been so strange if we'd ended up there.

**Norma** Ooh, that would have given me goosebumps, Jess. My mum stayed in that house until she died and by then she was the owner – we were so proud when she bought it because she really did love living there.

My mum and dad, Jessie and Tom, were hard up but they always managed to keep our heads above water. I certainly didn't ever feel we were 'poor' because everybody around us was more or less in the same boat. Dad worked for a drapery company. My mum had gone into service, looking after two little girls when she left school at 15, although once she'd had my eldest sister, she didn't go out to work again.

**Jess** There was a big age gap between you and your sisters, wasn't there?

# CHAPTER ONE

**Norma**  That's right. Joan and Betty were 16 and almost nine when I came along. My mother was 38 when she had me, so she was quite a bit older than most of the other mums.

**Jess**  So do you think you were an accident?

**Norma**  I beg your pardon?!

**Jess**  Do you think you were, you know … planned?

**Norma**  Oh, you are brazen, aren't you? To be perfectly honest, I think not. But I was very much wanted, Jessica.

**Jess**  A happy accident, then.

**Norma**  If you want to call it that. I was born just after lunchtime, 6 March 1934, delivered by a lady called Nurse Noble at the Mount Vernon nursing home in the east of Retford. And let me tell you, my mum had to walk herself all the way there while she was in labour with me.

**Jess**  Wow … How far was that from Nelson Street?

**Norma**  Well, I wouldn't like to walk it myself! It was a fair old way and especially for a labouring woman.

**Jess**  I guess women like your mum were made of tough stuff.

**Norma**  She had to be. She knew nothing else. Life was difficult back then, but people had no choice except to soldier on.

**Jess**  It can't have been an easy labour either, given the size of you. Tell our readers how much you weighed.

**Norma**  Jessica, I try to hide these things, as you know.

**Jess**  Go on, Nan …

**Norma**  I was a big baby. Let's leave it at that.

**Jess**  How big?

**Norma**  All nine-and-a-half pounds of me.

## CHILDHOOD

**Jess**  Ever so petite!

**Norma**  Stop your mischief-making.

**Jess**  Shall I change the subject before you clip me round the ear?

**Norma**  I think you'd better.

**Jess**  Those houses on Nelson Street are so sweet, real traditional British terraces.

**Norma**  Yes, they had good bones and people like my mum would take great care of them. There was a large open passageway down the side and we'd walk down there to come in via the kitchen at the back. The front door was only used for special occasions or when the doctor called. Mum was very particular about that.

Upstairs, Joan and Betty shared a bedroom at the front, and I had the little room at the back to myself. You had to walk through my parents' room and down two steps to get to that little bedroom.

**Jess**  A lot of people who live in those houses today have converted what would have been your bedroom into a bathroom. That was the case with the one me and Jake went to view.

**Norma**  When my mum bought the house herself in the sixties, she received a government grant to do just that. Up until then, the toilet had been outside.

**Jess**  If anyone needed the loo in the night, they had to use the potty, right?

**Norma**  You do like the nitty gritty, don't you, Jessica? It wasn't like a child's potty you see today; it was more of a large bowl. But what else were we to do? You couldn't very well go out into the garden in the middle of the night in the freezing cold, you'd catch your death.

# CHAPTER ONE

And I can promise you that my lovely mother was very hygienic about the potty. I'm quite sure we don't need to go into any more detail than that.

**Jess**   I'm just pulling your leg, Nan.

**Norma**   Next to the outdoor toilet we had a wash house, as we used to call it, where my mum had a copper, which was a large metal tank used for heating water. Monday was wash day and she'd get up at six o'clock in the morning to fill the copper up bit by bit with buckets of water carried from the kitchen. Then she'd light a fire underneath to heat it all up and add the laundry to the now-boiling water before fishing it out with a pole and transferring it to a tub.

Then she'd get her dolly-legs out.

**Jess**   Her what?

**Norma**   A dolly-legs was a long wooden pole attached to a small four-legged stool. Mum would plunge that into the tub with the laundry and then twist the clothes from side to side to get them clean. After that, she had to feed each item of clothing individually through her mangle to wring out the water and on wet days they'd be hung up to dry in the living room where we had a line running across wall to wall.

Gosh, it must have been backbreaking work and a tortuous life but, do you know, I never heard her grumble. People in that day and age were proud of what they had and they looked after it.

**Jess**   Did everything get washed on the Monday wash day?

**Norma**   Yes, including us! Once Mum had finished all her washing, we'd all take our baths in the tin bath in the wash house. She just kept topping the copper up while each of us washed so there would be enough hot water for everyone. Once we'd finished, we had to carry the bath between us to tip the used

# CHILDHOOD

water down the drain and then it would be hung back up on its hook on the wall.

**Jess** I can't get over the fact you all only had one bath a week! By the weekend everyone must have been humming. People must have stunk back in the day.

**Norma** Perhaps we did, but nobody noticed because that was the norm. We washed in between, you know.

**Jess** That's something at least.

**Norma** Because Mondays were always so busy, what with all the washing and bathing, Mum didn't have time to cook the dinner from scratch as she usually would. So our evening meal was always the leftovers of Sunday lunch from the day before, along with a jacket potato. She was a wonderful cook, my mum. Dad used to say she could produce a meal out of nothing. We had home-made soups, rabbit pie, and in the summer she'd make a Lincolnshire salad, which I loved. I don't know where it came from …

**Jess** … Lincolnshire, I'd guess.

**Norma** Thank you, Jessica. How fortunate we are that you're here to keep us right.

It was lettuce and pieces of onion with vinegar and a sprinkling of sugar on top. We'd have that with new potatoes – Mum's were the best I've ever tasted – and whatever meat there was. Dad had a vegetable allotment where he grew everything so that was very lucky for us, and on a Sunday when the joint was in the oven … oh, the smell was heaven. Roast dinners don't smell like that any more.

**Jess** Sounds like Jessie could have given Mary Berry a run for her money.

**Norma** You say that, but she wasn't terribly good at cake-making.

# CHAPTER ONE

She used to make the Christmas cake, but she never thought she'd done it properly or made it quite nice enough. Her sponges were a bit like yours, Jess. If you took a bath after eating a slice, you'd sink.

**Jess** Don't I know about it! You never bother to sugarcoat your verdict on my baking. I'm going to invest in a fancy food mixer to see if that helps keep my batter lighter.

**Norma** Well, you be careful with that. My good friend Niff Burton always said you can whisk too much.

**Jess** Sheesh, I can't win.

**Norma** My mum was a beautiful pastry-maker, mind. Her apple pies were especially good. I could just murder a piece right now!

And she worked so hard in the house. Whenever we had the chimney swept by Mrs Alvey the local sweep, I used to go outside and watch for her brush coming out through the top, which was fun. But poor Mum, no matter how well she'd covered everything up, then had to spend the rest of the day cleaning the soot from the whole of the house. The walls would have to be washed down from top to bottom and it would be late into the night before the place was beautifully clean and fresh again.

**Jess** This might sound really narrow-minded of me, but I'd always imagined the houses back then to have cement floors and bare brick walls.

**Norma** Not quite. We had plasterboard on the walls and because Mum was very house-proud, she would make rugs for the floors with rags. They called it rag carpet and it was strips of cloth cut to a certain length and then pushed or hooked through a large piece of hessian. It was hard-wearing and would keep our floors warm, although later on we had lino fitted, which Mum was awfully proud of.

## CHILDHOOD

But we had no modern appliances, no hot water and no fridge. We had a very small kitchen with a pantry for storage. Milk was delivered every other day by the milkman, who would bring a churn and a measuring jug. He'd dip the jug into the churn and then pour the milk into a basin my mum had brought from the kitchen and then she'd store it on the pantry floor to keep it cool. Meat and butter would be kept the same way. If the meat ever smelled a bit off, Mum would pop it in a bowl and cover it with vinegar.

**Jess** You what?

**Norma** I'd guess the vinegar freshened it up a bit. She wouldn't have cooked it if it had been crawling, obviously. She was a wife and a mum and she was excellent at both of those jobs. My word, she was lovely. She never complained, she never fell out with anybody, I never ever heard her say a wrong word about anyone.

I used to put my arms around her to kiss her on the cheek and her skin was always so soft and lovely. And always the smell of Cuticura talc. That's what she loved.

**Jess** Aw, Nan. That's gorgeous.

**Norma** I do know that I said to her once, 'Whatever am I going to do, Mum, when I'm too big to sit on your knee?' I suppose that had to come to an end one day. Especially having been a nine-and-a-half-pound baby!

**Jess** I love hearing you talking about Jessie. I can see the twinkle in your eye whenever you do; it just ignites something so special.

**Norma** I could talk about her all day. I only wish she could have had a bit of an easier life. I know after my dad died she grieved for him dreadfully.

# CHAPTER ONE

**Jess**   That must have been awful for the whole family. You lost your dad, Tom, when you were still very young.

**Norma**   He died just before my eighth birthday in 1942. I was thinking the other day about how I wish my dad could have lived that bit longer so I'd have had the chance to form solid memories of him. What I do have is so vague.

I know he loved his music and he could sing and play the piano. Not that we had a piano. And I remember he used to buy Pontefract cakes, cutting them in half for me and him to share. He would mend our shoes, patching up the leather and resoling them. But other than that, things are very hazy.

I do have a clear memory of one Christmas morning when I was about seven. I'd come running down the stairs, excitedly asking: 'Has he been? Has he been?' And my dad said, 'Well, somebody has!'

I can almost feel the excitement now; it had built up so much that I didn't know what to do with myself. There was a doll and a book waiting for me and I was thrilled to pieces.

**Jess**   Was that the Christmas you got so excited that you ended up on the loo with the runs?

**Norma**   Don't you have a way with words, Missy? Yes, it was, if you must know. My sister Betty told me I'd worked myself up into such a state of anticipation that I was shaking all over.

**Jess**   Do you remember when I was little, we used to go through the Argos catalogue around Christmas time and I'd circle the toys that I wanted? Creating that wish list is such a core childhood memory for me. And you, Grandad and my mum teamed up to make sure there were a good few presents from the catalogue to unwrap on the day.

**Norma**   You didn't do too badly, love. You know your grandad and I always loved treating you.

## CHILDHOOD

**Jess**  It's lovely for you to have that Christmas memory of your dad. Even though what you remember of him is blurry, your mind obviously associates him with positive, happy times like that. I think it shows how much you meant to each other.

**Norma**  I've been told that my dad's only thought every day was making sure that my mum and us girls were all right. On the day he died it was snowy outside, so bad that he'd said to my mum, 'You're not turning out in this to get the groceries, Jessie. I'll go instead.' That was typical of him, looking out for us like that. Off he went and he never came back. He dropped dead in the street.

**Jess**  That's so tragic. Was it a heart attack?

**Norma**  I think it must have been his heart, yes. I would like so much to remember more. I can visualise things in my head; I can see the policeman coming to the door to tell my mum the news and I can picture the snow. But it's all quite murky.

I wish I'd written some of it down, but I was too young at that age to understand what would be important later on. I suppose with my age being what it was, I was sheltered from a lot of the sadness. I know I left my bedroom and slept in Mum's bed with her for quite some time after he died. Mum just carried on, but the impact of losing him was huge. She went deaf for three months from the shock.

**Jess**  Poor Jessie. That's dreadful.

**Norma**  After Dad passed, Mum and I would take it in turns to make each other breakfast in bed on a Sunday. I'd do one week and she'd do the next, usually bacon and tomato and occasionally an egg. I like to think our closeness helped her through her grief.

And I know Joan, my eldest sister, was a rock at the side of our mother. She was in her early twenties by then and

# CHAPTER ONE

working as a teacher and she was such a wonderful help, emotionally and financially. When she was first widowed, Mum got ten shillings for herself and five shillings for me each week.

**Jess** Hang on ... with inflation that would be about £30 today. That's next to nothing, Nan!

**Norma** It bought the necessities – milk, butter, sugar, eggs and the like.

I know my dad had once confided in Joan that he worried about not living to see me grow up. There were 27 years between my parents – so it was always something that troubled him. Dad was 73 when he died. He'd been married previously, but his first wife died of cancer long before he met my mum.

**Jess** Twenty-seven years is a fair amount, though.

**Norma** I'm sure some people mocked the age gap, but my mum and dad were so happy together. If you're in love, age doesn't count.

**Jess** OK, if I wasn't with Jake and I introduced you to my new fella who was in his late fifties, what would you say?

**Norma** I'd say take him round to your mother's.

**Jess** Haha! I don't even know where I'd find a boyfriend in his late fifties, to be honest. How did Jessie and Tom meet?

**Norma** I don't know. That's sad, isn't it? It's things like that I wish I'd asked. There are so many things I never found out about my family and now there's none of them left to ask.

Mum had a lot of friends in the community who were a great support for her and particularly the ladies on the street whom she was pally with. They all had nicknames for each other. My mum was Deanie because our surname was Dean.

# CHILDHOOD

|   |   |
|---|---|
| | Mrs Irwin who lived immediately across from us was Irwie and Mrs Tootle at number 52 was known as … |
| Jess | … Stop there, let me guess. Tooty? |
| Norma | How did you get that? |
| Jess | Just a wild guess. |
| Norma | And my Auntie Mae – one of Mum's sisters – lived just across the road. She had nine children, so she'd been, er, busy. |
| Jess | I suppose they didn't have TikTok to scroll through of an evening back then. |
| Norma | No, they had to find some way to pass the winter nights. But as women and as a community, they really did pull together. It was that sort of a place. On a Saturday morning everyone would collect at a café called Howard's in the town centre – quite a well-to-do spot where the waitresses wore white pinnies and little hats. Everyone there knew each other and the women would all arrive with their baskets, dressed in their best outfits to have a coffee and a catch-up. |
| Jess | That's one of the lovely aspects of living in a small town. Everyone knows each other so it feels very together and familiar. |
| Norma | It also means that everyone knows your business. We all knew who had been doing things they shouldn't. Or, to be more specific, dabbling with people they shouldn't. Nothing stayed secret for long. |
| Jess | There is that. Were there no skeletons in your closet? |
| Norma | Chance would be a fine thing. |
| Jess | I loved the experience of growing up in a village where all my friends lived within walking distance. We'd play out until the street lights started to come on, which was the signal to stop |

# CHAPTER ONE

the game of Blocko or Kerby and head home for the night. Blocko, which I think is known by other names depending on where you are in the country (I've also heard it called 40-40 or Block One Two Three), was like a more challenging version of Hide and Seek – one person would stay at the base and count to 100 while the others hid. The aim for the hiders was to get back to base before being found and tagged by the seeker. And Kerby was a points-based game played with a ball while standing across the street from your opponent. You had to throw the ball, trying to hit the kerb on the other side, then catch it on the rebound. You scored points if successful.

Seems so simple and innocent now! I always felt safe and I was back and forth between your house and mine, which were only a few minutes' walk apart, the whole time.

**Norma** I don't think any of us appreciate the beauty of that freedom until we look back on it as adults. We both got lucky, Jess, growing up where we did. It's different for children in the big cities.

When I was little we'd go primrosing – flower picking – in the woods, which was perfectly safe in those days. We'd return home healthy, sunburned and hungry.

At the back of our house on Nelson Street, there was a small stretch of concrete, big enough for bikes but not for cars, and we'd spend hours there with our whip and tops and coloured chalks. The whip was a length of stick with a lead attached which you wrapped all the way around a wooden top. Then you'd whip it away, releasing the top, and just watch it spin.

**Jess** So a bit like a Beyblade of today.

**Norma** I'll take your word for that.

Another great love from my childhood – and one that has continued throughout my life – was our royal family. I was

## CHILDHOOD

fascinated by them as a little girl. Mrs Bell, who lived next door to us, had loads of big hardback books about all sorts of different topics and I used to go round and ask, 'Please could I borrow your royal books?'

Very kindly, she would allow me to bring them home where I'd sit and pore over them, looking at all the pictures and reading about the history of the monarchy.

**Jess** You were always a big fan of the Queen, weren't you? I guess being a similar age meant that you felt a connection with her although you obviously had very different lives. I mean, you've never been ferried about in a horse-drawn carriage while wearing a tiara and waving at the public, for a start.

**Norma** Sadly not. But you're right, Jess. She was just eight years older than me and I loved our late Queen to bits. I shall never forget her. She was lovely inside and out and I miss her very much.

**Jess** I was in Cyprus on holiday when I heard that the Queen had died in September 2022. My first thought was for you because I knew how sad you would be. I phoned you straight away to tell you to put the telly on and watch the news.

**Norma** I was ever so upset. Her passing had been expected for a couple of days before because there were reports that she'd been in poor health. We'd also seen Prince Charles and other family members on the news arriving at Balmoral to be with her. But it was still a dreadful shock when it happened.

**Jess** It did feel odd when she died. There was a strangeness in the air like there was something not quite right. Obviously for anyone to pass away, it's awful, isn't it?

**Norma** I don't know, I've not tried it yet.

**Jess** Nan, honestly! What are you like?

# CHAPTER ONE

**Norma**     I couldn't resist that one.

**Jess**     Anyway, I know how much the Queen's death impacted you and I could see you were grieving.

**Norma**     It was grief, yes. I just felt the loss very keenly because she'd been there the whole time. She was part of my life. One of my proudest moments has always been the day I saw her in the flesh from just a few feet away. It was 1953, so I'd have been 19, and a cousin of ours asked me and Betty if we'd like to go along to the St Leger in Doncaster. We'd never been anywhere like the races before – we had no money to spend but, my goodness, the thrill of it all!

As we came off the racecourse, we stayed on the pavement to watch Queen Elizabeth, who always attended the Leger, drive past. She looked so beautiful with that fabulous complexion of hers. She was a vision. And with her in the backseat was Sir Winston Churchill. What an honour it was to witness a spectacle like that.

**Jess**     That's more than 70 years ago but you remember it so clearly.

**Norma**     Like it was yesterday. You don't forget things like that. We all loved the royals in our family. They are intrinsically part of the fabric of this country. I really do think that whenever there's a jubilee or a royal wedding, we come into our own as a nation. Nobody does all that pomp and ceremony like we do.

Betty even went down to London for the royal wedding when Princess Elizabeth (as she was then) got married to Philip in 1947. I'd have only been 13 so couldn't go with her. Betty lined the streets alongside thousands of other well-wishers all hoping to catch a glimpse of the newlyweds. When they drove past in the carriage heading off on their honeymoon, this woman – a Londoner – who was standing next to Betty shouted out, 'What colour's your nightie, love?'

## CHILDHOOD

|       | I mean, really. But that's London for you. |
|---|---|
| Jess | I'm just picturing Betty all horrified! |
| Norma | Oh, she was. Imagine shouting a fruity comment like that at the future Queen! She was wonderful, our Queen, and she worked so hard right to the end, always kind, thoughtful and diplomatic. |
| Jess | I completely appreciate that she was incredible for her age, and managing the pressure of all those public appearances and speeches well into her nineties was amazing. If it was you, I think you'd say, 'Ring 'em up and say I'm not doing it.' |
| Norma | You don't know that. Try me. |
| Jess | OK, Buckingham Palace on the balcony, tomorrow at midday. |
| Norma | I'll see you there. |
| Jess | I'm always telling you that you're the nation's true queen. So when you weren't delving into Mrs Bell's royal family books, what did you spend your time doing when you were younger? |
| Norma | I was often with my best friend, Pat Gregory. She was two years older than me and used to eat raw potatoes. Isn't that odd? Whenever her mum was peeling them for lunch, she'd always ask for half of one and she'd eat it just like that. I tried it once myself but never again! |
| Jess | I know you and Pat each had a nickname … |
| Norma | Jessica, you are so naughty. You see, Pat was very thin … |
| Jess | … And Nan was quite plump. So all the kids used to call them Barrel and Matchstick! |
| Norma | Isn't that cruel? I can just about see the funny side of it now … |

# CHAPTER ONE

I also had a second cousin called Dinah who was the same age as me and we were great friends when we were younger. It was a super neighbourhood to be part of although I did take issue with the local Salvation Army brass band who used to come round and play right outside my bedroom window at the weekends, which often spoiled my Sunday-morning lie-in.

**Jess** Was it church every Sunday?

**Norma** Absolutely. My dad was a religious man – he didn't flaunt it, but he was a big believer and he'd have gone anywhere to hear Handel's Messiah. So it was morning church, Sunday school and then evening church.

**Jess** That's a lot of church!

**Norma** We had to treat Sunday as the Sabbath; we weren't allowed to play and had to go on long walks in the countryside as a family. My mum relaxed the rules a bit after he passed – he was a loving dad, but he was set in his Methodist ways. I think my poor father would turn in his grave if he knew you and I sometimes go up to Meadowhall shopping centre on a Sunday.

**Jess** Er, Meadowhall on a Sunday is probably the least of his worries, let's be honest. He'd surely be spinning at all the innuendo that makes you giggle.

**Norma** Is that what they call it?

**Jess** What about us doing a Facebook Live on a Sunday? Or eating fish and chips in the car?

**Norma** I should think he'd be horrified.

I did a bit of a naughty thing in church once which I'm relieved my dad didn't ever find out about. We had a Methodist preacher who came to deliver a sermon and he told us all to shut our eyes so that we couldn't see each other and to put our hands up in the air if we wanted saving. I took a little peek and I saw a lady we knew well with her hands up. I told my sister Betty about that later and she thought it was hilarious.

Jess   I wonder what that woman had been up to that was so bad she thought she needed saving …

Norma   We'll never know! So yes, it was a tight-knit sort of place on the whole. And of course, that community spirit counted for an awful lot when the war broke out.

Jess   That must have been a terrible time to live through. I can't even imagine. You were born in 1934, just five years before the Second World War started.

Norma   Yes. When war broke out we were all given gas masks and had to go to school carrying them over our shoulders – I would only have been five or six but I can still smell the rubber. And I can still feel the fear that came over me whenever I was awoken by the air-raid siren in the night. My tummy would sink and we'd all have to come downstairs and shelter in the little cupboard area where the brushes and gas meter were stored. We had to stay there until we got the all-clear.

It was awful, but we were lucky because we didn't ever suffer a hit. There was once a bomb dropped in the school playground just a few minutes from where we lived, but there was no one there at the time and nobody got hurt. Thank heavens.

They'd built Anderson shelters on Retford's Spa Common, which was just across from the school, and if there had ever been an air raid during school hours, that's where we would have gone. We did a few practice runs but I'm eternally grateful that we never had to use them for real. Those shelters smelled of damp and concrete.

# CHAPTER ONE

We were just a quiet market town so we didn't have it anything like as horrific as they did in London or down the road in Coventry. And because we were relatively safe, Retford became one of the places children were evacuated to. So we'd get little kiddies arriving from Liverpool, Sheffield and Manchester – Joan spent her 21st birthday in 1939 looking after the incoming evacuees and taking them to the various places they were going to stay.

My auntie Con took one in, a little girl called Ellen who had come down from Leeds. She had a frightened look on her face and was clutching her suitcase. And you know, when Connie died in the 1980s aged 92, Ellen (who was now a woman in her fifties) came to the funeral. She'd kept in touch with the family all those years.

**Jess** That's amazing, Nan. It shows what fantastic, kind people your family – our family – were.

**Norma** Yes, I think so too.

**Jess** Do you remember your mum and dad being scared?

**Norma** I think they did a good job of shielding me from the worst of it, but I do remember one day at school my teacher asked how my mummy had been during the air raid the previous night. And I said, 'Oh, she didn't like it, Miss. But my daddy gave her a bottle of whisky and she was OK after that.'

She'd actually only had a little tot, but there I was telling the teacher it was a whole bottle. I'm sure my mum was mortified when I told her what I'd said.

**Jess** Everyone at school would have been thinking poor Jessie was an alcoholic!

**Norma** Mum did enjoy a glass of Guinness because she said it was good for her … but that was as far as it went, I promise you.

# CHILDHOOD

**Jess**  I really can't get my head round how people managed. It must have really shaped your generation in every way. Mentally, psychologically and emotionally.

**Norma**  I'm sure it did. Everybody had to be there for each other and so we matured into people who were kind, helpful and resilient. Women went to work in the munitions factories having said goodbye to their husbands, not knowing when or if they'd ever see them again. That takes steel.

We also got used to having very little. When you've lived on rations for as long as we did, having to spin it all out over the week teaches you to make the most of what you have. And to value it. We'd get four ounces of butter per person for the week and Mum would always ask if I'd like mine all in one go or little by little. I'd say to slather the lot on one slice of toast and then I'd suffer with margarine for the rest of the week.

**Jess**  That's how you take your toast to this day. More butter than bread.

**Norma**  I've a sneaky feeling Mum gave me her share as well, you know. That's the sort of thing she would have done. I must tell you, my mum's sister Ethel was a prolific letter writer and during rationing, she'd write, 'Jessie, I haven't got a skerrick of butter in the house!'

Mum would be reading the letter with a withering look on her face. 'Really?' she'd say to me and my sisters, with a roll of the eyes. 'Does she think she's the only one?!'

**Jess**  So that's who you inherited your sassy eye roll from! It's Jessie. Do you know your eye rolls and side eyes are internationally famous now? If your mouth doesn't say it, your face will.

**Norma**  I don't even know I'm doing it.

# CHAPTER ONE

**Jess**  The most epic eye rolls are saved for when my mum, Kate, wears her hat.

**Norma**  Oh, that hat …

**Jess**  It's seen better days, let's put it that way. Whenever she arrives anywhere wearing it, you're like, 'Eh up, the hat's back.'

**Norma**  She gardens in it, she walks the dog in it. Luckily she's never met me in town wearing it otherwise I would have turned on my heel and left.

**Jess**  It's shocking.

**Norma**  Enough about that hat. When it came to rations, people just got on with it and I never heard anyone grumbling. Barring Auntie Ethel, that is.

**Jess**  Well, I wouldn't be able to cope with rations and living in fear. And I can tell you that I certainly would grumble!

**Norma**  I don't doubt it, Jessica. You'd have packed up as soon as the sirens went off.

**Jess**  I'd have been sat on the toilet with the squits like you on Christmas Day!

**Norma**  You'd have been utterly hopeless. But it's just the way things were and we had no choice but to make the best of it. Such tragedy, though. There were so many young boys who went off to fight. Some of them pretended to be older than they were just so they could join up. That's how we ended up losing kids who weren't much older than myself.

**Jess**  Do you remember the end of the war?

**Norma**  My memories of VE Day in 1945 are a bit foggy, but I do recall the street parties and everybody dancing around because they were so happy the war was over.

## CHILDHOOD

There were celebrations when the men came home – some of them had left their wives to fight and didn't return for years. Of course, some never came home at all. So there was a lot of sadness around, but I always say we were the lucky ones living where we did. And my dad was 70 when the war broke out, so he was too old to be conscripted, which was something else to be thankful for.

**Jess** You've told me a lovely story about your sister's wedding dress which I think shows the generosity of people at that time.

**Norma** When Joan got married in 1946, she so wanted to have a nice gown, but she didn't have enough coupons for the fabric. The man who lived next door, Mr Bell, gave her his so that she could have the beautiful dress she'd dreamed of.

**Jess** That's so thoughtful. Until you told me that story I'd always thought that rations were just for food. And I hadn't realised they carried on after the war ended.

**Norma** Oh yes, it wasn't a case of the war being over and everything immediately going back to normal. Not at all.

Joan married a Polish man called Kazik and it was a true love story with those two. They had a beautiful wedding day in the February although it was bitterly cold.

Kazik had managed to escape Poland at the start of the war when Hitler invaded. I don't know enough about his story or how he managed to flee, but I do know he was only 19 when he left and he had to spend several nights hiding in an open grave. He was later given the *Croix de Guerre* medal, which was France's version of our Victoria Cross – the French awarded it to members of the allied countries as well as their own.

**Jess** It's so fascinating talking to you about your wartime

# CHAPTER ONE

|  | |
|---|---|
| | memories. Everything seems so easy for us now by comparison. |
| Norma | You say this, Jess, but I still think it's a hard world for the youth of today. I'm not sure I'd have liked to have grown up in modern times. |
| Jess | Some older people take a 'you don't know you're born' kind of attitude and think the younger generations have everything handed to them on a plate. But one of the things I love most about you is that you've always been really good at looking at everything with empathy and from a wider perspective. |
| Norma | I just think you lot face different challenges. We didn't have mobile phones, which are the cause of so much trouble now. Our pace of life was much slower, more manageable, and we didn't compete with one another. Things were simpler. |
| Jess | It's certainly true that I was born into a very different world … |
| Norma | Oh, I remember so well the day you were born, Jess. Your grandad was in the garden and I came off the phone and said to him, 'Michael, we've got a little granddaughter, and she's going to be called Jessica.' |
| | The chap from across the road called over, 'That's my favourite name!' And one of his grandchildren was later named Jessica, too. |
| Jess | Funnily enough, I wasn't named after your mum Jessie. |
| Norma | No, you were named after a poster in the hairdresser's for Jessica nail polish. |
| Jess | So glam. |
| | For context, my mum is a hairdresser and my dad popped into the salon to tell her colleagues that she was in labour, but added that they hadn't picked a name yet. There was a poster |

# CHILDHOOD

on the wall advertising Jessica nail varnish and my dad said, 'That's it!'

So that's where Jessica came from. Not exactly the most romantic story, is it?

Norma    It's a lovely name, though, and it's always suited you. I can't imagine you being anything else.

Jess    And my middle name is Mae but that wasn't after Nan's Auntie Mae (the one with the nine children), it was just because my parents liked it paired with Jessica. I think it's all a nice coincidence anyway – sometimes Nan calls me Jessie and it always makes me smile.

Norma    They do go together well, Jessica Mae. I used to call you Jessica Mayhem. You were such a fidget as a child; you never sat still. Just like your mum, always dashing about.

Jess    Nan used to say to me, 'Stop orming around!' That's a good Retford word, orming. It basically means having ants in your pants.

Norma    You must have had a colony in there! You were always faffing about, right from the day you were born.

Jess    That was on 8 June 1996 at Bassetlaw Hospital in Worksop.

Norma    You arrived quite early, which was a pity because we could have all done with a few more nights' sleep. But I didn't mind, really. We've got a photograph of me and your grandad coming to visit you in the hospital for the first time. You were laid there with your tiny hands on your tummy and I thought they looked like stars. You were so beautiful and perfect.

Then, of course, you became difficult! As soon as you could speak, we had our work cut out.

Jess    Hang on a minute, this is where you're supposed to say nice things about me …

# CHAPTER ONE

**Norma**  You were a little monkey, you really were. Very mischievous.

**Jess**  My mum has told me I had a habit of waiting in shop queues with her and then running off just as she got to the front.

**Norma**  You were exactly the same when I picked you up from school, rushing off in the opposite direction while I chased after you, pushing your little brother in the pram. I remember one woman saying, 'You shouldn't be doing that, you'll give yourself a stroke!'

But we loved you with all our hearts. Your grandad adored you.

**Jess**  Grandad had a big greenhouse in the garden and he'd show me his tomatoes, which he was so proud of. He grew mint and runner beans as well and he was always in the garden, the garage or the shed, tending to things, pottering about or making something.

**Norma**  He was very talented with things like that, especially wood turning. He was an amazingly gifted man.

**Jess**  We used to sweep up the sawdust from his shed and take it down to the school in a bag because it always came in handy if one of the children had been sick and they needed to cover up the vomit!

I also remember me and Grandad rolling out Chewits sweets together using a pen as a rolling pin to flatten them before I ate them. I have no idea why.

He taught me how to wash my hands properly, going round every finger individually. He used to measure my height and record it with a date on the white brick wall in the garage. That's still there now, his distinctive writing in pencil, charting my growth up until I was seven, which is when we lost him. And he used to make me little hats in the summer out of his handkerchief, twisting each corner into a knot and then placing it on my head to protect me from the sun. I remember day trips to Creswell Crags, exploring the caves, and bike rides down the lane where, years later, me and Jake would share our first kiss.

Norma   Do you remember that day we went to Daneshill Lakes and the swan turned nasty on your grandad?

Jess   Yes! We were walking back towards the car and one just went for him.

Norma   They can be nasty, swans.

Jess   We had to run as fast as we could to get to where the gate was and escape! I was petrified at the time, but we couldn't stop laughing once we got back to the safety of the car.

Norma   It still makes me chuckle now.

Jess   Nan and Grandad were very central to my life from day one. My parents got divorced when I was two; I didn't see my dad much, and when I say my mum worked every hour God sent, she really did. She's still like that now, never stops.

Norma   She always did her best in difficult circumstances, your mum.

Jess   And you didn't hesitate to step in and help us out. It meant that I spent so much time with Nan and Grandad – they were the ones who would take me to school and pick me up, give me my dinner and read me my stories. Nan always used to bring me a Cadbury's Fudge at the end of the school day.

Norma   And when your brother came along, I'd bring him a pint of milk. That's what he wanted, strange boy.

Jess   At least he'd have looked cute while drinking it, with his blonde bouncy curls.

My little brother Cadan was born when I was seven. Mum had him with a new partner. We lived just around the corner

CHAPTER ONE

from Nan, so I'd be there after school to have my tea – her chicken casserole was next level. She would do it in the slow cooker and I used to absolutely love it. Such a good, hearty meal, even if the mashed potato was a bit lumpy.

**Norma**  Pardon me? Lumpy? I'll deal with you later.

**Jess**  We loved it lumpy! It made it special.

**Norma**  I'd make a big batch of that and freeze it into portions that would last for a whole week. Cadan used to go to a local childminder called Louise and I'd send him with a portion of the casserole for his lunch.

**Jess**  We saw Louise quite recently and she said she still remembers Nan's chicken casserole because it smelled so good. So it's famous! You can find the recipe on page 45 of this book if you want to try it yourselves.

I loved dinnertime at Nan and Grandad's. I remember Grandad used to have the same plate for every meal, brown with a little rim around the edge.

**Norma**  That was his favourite plate. I can't think of where it came from, but he took a shine to it for some reason. It was accidentally smashed a few years ago, sadly. I can't remember how it broke now.

**Jess**  Don't look at me!

**Norma**  I wouldn't dream of it.

**Jess**  Do you remember I had that special chair which started off as a highchair and then converted into a little seat and table?

**Norma**  I do.

**Jess**  And I'd sit there eating my chicken or beef casserole or fish and chips if we'd been to the takeaway. After tea we'd play games like Hungry Hippos, Snakes and Ladders and Snap.

## CHILDHOOD

**Norma**  Buckaroo. That was another one you loved.

**Jess**  Ludo, Jenga, Operation …

**Norma**  All of which you had to win. We didn't finish many games because you were such a sore loser and you'd chuck it in if you weren't winning.

**Jess**  Fair enough, I'll plead guilty to that.

We'd also play shops and you'd teach me how to add and subtract. Grandad would be sitting in his favourite chair in the lounge, the green leather one by the front window, which is still there today. And we'd watch a bit of TV together – *Brum*, *Teletubbies*, *The Tweenies* and *Rosie and Jim*.

**Norma**  *The Woodentops.*

**Jess**  No, that would have been my mum!

**Norma**  Are you sure?

**Jess**  Positive. I'm not that old! You'd walk me home between six and seven o'clock. As I got older you gave me a front door key.

**Norma**  You came and went as you liked and we always loved having you. Even if you were a handful. I was happy I could do it. I enjoyed it.

**Jess**  I loved it if I had a day off school with you. I'd lie on the sofa watching *Jeremy Kyle* and *Bargain Hunt* while you fed me toast. Can you remember how I liked my toast? Jam with marmalade on top on one side and marmalade with jam on top on the other.

**Norma**  I must have been stark raving mad to do that.

**Jess**  You also used to keep dummies – which we called noonies – in the fridge for me and I'd put them freezing cold in between my fingers and toes and another one in my mouth,

# CHAPTER ONE

        while nestling with shawlie, my comfort blanket. God, I was a nightmare, wasn't I?

**Norma**    That went on until you were about 11.

**Jess**    It was my mum who pulled the plug on the dummies in the end, saying I was far too old and I'd get bullied at secondary school if anyone caught on. I was a strange child in a lot of ways.

**Norma**    You were, but it was a sensory thing and it was very calming for you. Even if it meant I had a fridge full of noonies for years.

**Jess**    I don't know who was more stupid, me for doing it or you for entertaining it.

**Norma**    Let's not answer that one.

**Jess**    Nan and Grandad were always there at my sports days, my school plays and parents' evenings. Because of that, I felt like Nan was a second mum.

**Norma**    But that's the way it had to go. Your mum was so busy trying to stay afloat.

**Jess**    I saw it as having two homes. I never knocked on the door or rang the doorbell at Nan's; I always came running in and I had my own little bedroom upstairs where I'd stay for sleepovers on a Saturday night when Mum went out with her friends. I treasured those sleepovers.

**Norma**    I'm glad somebody did! I'd be reading you stories until I was dropping to sleep myself.

**Jess**    Nan used to make up these stories about mice – one of them was called Mickey and another called Minnie, but they weren't like the Disney characters. They were actual mice with tails, they ate cheese and only came out to play when

# CHILDHOOD

|  | everyone in the house had gone to sleep. There were quite a lot of characters. I remember Smoky, Bluey and Cheesy. |
|---|---|
| Norma | I sometimes used to dread you coming round because you always wanted the mouse stories and I'd have to think up a new adventure from nothing. I was often running out of ideas. |
| Jess | You always managed it, though. You'd sit on the edge of my bed and tell me these stories and it was just the most special time ever. We'd also read *The Magic Faraway Tree* by Enid Blyton, which I loved. I was spoiled by you and Grandad. Not with materialistic things, but with love and time. |
| Norma | You got away with a lot of things because we loved you so much. I was soft with you and although Grandad was firmer, he was never sharp. |
| Jess | You were definitely more of a pushover. I knew I could get away with murder! |
| Norma | Maybe I should have been a little more stern, but I didn't have it in me. |
| Jess | I think I turned out all right! |
| Norma | You're not too bad, I suppose. |
| Jess | I always say that Nan and Grandad made my childhood magical. In the bathroom, there's a little ledge underneath the towel rail and at night we'd sprinkle a pile of talcum powder there. Nan would tell me it was fairy dust and that if the fairies were real, they'd come and collect it. In the morning it had always been cleaned away. |
| Norma | And you really did believe it was the fairies, which amused me and your grandad no end. |
| Jess | I used to come and lie in bed with Nan and Grandad sometimes. They had a telly in their room and on a Saturday |

# CHAPTER ONE

           night we'd watch *Casualty* together, which felt like such a treat.

**Norma**    They were terrific times. You have always been here with me and we've made some lovely memories over the years. And we've never been short of conversation, have we?

**Jess**    We both love a good chat. I could listen to the stories from your childhood over and over again. I never get bored. You're so strong and inspiring for what you've been through.

**Norma**    You're not so bad yourself, love.

**Jess**    The way you describe your mum and all her values and lovely nurturing qualities and the soft skin, you could be describing yourself.

**Norma**    You and I are both products of the love we had in our childhoods, Jess. Being loved unconditionally and knowing you're cherished and good enough just the way you are … that stays with you forever.

**INTERLUDE**

# Norma's famous slow cooker chicken casserole

### Ingredients

2 tbsp plain flour
5 chicken breast fillets
Knob of butter
2 large carrots
2 brown onions
2 sticks of celery
2 chicken stock cubes
2–4 tbsp chicken gravy granules
500g potatoes
Salt and pepper

### Method

1. Preheat the slow cooker to high.//
2. Put the flour on a tray, add a generous grind of salt and pepper and mix it all together. Coat each chicken breast in the salt and pepper flour.
3. Add a knob of butter to a frying pan on a high heat. Brown off the outsides of the chicken breasts in the pan, then set them aside (keep the pan handy).

## INTERLUDE

4. Chop your carrots, onion and celery into small dice.

5. Boil a kettle, then pour a splash of boiling water into the chicken pan to scoop up the flavours.

6. Put your chicken breasts into the slow cooker and cover with the water from the pan. Add the chopped veg and a generous grind of black pepper, then cook for 30 minutes.

7. When the 30 minutes is nearly up, dissolve the stock cubes in 500ml boiled water and mix well. Pour the stock over the top of the chicken and veg, then stir.

8. Leave the slow cooker to work its magic.

9. After 3 or 4 hours, chuck in a couple of tablespoons of chicken gravy granules and mix to dissolve. Keep adding and mixing the granules until you get a good consistency, then cook for another 30 minutes.

10. Meanwhile, boil the potatoes until tender, then mash. Add 2 tablespoons of this to the mix for the last 15 minutes and serve the rest as an accompaniment to the casserole.

CHAPTER TWO

# School

**Jess** You don't realise it at the time, but life will never be as uncomplicated or as pure as your early years at school. My primary school days were probably the happiest I've ever been. Imagine being that innocent and carefree again!

**Norma** If only we could bottle that feeling, eh? Although if I close my eyes, I can take myself right back there. I did so enjoy my primary school days and felt excited to go in each day. School was full of fun, friendships and freedom.

**Jess** We had a big field where they had an installation of car tyres which we used to climb on. I had lots of friends and loved learning, playing and being outside. There were harvest festivals every autumn. Sports days with the egg and spoon race. Summer fairs with the stocks where the kids could pelt the teachers with wet sponges. It was uncontrollable giggles with friends, making up silly dances in the playground and cosy class storytimes on the carpet.

**Norma** Is the stocks the contraption where you put your head and hands through the holes?

**Jess** Yes. You'd fit into a set of stocks very well because you're nice and bent over, Nan. You'd go straight in.

**Norma** Don't you be getting any ideas.

**Jess** Ooh, would I do something like that?

**Norma** And here's me thinking you were a good girl, Jessica.

## CHAPTER TWO

**Jess**    I am ... most of the time. Mind, I bet you were a right goody two-shoes teacher's pet at school! I can't imagine you being a rebel.

**Norma**    I wouldn't say the teacher's pet exactly, but I was very well behaved because the teachers in those days didn't tolerate any silliness. And the way they dealt with us children ... well, it was a different time and you couldn't do any of that now.

**Jess**    Sounds like you experienced just how different. Did you ever get the cane?

**Norma**    I did once, at senior school. We weren't allowed sweets and I was caught chewing a bit of gum.

**Jess**    Knowing you, I'm surprised you didn't have a full bag of Werther's Originals in your pocket.

**Norma**    I was hauled out for it and given three strikes on the hand by the headmistress Miss Lee, a very tall woman who carried herself so majestically. She was very strict.

**Jess**    Like Miss Battle-Axe from *Horrid Henry*.

**Norma**    A bit like her. I didn't think it was such a terrible thing to have done and the punishment seemed a little harsh, but those were the rules and woe betide you if you stepped out of line. And I certainly didn't do it again.

**Jess**    I think it's awful that you got the cane for something so minor. If that had happened to me as a child, I think it would have damaged me mentally.

**Norma**    Well, it was 78 years ago so I think I'm just about over it now! I don't like the thought of corporal punishment one little bit and I'm glad we no longer have it in schools. I could never cane a child myself.

**Jess**    I can believe it. When I was growing up, you never smacked me on the bum, did you?

# SCHOOL

**Norma**  No, but I was tempted now and again!

**Jess**  Discipline when I was at school was getting minutes knocked off your 'golden time' and having to stay in during break. Not getting the cane! I actually feel really sad that you got slapped on the hand three times just for chewing gum.

**Norma**  That was the only time that I got hit, but I had a very lucky escape one morning which I shall never forget. At the start of each day, we'd be brought into class, where we had to stand in a row to show the teacher that we all had a handkerchief with us. Unfortunately for me, I'd forgotten mine one day and I was ever so worried about her reaching me in the line and having to admit that I didn't have it.

There was a little lad called David Taylor who saved my bacon. After he'd shown his hankie, he passed it down the line behind everybody's back until it reached me and the teacher was none the wiser. What a lovely act of kindness that was. I've never forgotten it.

**Jess**  I don't understand why you all needed to carry a hankie.

**Norma**  To blow our noses! But you're right, putting a hard and fast rule on it does seem silly. There are many codes of conduct from the past that we would laugh at now.

I can't recollect being scared of the teachers, but we were on our toes all the time. I think nowadays they'd talk to the children with a bit more fun in their voice. Back then they were just cross a lot of the time.

There was a little ditty we used to sing at primary school:

*Miss Hudson stood on the burning deck,*
*Miss Norman blew the hooter,*
*And who do you think came riding by?*
*Daddy Goodall on his scooter!*

## CHAPTER TWO

Now, you might have thought that the teachers would've had a bit of a giggle about this, but no. They were so angry with us. The whole class was lined up and the first child was asked who they'd learned it from. Then the teacher went to whoever they'd blamed and asked the same question until she got to the original culprit. And we were really in trouble. They had no sense of humour.

**Jess** Was Mr Goodall the headmaster at your primary school?

**Norma** That's right. From 1938 I went to Grove Street Methodist Primary, which was near to where we lived on Nelson Street. I could walk there easily in ten minutes if I wasn't dawdling which, admittedly, I was prone to – my friend Sheila would knock for me every morning and we'd go in together. There was a little corner shop we'd pop into on the last bit of the journey and do you know what Sheila would do? She'd buy herself an Oxo cube for a penny and she'd chew on that until we got to school.

**Jess** An actual Oxo cube?!

**Norma** Yes, it's unbelievable, isn't it? I suppose it was an acquired taste, a bit like Marmite. But I did find it very strange.

**Jess** So you had one friend – Pat – who liked raw potatoes and another one who ate Oxo cubes.

**Norma** A bit bizarre.

**Jess** Maybe you attracted strange folk.

**Norma** Well, you're here with me every day, so what do you think that says about you?

**Jess** Ha! I'm not sure … Did you wear a uniform for school?

**Norma** Not in those days. In the summer we'd wear an everyday dress with a cardigan and during the cold season we'd get wrapped up because we did have some very hard winters.

# SCHOOL

My mum sometimes had to shovel the snow away from the back door so I could get out of the house.

In the infant class, we had a huge open fire with a very big guard round it and that kept us warm.

It's funny, I can picture that classroom very clearly, but I struggle to call to mind much at all about the next class up.

I know we all had our own desks with a lid and a little inkwell at the top and we sat in rows. We were so tightly packed into the classrooms that if there was a girl in front with long plaited hair, the plaits would come over and sit on the desk behind, which my mum thought posed a risk of catching nits. And some children really were eaten up with the things, so she was right to be wary!

Every Friday night when I got home from school, Mum would be waiting with newspaper on the dining table and a nit comb at the ready to make sure I was all clear.

That would be followed by – and don't you laugh at this, Jessica – my dose of Epsom salt to keep me regular, as it were.

|       |   |
|---|---|
| Jess | You're so cute trying to phrase these things politely. What you mean is, it helped stave off constipation so you could drop the kids off at the pool. |
| Norma | We can always rely on you to lower the tone. Mum used to put a spoonful of the salt on a saucer and pour a bit of boiling water on top so it melted. It wasn't a very nice thing to take at all. |
| Jess | But did it keep things moving? |
| Norma | I would think so. |
| Jess | We should try that now when you're bunged up. I'll add Epsom salt to this week's shopping list! |

## CHAPTER TWO

**Norma**   I'm so proud of you most of the time, Jess, but you really can be quite coarse.

**Jess**   We were talking the other day about the songs we both used to sing at school – I went to the local village primary – and a lot of them are the same. Classics like 'All Things Bright and Beautiful', 'He's Got the Whole World in His Hands' and 'When I Needed a Neighbour (Were You There?)'. We actually use a lyric from that one when I'm getting you washed, don't we?

**Norma**   'I was cold, I was naked …'

**Jess**   '… Were you there, were you there?' We sing that line every time!

**Norma**   I did so love singing songs when I was at school. I can remember one song I particularly liked called 'Mary of Argyle (I Have Heard the Mavis Singing)' – a mavis is a bird. And the lyrics went:

*I have heard the mavis singing her love song to the morn,*
*I have seen the dewdrops clinging to a rose just newly born,*
*But a sweeter song has cheered me at the evening's gentle close,*
*And I've seen an eye still brighter than the dew drop on a rose,*
*'Twas your voice, my gentle Mary, and your artless winning smile,*
*That made this world an Eden, Bonny Mary of Argyle.*

I think the words are absolutely beautiful.

**Jess**   I used to like the tiny ant song.

**Norma**   The what?

**Jess**   'From the tiny ant to the elephant, from the snake to the kangaroo.'

Not quite your 'Mary of Argyle', but it was all about what God had created so the idea was the same.

## SCHOOL

**Norma**  I suppose I can see that. At a stretch.

**Jess**  I loved it when I got to year six in primary school because, as the oldest, it meant we got to sit on a bench at the back of the hall during assembly. All the little ones would be sitting cross-legged on the floor singing their hearts out, but we had a bit of extra importance.

**Norma**  Ah, all this is bringing back so many memories of music in school. That was probably my favourite subject. I loved English as well because I've always been a bookworm. But the less said about my maths the better.

**Jess**  Your maths is good! You taught me everything I know to do with numbers.

**Norma**  I'm not too bad at mental arithmetic and working out what change I need in a shop. But ask me about algebra and I'm all at sea. My mother died two years before decimalisation came in in 1971 and I've always said I don't think she would have coped with it. She didn't like change, which I think is the same for all of us as we get older.

**Jess**  Did you get any sex education?

**Norma**  Not at school, no. And I know my mum meant well, but she didn't discuss it with me either.

**Jess**  So where did you think babies came from?

**Norma**  I figured it out gradually, I suppose. My sister Betty used to think she'd come out of one of our mum's breasts! Parents back then didn't push anything onto us because they thought we weren't old enough.

**Jess**  I can remember my mum sat me down when I was still quite young, drew me some diagrams of the reproductive system and told me how everything worked. I mean, it was slightly embarrassing, but I was also completely fascinated. It's very

## CHAPTER TWO

                normal to be curious and I was always quite proud that my mum had had that conversation with me.

**Norma**    I think my mother would have run a mile and then run some more if she'd been told she had to tell me about any of that.

**Jess**    Did she not even tell you about periods?

**Norma**    Not until I'd started. I knew a bit about them, though, probably because I'd discussed it with my friends. We'd have these little talks between us.

                I remember as a young girl having to go and get some sanitary towels from the little draper's shop. But there was a man behind the counter and so I came out with a reel of cotton.

**Jess**    Bless!

**Norma**    And Betty once told me that the reason men had more strokes than women was because we menstruated to get rid of dead blood. I mean, you work that one out.

**Jess**    But that's what happens when people are too awkward to talk about these things and keep them private. We end up with these ridiculous myths and confusion.

**Norma**    My mum just didn't want to discuss things like that. It would have been the same for her as a girl, too.

**Jess**    She probably wouldn't have appreciated some of the banter we have in this house in that case.

**Norma**    Oh, she would have gone barmy, Jess! I can't even believe we're writing about it here.

**Jess**    Times have changed, Nan. I like to drop cheeky comments in front of you because I can see you trying not to laugh.

**Norma**    I don't know what you're talking about.

**Jess**    I can always see your shoulders shaking.

## SCHOOL

**Norma**    Don't drag me down to your level. I just sometimes think it's gone too far the other way. Children seem to know about everything as soon as they can talk. Goodness me, you only need to look at some of the adverts we see today on the telly.

**Jess**    Are you talking about the one we saw for tampons?

**Norma**    That's one of them. They go into such graphic detail.

**Jess**    You're not keen on condom adverts either.

**Norma**    Is there really any need? Adverts, telly programmes, whatever it is, everything seems to come round to sex nowadays.

**Jess**    You think the world's gone sex mad, don't you?

**Norma**    It just seems to me that it's whichever way you turn. And I'm sorry but it starts a bit too young in schools for children.

**Jess**    Sex education is all very factual, Nan. They teach them about the fallopian tubes, ovaries and testicles and how babies are made. It's not about sex positions and what you would call 'canoodling'.

**Norma**    My eldest sister Joan was a teacher, as you know. And the headmaster told her one day, possibly during the seventies, that she had to give sex education lessons and she really, really didn't want to.

**Jess**    Do you remember we had some sex education ourselves when we went to Yorkshire Wildlife Park for your birthday?

**Norma**    Oh, the wallabies!

**Jess**    We learned that the male wallabies have a double-ended penis and the females have three vaginas.

**Norma**    Yes, and you were dead jealous!

**Jess**    Nan! I just found it really interesting …

**Norma**    Shall we take this chapter out of the gutter?

## CHAPTER TWO

**Jess**  We better had. Who was your favourite teacher at school?

**Norma**  At primary school it was a lady called Mrs Markham. She used to be quite friendly with my mum and she was a comfy, cosy sort of person who absolutely loved her job. The kiddies were her family in a way because although she was married, she didn't have her own children.

I also adored Miss Delaunt. She always read beautifully to us and if we'd behaved well, we would get an extra ten minutes, which was a real treat. I used to sit there entranced with the way she told a story.

Our headmaster at primary school was Mr Goodall (from the previously mentioned song) and I've still got the Bible he gave us all when we left, signed by him. He was a good man – he alerted my mum to the fact I wasn't seeing things properly and I was sent to the eye clinic, where they found that I needed glasses very badly. I've worn them ever since and lessons were so much better when I got them.

But dear me, that first pair of specs was so clunky! It was like having a piece of wire wrapped around my head and I'd get very sore. I used to bleed because they were cutting into me. And I looked positively dreadful in them.

As soon as Joan got on in her job, she bought me a new pair which were much more comfortable.

**Jess**  Did you have a sports day? I think you'd be good at the sack race.

**Norma**  Do you really? I can't tell if you're winding me up or not.

**Jess**  Well, you can't walk so maybe if we tied you up in a sack, you'd be a bit more mobile.

**Norma**  Jessica, I can't jump either.

# SCHOOL

**Jess**  If we put a packet of Werther's at the finish line, you might just manage it.

**Norma**  I'm going to have you removed in a minute, you cheeky beggar.

But no, there was nowhere to have a sports day. We didn't have a school field, just an ordinary playground where we'd play skipping games and hopscotch. There was something about those years at infant school that was safe and warm.

**Jess**  I have great memories of being at primary school, too. Mrs Walker and Miss Oliver were my favourite teachers. Our head was Mr Bacon, and he was brilliant. If anybody got sent to Mr Bacon's office, they knew they were in trouble, but he wasn't scary.

**Norma**  You were always more than happy to go to school.

**Jess**  Do you remember when I was the lead role in the school nativity? I was the Whoops-a-Daisy Angel who kept doing things wrong and saying, 'Whoops-a-daisy!' I had a silver tinsel halo on my head and was dressed in a big white sheet. Very angelic.

**Norma**  Angelic, yes. It took the performance of a lifetime to pull that one off. We all came to watch it, and I shan't forget it. I was sitting there with everything crossed that could possibly be crossed, wishing you well. I think you were a bit nervous. You said to me, the night before, 'Am I going to be all right, Nan?' And I said, 'I'm sure you are, just try to keep calm and it'll all be fine.'

**Jess**  See, you've been there pushing me on since day one. I actually went into a pet shop recently to buy some food for my dog Joey, and the lady behind the till was an old teacher from school. She said, 'Ohh, you were Whoops-a-Daisy Angel!' She could remember!

## CHAPTER TWO

**Norma**    I'm not surprised because you were awfully good, Jess. I think it must have been a memorable performance. And you were very well behaved at primary school. I can't recall you ever getting into trouble.

**Jess**    Hmm, there was one time I was passing love notes to a lad across the class when Mrs Walker spotted what we were up to. It said something like, 'Do you want to snog in the toilets after school?' I quickly ripped it up into tiny pieces and put it in the bin before she got her hands on it and read it out to the entire class.

**Norma**    A snog in the toilets? Jessica, I despair.

**Jess**    Another thing I remember is that when you used to pick me up at home time you always said that I smelled of school.

**Norma**    In the nicest possible way. Schools have such a distinctive, nostalgic smell, don't they?

**Jess**    A bit stuffy, a bit musty with a distinct whiff of vinegar and gravy.

**Norma**    A perfect description of good memories.

**Jess**    Do you remember the hedgehog story?

**Norma**    Oh Jessica, only you.

**Jess**    When I was in year seven, we went on a school camp – I can't remember where it was, only that I hated it. I don't like camping. When we got home, me and my mum were in my bedroom and I saw this thing in the corner of the room. I let out a scream.

            There was a live hedgehog in my room. Mum had to get a neighbour to come round with these big gardening gloves so we could pick him up and set him free.

**Norma**    You must have brought him back in your rucksack.

## SCHOOL

**Jess** That's the only explanation. Otherwise how would a hedgehog have got into my bedroom? I was scared to death – he was so prickly!

**Norma** It's funny, the stories you remember when you start thinking. I have to say that I wasn't quite as happy at senior school as I had been at primary. It was quite an adjustment for me, meeting all sorts of different children. Plus, as I've already said, Miss Lee the headmistress – the one who gave me the cane – was very stern.

I hadn't passed the eleven-plus and so hadn't got into the grammar school. I'd sat the exam before I got my glasses and my poor eyesight meant I struggled to distinguish between a plus and a minus sign. Perhaps I would have got through if it hadn't been for that, I don't know. Regardless, I ended up at Hallcroft Secondary School on West Furlong.

**Jess** Was that girls only?

**Norma** It was. More's the pity.

**Jess** Nan, you do make me laugh!

**Norma** I managed the lessons OK, as long as it wasn't needlework. And I have to confess that I didn't come away with flying colours for my cooking in domestic science either.

**Jess** Tell us about your sewing, please. Just now you've mentioned it …

**Norma** Oh dear. So while my sister Joan was a very handy needlewoman and actually made a lot of my clothes, whatever sewing gene she'd been given missed the rest of us out. I remember being shamed into showing the class how long my tacking stitches were. Then the teacher made me get a ruler to measure the length of cotton I'd used in one hemming. They were three inches. Huge. I just didn't take to it. Your grandad's mother was a professional dressmaker and, when

## CHAPTER TWO

we married, he used to encourage me to try. I'd say, 'Michael, I haven't got that gift.' And it is a gift.

Betty had been exactly the same at school and she'd eventually been excused from her needlework lessons and permitted to do art instead. She was ecstatic because Betty could draw.

**Jess** Could you draw?

**Norma** Nope. The most I've ever been able to draw is a cat with a round tummy, a round head, a tail and whiskers. I've always wished I'd been blessed with some artistic or creative skills, but I'm afraid I have none. Maybe I passed them all down to your mum?

**Jess** She can turn her hand to anything, can't she? She makes me the most beautiful wreaths. The creativity gene skipped me too, sadly.

I'd have loved to have spent more time being taught needlework at school. It's a dying art. Things like that and woodwork and cookery are important life skills and should be up there with maths or English. They put so much pressure on learning algebra, which I've never used since I left school.

**Norma** If you'd had a few more cooking lessons maybe you wouldn't have burned my jacket potato that time.

**Jess** On the other hand, I was offered more choice with subjects than you, like psychology and sociology, which I went on to do at A level.

**Norma** I think I would have enjoyed learning about all that and finding out how the mind works. That might have come in handy, but obviously we didn't get the chance or have the luxury of choice. I left Hallcroft at 14, which was perfectly normal back then, and went to technical college in Worksop to do a two-year secretarial course. There were a few of us there from Retford and we had a little friendship group – me, Pam Woodward, Jean Watkinson and Gill Hopkins.

I loved the people, but I didn't feel I was in the right place. I wasn't suffering in any way; I just didn't click with the course. We learned skills like shorthand, but I don't think I caught on as quickly as the others. To me it was very confusing.

I was a bit lost at that stage and didn't really know where my future lay. I'd always wanted to be a nurse until I realised I couldn't stand the sight of blood and wouldn't have had the stomach for it.

**Jess** Maybe you just wanted to wear the sexy uniform.

**Norma** Possibly.

**Jess** Wasn't there a story about you getting into trouble for missing the train to college?

**Norma** That was the day I was unwell and so my mum had kept me at home. I was genuinely ill in bed, but someone said they'd seen me on the station platform running to try and catch the train and missing it. They said that was the real reason I was absent and I'd made it up about being poorly. It was a case of mistaken identity.

**Jess** How did you work out what had happened?

**Norma** There was a girl about my, er, 'build', shall we say …

**Jess** Are you trying to say you were quite sturdy back in the day?

**Norma** I believe they'd have called me 'curvy' nowadays. Anyway, this girl went to a college in Sheffield and she'd been the one who had missed her train. It wasn't me – it couldn't have been – but I got a severe talking to when I went back the next day and they didn't give in. I was horrified.

## CHAPTER TWO

It still rankles a bit even now because I was innocent and it was so, so unfair. Especially being such a young girl, that sort of thing stays with you.

**Jess**  Those years of your life are so formative, aren't they? It all feels so make or break and the experiences can have a lasting effect. My move to secondary school really sticks in my head, and not in a very positive way. I struggled with it like you, Nan. Everything was much more formal, from the uniform to the style of teaching, and I was immediately out of my comfort zone. I found it quite difficult to navigate, I felt uneasy and like I didn't fit in. I used to get lost around the building – it was so big. And then things started to go, well, a bit wrong.

**Norma**  They did, but none of that was your fault, Jess.

**Jess**  I went into myself at first, becoming quite shy and nervous and embarrassing easily. But later I started misbehaving and chatting back to teachers.

**Norma**  But it was a very difficult time in your life away from school. You had a lot to cope with and it was all quite traumatic. We can see that now.

**Jess**  There were several things going on at the same time and they definitely impacted those years of my life.

My dad and my mum had split up when I was two, which was tough, and my mum had met another partner, whom she had my brother Cadan with when I was seven. A couple of years after he was born, Cadan's dad brought his children from a previous marriage to live with us. Suddenly everything at home changed and became difficult. My relationship with my mum was strained and we'd often clash. I started to struggle with feelings that I didn't understand at the time, but that I now know were adrenaline and nervous energy. I'd have to get in the shower just to try and calm myself down.

## SCHOOL

I'd gone from being so happy and having had this lovely experience whilst at primary school, to everything feeling disrupted. I was really unhappy, so after a few years I made the difficult decision to move in with my dad, which meant moving away from my nan.

He had a partner and a new baby at the time, my sister, and at first it was great. I was settled and happy. But then his mum – my Nanny Margaret – passed away and dad sort of spiralled.

He stopped working, split up from his partner and I moved with him to a flat. I spent a lot of time on my own and started to experience those same feelings of anxiety and adrenaline, but again, I didn't know what they were or how to regulate my body to control them. Having felt unsettled at both my mum's and my dad's house, I started to feel as though I didn't belong anywhere unless I was with Nan. It really impacted me and my secondary school experience.

**Norma**  When you came to visit, I used to put my arm around you and rub your arms, just stroking them up and down. That helped calm you, but those times were awful. I was so frightened for you.

**Jess**  You were always my comfort, Nan. My safety and security.

Poor sleep led to poor concentration led to poor attendance at school. My moods were unpredictable and sometimes I wasn't very kind to my schoolmates. My friends never knew which Jess was going to come to school that day. Was I going to be quiet? Was I going to be snappy? Or was I going to be happy and fun? It was an awful time. I was too young to connect the dots. I had no idea that the environments around me were the root cause of all this.

**Norma**  I don't think any of us connected the dots. We didn't realise how difficult things were for you and I feel so cross with myself that we didn't pick up on it more quickly.

## CHAPTER TWO

**Jess**  Nobody picked up on it. Everybody just thought I was naughty. I didn't tell you much, Nan, because I didn't want to worry you. I'd always been capable at primary school and somewhere near to the top of the class, so it's weird that no one questioned why this previously bright kid was all of a sudden dropping grades, chatting back to the teachers and getting detentions.

But despite everything, I managed to get my GCSEs. I got Cs and above in every subject and even managed an A star in history. Nan's support helped push me through, and something else did too – I think at least part of it was a determination not to have the same life as my parents. I'd seen my dad in and out of work and my mum graft so hard only to scrape by. I knew I wanted more for myself. So I'd stay back after school and catch up on revision.

**Norma**  You did brilliantly and I was so proud of you. What you managed to achieve despite everything you had to contend with was nothing short of marvellous.

**Jess**  I stayed on to do my A levels and my psychology teacher Mr Simpson noticed there was something wrong. He was the first person at school to ask about what was going on at home and I ended up telling him about everything.

As a teacher, Mr Simpson was quite scary and strict, but now I saw a different side to him and realised he was actually really kind. Things had become so normalised that I was worried if I told anyone they would think I didn't have anything to complain about, but Mr Simpson understood. He showed me empathy and made me feel heard.

After living at my dad's off and on for three or four years, I ended up moving back to live with my mum full time. I was about 17 by that point, Cadan's dad had left and Nan was just around the corner. Things were still rocky, and I needed to

## SCHOOL

|||
|---|---|
| | stay on an extra year to complete my psychology, sociology, and health and social care A levels, but I did it. |
| Norma | As things became more stable, you blossomed. You really did. We'd been so worried that you would struggle to get your grades and then find it hard to get work, but now you had such a bright future ahead of you. |
| Jess | When life was chaotic and uncertain, I still saw Nan regularly and she was my rock. She has loved me unconditionally throughout everything, even when I was, at times, speaking to her not very nicely. Because I could be so rude to you sometimes, couldn't I? |
| Norma | You were in quite a bad place, love. You were very troubled at that time and we were all concerned about you. |
| Jess | No matter what happened, Nan was patient and loving. I'd walk through her front door and feel like I was at home. Everything that happened during those years is a massive part of our story and goes a long way to explaining why we are so close. It has shaped us and our relationship and made our bond unbreakable. |

INTERLUDE

# Our favourites

### Favourite film?

Norma    *Gone with the Wind*. A real weepie but I've always loved it.

Jess    *Pretty Woman*. That shopping scene! 'Big mistake. Big. Huge.' I've lost count of the number of times I've watched it.

### Favourite book?

Norma    *Rebecca* by Daphne du Maurier. Sad and haunting but captivating and beautifully written. I've read it again and again.

Jess    I've recently read *Verity* by Colleen Hoover and loved it. As a kid it was *The Magic Faraway Tree* by Enid Blyton.

### Favourite musical?

Norma    I'm not mad on musicals but I did see a show in Paris called *Waltzes from Vienna*, which was the story of Strauss and was very pleasurable. It was all in French so I didn't know what they were talking about, but the music was beautiful.

Jess    I went to see *Billy Elliot* in the West End and absolutely loved it.

# INTERLUDE

### **Favourite singer?**

Norma     I do love Westlife's version of 'You Raise Me Up'. It's an absolutely wonderful piece of music and it makes my heart soar when I hear it. I also listen to a lot of Alfie Boe and Susan Boyle. Susan has such a calming, pure voice.

Jess     I've got a really varied taste. I've been to see Adele live – I absolutely adore her. I love music from the noughties, especially R&B. I'm a huge fan of N-Dubz and have been since they started out.

### **Favourite meal?**

Norma     My mum's Sunday roast. It will never be beaten.

Jess     Anything Japanese. Obsessed.

CHAPTER THREE

# Love

**Norma**     For me, being in love is a wonderful kind of warm feeling.

**Jess**     Yes! It feels fuzzy but also comfortable and safe. You don't think about anyone else. You can't think about anyone else!

When Jake used to pick me up to go on dates, I'd forget about everything else in the world.

Even now when he goes away, I count down the days till he comes home. I think about him before I go to sleep, when I wake up and throughout the day.

**Norma**     Can you spare a little place for me as well?

**Jess**     I have no choice but to think about you!

**Norma**     Those butterflies in your tummy come with the first flush of love. It takes a very special kind of love to last throughout the decades, like me and your grandad. We were married for over 40 years before he passed. The key ingredient for a long and happy marriage, I believe, is trust. It's the be all and end all. Without trust, there's no hope.

**Jess**     Laughter is really important, too. If you can make each other laugh, you can get through a helluva lot together.

**Norma**     Very true, and communication is another one. You should never let the sun go down on your anger. In other words, don't get mardy and turn your head away – keep talking and sort your nonsense out.

## CHAPTER THREE

**Jess** And I'd add compromise to all of the above. There has to be give and take and that's something me and Jake are good at.

**Norma** Does the giving mean allowing that lad a day off from you now and again to recuperate?

**Jess** Don't give me that, Nan! Jake is on the golf course more often than you have marmalade on toast.

**Norma** It all comes down to sharing your problems and always being there for one another. And I think I was extremely lucky because I had all of that and so much more with Michael during our 41 wonderful years of marriage. I only wish it could have gone on a bit longer.

**Jess** I was only seven when Grandad passed away, but what I do remember is that the two of you went everywhere together. Anything I was doing with you, I was also doing with Grandad. You both made the most of every minute you had with each other.

**Norma** The only time we were apart was when he took his weekly trip to the junk market on a Friday, which I had no interest in.

**Jess** Grandad made sure that you were comfortable in every aspect and I find the love you had for each other pretty inspirational. The only thing that mattered to him was your happiness and providing for his family.

**Norma** He had good, strong values, which all came from his upbringing, and he was on the lookout for me the whole time without ever being overbearing or finicky. And he was so kind. If we were ever shopping in town and I saw a dress I liked, he'd say, 'Norma, if you want it, let's just get it.'

**Jess** You were spoiled, basically!

**Norma** I was. But I'd only ever wanted Michael. I'd had the odd one or two boyfriends before he came along, but nothing serious.

He was my first love and I've been on my own since he died in 2004. I couldn't imagine so much as looking at another man and there has never been anything drawing me to anyone else. Lucky for them, eh?

Jess  You and Grandad never used to argue.

Norma  We sometimes had different opinions, but we didn't row. If I felt strongly about something I'd say, 'I'm sorry, Michael, I just don't agree with you,' and we'd talk it over. I can't remember him ever raising his voice to me. There's not a day goes by when I don't think of him.

We met in a club on Christmas Eve in 1960. I was 26 – he was a little older at 30 – and when I say club, it wasn't like the clubs as you know them, Jess. It was a lovely, big hotel in Retford – very smart – and it was run by Michael's boss at Clark's Dyeworks, where he was in charge of a department that dealt with washing machines that weren't working properly. Clark's was a huge employer round these parts.

Jess  What we've realised since is that you and Grandad must have crossed paths when you were younger because you went to schools that were right next to each other.

Norma  Yes, he went to the National School, which was opposite Grove Street Primary. So, you could say that he was right under my nose all along.

Jess  That's a bit like me and Jake. He was three years above me at school, but I always knew who he was. Jake was what you'd call the 'It' boy: into his sport, hugely popular, very good looking. He would get the same school bus as me and I thought he was completely gorgeous, but never in a million years did I think I'd stand a chance. I was a bit of an ugly duckling at school, wasn't I?

Norma  Less of an ugly duckling, more of a tiresome little monkey.

## CHAPTER THREE

**Jess**  Whatever. I just admired him from afar. It wasn't until several years after we'd both left school that things happened.

**Norma**  Life has a funny way of doing that, doesn't it? I'd probably walked past your grandad many times when we were youngsters, never knowing he would be my future husband. That's just given me a little tingle.

**Jess**  Who approached who on that first night you and Grandad met?

**Norma**  One of my friends, Niff Burton, who worked at the post office, introduced us and, while I'm not saying it was love at first sight, we had a drink and a chat and it was all very pleasant. With it being Christmas Eve, there was a lot of music and dancing and high spirits, but I promise you I wasn't looking around to see if I could pick anyone up.

**Jess**  So it wasn't a swingers' party?

**Norma**  Absolutely not.

**Jess**  I bet you played hard to get.

**Norma**  I wouldn't know quite how to do that, Jessica. But I thought he was a very nice chap and I saw him again a week later on New Year's Eve. I met him in a local pub, the Chequers, for a drink before heading back to the club together where we all used to gather.

We talked some more over a glass or two and we must have liked each other because the following week he rang me at work to ask me out. At the time, I was in charge of the GPO telephone exchange – that was my job – and one of the telephonists took the call, saying, 'Yes, I'll put you through,' while grinning at me.

It was Michael on the end of the line asking if I'd like to go to the cinema. Of course I accepted. He came to pick me up in his car and we drove to the Odeon in Doncaster. Don't ask me what we saw because I've racked my brains and I can't remember. I do know that I didn't think much of the film, but I was rather taken with Michael.

**Jess**   Did he make you feel young and excited?

**Norma**   How excited do you mean, Jessica?

**Jess**   I mean did he make you feel giddy inside?

**Norma**   Oh, no, no, no! We weren't like that. It was a different time, Jess, we didn't do that sort of thing. Our courting days were quite plain – they weren't what you'd describe as 'hot'. We used to go over to Derbyshire a lot and have a nice drink together in a pub. We also liked visiting Nostell Priory, which is a stately home between Doncaster and Wakefield.

But while I wouldn't use the word 'giddy', whenever he was coming to pick me up, I'd be looking at the clock and I'd feel all nervous if he was a bit late. I always looked forward to seeing him. He made me feel comfortable. Your grandad was comfortable. I like comfy men.

**Jess**   Comfy men! I love it! When did it get, ahem ... interesting?

**Norma**   When we got married in 1962.

**Jess**   Nan, you little minx!

**Norma**   He was reliable and dependable and the whole family approved of him. My mother liked him very much although when he took me out for the evening, she never settled until I was home safely. I remember one night after Michael and I had been courting for quite a while – in fact I think we were actually engaged and planning the wedding by this point – I arrived home and shouted upstairs, 'I'm in, Mum!'

She called back, 'Oh Norma, you *are* late!'

# CHAPTER THREE

Do you know what time it was? Quarter to 11. Can you believe that? I was hardly tearing round the streets in the early hours.

**Jess** I love that you and Grandad got together in a very traditional way, meeting on a night out and then slowly getting to know each other. That's almost medieval in today's world of dating apps and social media.

**Norma** That's how everyone got together back then. You met or were introduced and had a drink and a dance. Not that you'd ever catch your grandad on a dancefloor, he'd much rather be sitting down with a quiet drink, but you get what I mean.

I remember the American airmen who were based at Scofton, which was about ten miles away, would approach the girls very confidently.

'You dancin'?' they would ask.

'You askin'?'

'I'm askin'.'

'We're dancin'.'

And away they went.

**Jess** And did you ever dance with one of them?

**Norma** No. They never asked me. Probably for the best, given the things I heard about those American boys.

**Jess** That whole 'you dancin'?' chat-up-line routine seems so old-fashioned and lovely. Is 'quaint' the right word? A world away from how people approach others now on Tinder!

**Norma** Tinder ... Remind me how that works.

**Jess** OK, it's a dating app and you see a series of photos of people on your phone and alongside that is a bit of information

# LOVE

        telling you more about the person. You swipe one way if you're interested, and the other way if you're not. If you've both swiped that you're interested, you get a 'match' and then you're able to start communicating with each other.

**Norma**    Isn't that clever?

**Jess**    Are you saying you'd like me to sign you up?

**Norma**    If you think we could find someone who likes hearing aids, false teeth and dodgy knees.

**Jess**    Nan, there's someone for everyone out there.

**Norma**    Is that how you and Jake found each other?

**Jess**    No, it wasn't through a dating app, but we did sort of get together through social media. It was in the summer of 2020 and one of my friends was seeing one of Jake's friends. Jake had followed my friend on Instagram and having seen me on her stories and posts, he requested to follow me.

**Norma**    You've lost me already.

**Jess**    I can remember ringing my best friend saying, 'You'll never guess who's just requested to follow me? Jake Scott from school!'

        Obviously, I accepted straight away and followed him back. A few weeks later it was my birthday and he messaged me asking if I'd had a good day. Well, that was my birthday made. I was absolutely buzzing. I thought Jake was way out of my league, I couldn't believe he'd even messaged me. The conversation moved from Instagram to Snapchat – how cringe – and then to WhatsApp.

        To cut a long story short, he eventually said he'd love to go for a drink one time if I fancied it. I mean, did I *fancy* it? Are you kidding me? That's when I realised, OMG I'm in here!

## CHAPTER THREE

But we were both not long out of relationships and neither of us was looking for anything serious.

Norma   I remember you telling me there was a boy you'd known years ago from school who was absolutely gorgeous, he'd asked you out but didn't want anything serious. You said to me: 'Do you think I should go, Nan?'

Jess   And you said, 'You go, love. When he realises what you're like, he will want something serious.'

Norma   And I was right, wasn't I?

Jess   You're rarely wrong. Before the date, I was pacing the floor. I was so nervous. I had a dickie tummy from the nerves and by the time Jake came to pick me up, my legs were weak and I was shaking.

Norma   It was Doncaster he took you to for that first date, wasn't it? Same as me and your grandad.

Jess   Yes. We went to Urban Burger, got some food and sat outside on a bit of grass, where we talked and talked. Before we knew it, it was dark and we'd been there for hours.

My friend had been watching where I was on the Find My Friends app, so she knew it was going well. She messaged me saying: 'You've had the best night ever, haven't you?' And I had.

Norma   I think you fell for him on that first day out, love.

Jess   I was definitely walking on air. The way he treated me and spoke to me, I'd never had that from a boy before. I just felt so comfortable with him and he made me feel really looked after. He still does. He'll get the door for me; he pulls my chair out for me; if we're walking together on the pavement he makes sure he's on the outside and I'm on the inside.

Norma   That's just extra special, isn't it? Chivalry. You don't get a lot of that in this day and age, not like in years gone by.

Jess    I love the little things that Jake does for me, but not all women want to be 'looked after' in the same way as they were in your day, Nan. I'm quite happy to not be considered the 'fairer sex'. Until it comes to the 'boy jobs'. Picking up the dog poo and dealing with the bins are boy jobs. If there's anything heavy to lift or we need to get something down from the loft, that's a boy job. And before we had our artificial grass put down, mowing the lawn was a boy job too.

Norma    You'd best stop there, Jess, otherwise Jake will twig that he's got the raw end of the deal here.

Jess    Good point. I'm pretty happy with the arrangement we've got! I'm all for Girl Power …

Norma    … Until the bins need taking out.

Jess    You said it! In all seriousness, I have always felt as though Jake is a little too good to be true. He was really popular and I'd always assumed that men like him would be players or really full of themselves. I worried that it would all come crashing down and I'd discover he wasn't really interested, but he was the complete opposite. It just got better and better and I started to understand that this was real.

I kept a diary of that time, because I knew this was significant.

Norma    That diary sounds interesting.

Jess    There's hot stuff in there. Trust me, Nan, you do NOT want to read it.

Norma    It might give me some ideas.

Jess    Nan, you'd have a heart attack if you saw what's in there. But I was head over heels. Jake was just everything I could have wished for in a partner but never believed existed.

Norma    Every woman deserves a bit of romance.

## CHAPTER THREE

**Jess**  Was Grandad romantic?

**Norma**  I suppose he was, in a certain sort of way, because of the care that he took of me. Anything that needed doing in the house, he'd sort.

'I tell you what, Norma,' he'd say, 'you could do with another shelf in this kitchen.' And he'd go out to his shed, make it and then put it up. He would spot little things to make my life easier and he'd fix them.

**Jess**  But he didn't used to put flower petals on the bed or anything?

**Norma**  Oh no, nothing like that. Although when your uncle was born, he bought me some beautiful red roses.

**Jess**  Ah see, now that's romantic!

**Norma**  And when your mum came along four years later, he bought me a heated tray so I could warm the baby bottles. Make of that what you will.

**Jess**  Did he at least get down on one knee to propose?

**Norma**  No, and I've often thought about this. I think marriage was a decision we came to between us; there was no grand gesture of a proposal. It was just a lovely time and we grew into each other in a funny sort of way.

Michael put the money down for a mortgage and I was able to claim a marriage dowry from my employer, the General Post Office. Back then you could choose whether to take a dowry – which was a one-off lump sum – or have a pension and I chose the money because we had a new house which we needed to furnish. We bought some beautiful new furniture from Eyres in Worksop.

**Jess**  That's a posh one!

**Norma**    Isn't it just? It meant we had a house ready to move into once we were married. Because of course, we didn't live together until we were wed.

**Jess**    That wasn't the done thing at all, was it? Jake and I live together now. How do you feel about the fact that we're not married?

**Norma**    That's just how it is these days. I would never have tried to stop you, what would be the point? And it probably helps couples learn of each other's faults and stops some from pursuing the relationship any further before they become legally bound.

**Jess**    Exactly: try before you buy. Surely it's healthy to live together first because marriage is such a serious commitment and you should really know the person beforehand. Sharing a home will make some people realise, 'Flippin' 'eck, I can't cope with this!'

**Norma**    I do believe that you need to summer and winter with a man before you truly know him.

**Jess**    That's one of your mantras. It tickles me, but I reckon there's a lot of truth in it.

**Norma**    I still have mixed feelings about 'living in sin', if I'm quite honest. But you and Jake ended up living with me at one point, so it's obviously not something I feel too strongly about any more.

**Jess**    That was a lifesaver for us. After me and Jake had been together for about a year we decided to start saving for a place of our own. We stopped going out drinking, cut down on spending and put as much money aside as we could. I'd lost count of the number of houses we went to view – it was post-lockdown when the market was going crazy and so in the end we decided to go with a new build. While we were

## CHAPTER THREE

waiting for it to be built, Jake moved in with me at my mum's and I'm not going to lie, there were 'challenges' with the new living arrangements.

**Norma** You and your mum had some right humdingers, didn't you? I don't think it ever works with two women in the kitchen.

**Jess** About three weeks before we were due to complete on the house we were buying, I had an almighty bust-up with Mum. Me and Jake packed our bags and turned up at Nan's until we moved into our own place.

Jake can't do any wrong in Nan's eyes. If I'm ever annoyed at him, she'll say, 'What you two have got is good and you need to look after it.'

**Norma** He's a good lad, that one. You make sure you look after him.

**Jess** He could go out and probably murder someone and you would tell me to give him a break.

**Norma** Well, he's got to have someone sticking up for him to make up for all your demands!

**Jess** That's outrageous, Nan! Would you like to see me and Jake get married?

**Norma** I would love to see that, but obviously I keep my mouth shut. And I wouldn't say anything at all in front of Jake.

**Jess** We don't want to put any pressure on him, do we? It's funny because when I was younger I used to dream of the big white wedding, the beautiful dress and the massive party. But now, if me and Jake ran away together and it was just the two of us, I wouldn't give a monkey's, because us being together is what's important to me. I'd love to get married to him, but I'm not desperate for it.

**Norma** So you've not put a little bag of confetti on the breakfast table yet? Hint, hint …

# LOVE

**Jess**     If we never got married, I wouldn't be rocking in a corner. I don't feel the need to prove anything.

**Norma**     Some young people go ahead and then a year later they're divorced or with another partner. That's terribly sad.

**Jess**     Do you think people are too fickle and give up too easily today?

**Norma**     I do. People can be awfully flighty and sometimes they start looking around and eyeing everybody else up, wondering if they might find something better. People think the grass is greener. They'll have someone one night and somebody else the next.

**Jess**     Sometimes they have more than one person in the same night!

**Norma**     Do me a favour, Jess. I should be worn out.

**Jess**     I reckon a lot of relationships fall down now because of social media.

**Norma**     You do hear a lot of that. You've told me stories of people rekindling old romances on Facebook and whatnot and leaving behind partners and families because they reckon they're onto something new and exciting.

**Jess**     I take it you've never slid into anybody's DMs, Nan?

**Norma**     What's a DM when it's at home?

**Jess**     A direct message on social media. It's a way of approaching someone you've got your eye on.

**Norma**     I don't think so. Not knowingly, anyway. What I'm saying is everyone wants things yesterday instead of being patient and waiting for tomorrow. I'm only surmising, but people seem less willing to put the time, effort and communication into making a marriage work. A marriage is an adventure. Every marriage will have its ups and downs, but that's all part of the lovely journey.

## CHAPTER THREE

**Jess**     But maybe in the past, people were forced to stay in unhappy marriages because divorce was so frowned upon.

**Norma**     Unfortunately, I think they did. I know of a married couple who continued to live in the same house but never spoke a word to each other and it was awful. That's no way to live a life.

**Jess**     What was your wedding day like?

**Norma**     We married on 27 August 1962 at half past midday at St Saviour's Church in Retford. We had 40 guests – I had made a silly mistake with the invitations because I ordered one for every person, forgetting that most people came as a pair. I did feel sheepish when I realised! More than 60 years on, I've still got a whole box of unwritten invitations … you can have them for your wedding if you like! We can just cross mine and your grandad's names out and replace them with yours and Jake's.

**Jess**     I might take you up on that. Wedding invitations are eye-wateringly expensive nowadays.

**Norma**     Some weddings today I've heard can cost as much as £15,000.

**Jess**     And the rest, Nan! The wedding industry is a huge business. We found the receipts from your wedding recently, didn't we? The prices are crazy compared to now.

**Norma**     I paid just £2 for both bouquets. Mine was pink roses and our bridesmaid – Michael's sister Caroline, who was only 14 – carried a posy of sweet peas. I'd have preferred camelias, but the chap at the nursery said it would be impossible trying to get hold of them.

**Jess**     A few years ago, a family member had Nan's wedding photos, which had been black and white, converted into colour and I love flicking through that album and seeing how smart everyone looked. Especially the ladies in their twinsets. Nan's mum has some beautiful gloves which match her bag.

**Norma**   Yes, the colour brings it all back to life and means you can see everyone's outfits properly. I wore a lovely rich cream, heavy satin gown made by Michael's mother, who I mentioned earlier was a professional dressmaker.

**Jess**   Do you remember how you felt in your wedding dress?

**Norma**   It was a bit unreal, as if I was floating. I'd been to get my hair done in the morning and my makeup was just a bit of powder on top of my moisturiser.

**Jess**   Astral, no doubt.

**Norma**   Don't you scoff, Jessica. You've been glad enough of my Astral in the past and your mother has, too. It's a lovely cream, you can't beat it.

**Jess**   Did you all have a big party to celebrate afterwards?

**Norma**   We had a small buffet reception in a hotel on Queen Street and my mum bought some cooked chickens from the butcher for people to eat after Michael and I had left for our honeymoon.

There was no such thing as an 'evening do' like people have now where they carry on long into the night.

**Jess**   It was the norm for the bride and groom to go off on their honeymoon straight after the ceremony, wasn't it?

**Norma**   Yes, later the same day. After the buffet, Michael and I went to my mum's to change into our honeymoon outfits and we headed off on a three-day holiday.

We drove to Harrogate to start with and then on to Barnard Castle, where we stayed in a hotel. The following day we moved to Wensleydale and then to the Wild Boar Hotel in Kendal. We finished up in Morecambe before heading back to Retford and moving into our first home together on Harewood Avenue.

## CHAPTER THREE

When we arrived back and parked outside, we saw that the girls I worked with had decorated our front gate with streamers and all sorts. Michael wasn't thrilled about it, I have to say. He didn't moan, but he told me to stay in the car and he didn't half move it quick.

**Jess**     He wasn't like that, was he? Grandad wasn't a big showy person. He preferred a quiet life.

**Norma**     He never asked for much and he definitely didn't like a fuss.

**Jess**     He was very regimented.

**Norma**     A lot of people were like that back then. His father had died when he was 19 and he'd also done his national service, so there were reasons for him being that way.

**Jess**     Your first home together, though. How exciting! Although I bet your mum missed you when you moved out.

**Norma**     I still saw her all the time because we weren't too far away, just a couple of miles. She would get the bus to our place and I'd bike over if I was going to her. Until I had the children, that is. I couldn't really pop them in the bike basket.

But, you're right, she definitely felt it because I was the last one to go. She'd packed my suitcase for me before I left and when I opened it, she'd placed my favourite dolly Topsy on the top of all my clothes. I've still got her. She has two arms that don't match and one leg wider than the other. Poor little Topsy. I can't bring myself to put her in the dustbin.

**Jess**     You can't ever get rid of Topsy, Nan! She's not fit to be seen but you have to keep her.

**Norma**     She was my reminder of home. Although obviously I had a new home now with Michael and he was my safety, my security.

**Jess**     That's how I feel about Jake. I've never felt so protected

|       |                                                                                                                                                                                                                                                                                                                                                                                                                                                                                   |
|-------|---------------------------------------------------------------------------------------------------------------------------------------------------------------------------------------------------------------------------------------------------------------------------------------------------------------------------------------------------------------------------------------------------------------------------------------------------------------------------------------------------|
|       | before. I can be fully myself around him with no judgement at all, he's so supportive and caring. And we're pretty much inseparable.                                                                                                                                                                                                                                                                                                                                                              |
| Norma | Just like your grandad and me.                                                                                                                                                                                                                                                                                                                                                                                                                                                                    |
| Jess  | We'd been dating for a few months when Jake told me he loved me for the first time. He'd taken me to Leeds to celebrate my graduation and he'd paid for a hotel for the night – I'd never been taken out and treated like that before. I'd bought him a Thomas Sabo bracelet with the date of our first date engraved in it – he still wears it every day – and although this all sounds super-romantic, the truth is we were both really bladdered. I'd had one too many porn star martinis. |
| Norma | Excuse me?                                                                                                                                                                                                                                                                                                                                                                                                                                                                                        |
| Jess  | It's a drink, Nan, don't worry! I didn't turn into a porn star.                                                                                                                                                                                                                                                                                                                                                                                                                                   |
| Norma | I think we can all be thankful for that. I do know what a martini is. I used to rather like them.                                                                                                                                                                                                                                                                                                                                                                                                 |
| Jess  | Anyway, we'd been hammering the two-for-one cocktails and I can't remember how I worded it, but I said there was nothing I'd change about him other than our relationship status … So I basically asked him to be my boyfriend.                                                                                                                                                                                                                                                                   |
| Norma | Did you really? He didn't manage to think up an excuse quick enough, then.                                                                                                                                                                                                                                                                                                                                                                                                                        |
| Jess  | He turned around to me and said, 'What would you say if I told you I loved you?' And I replied, 'I'd say that I loved you too.' We both burst into tears and that was it.                                                                                                                                                                                                                                                                                                                         |
| Norma | I remember when I met Jake for the first time. We went for a meal, all the family together, and I told him that it would have been my 58th wedding anniversary the next day. He was very shy and reserved, which I think is an asset in this day and age.                                                                                                                                                                                                                                        |

# CHAPTER THREE

**Jess**  He was sooooo nervous because I'd told him how important you were to me and he knew all about our relationship and our bond. He'd met my mum, my dad and my brother and he was fine with them, but he was really eaten up about meeting you.

I remember him saying to me before that meal, 'What shall I wear? Will your nan be offended if I wear a cap?'

I said, 'Just be you.'

**Norma**  I thought his quietness was lovely. I don't care for people who are loud and try to dominate. He was polite and he listened and he had a lot of time for me. He's so caring and thoughtful and what he does for me is wonderful.

**Jess**  Watching the amount of effort Jake puts in with my family and especially with Nan is incredibly special. It's never been any bother to him that I come with a bit of baggage – that baggage being Norma.

**Norma**  Charming.

**Jess**  He doesn't only take it in his stride, he actually embraces it.

**Norma**  It's not very often that you get a young man who would be bothered with their girlfriend's nan. I don't think many people find what you've found with Jake.

**Jess**  When I met Jake, I realised what true love was for the first time. I think because neither of us had been looking for a relationship, our guards were down from the start and we were really open with each other about our pasts. We told each other everything and it didn't hurt us to hear it. With hindsight, that was a really important thing to do because it meant there was nothing to come out of the woodwork and we both knew each other inside out.

## LOVE

I've always known exactly where I stand with Jake and he's made it clear that I'm his priority – it's such a comforting feeling not to be constantly doubting and questioning yourself or analysing everything to death. I'm no longer clinging on to a few tiny positive crumbs in the hope that things will come good because with Jake, it's all positive. He just makes me so happy.

He's just a brilliant influence on every part of my life. He knows exactly what to do when I get anxious about things. I don't know where he gets the patience from.

**Norma**  Somebody must be paying him.

**Jess**  Is it you?

**Norma**  No comment.

## INTERLUDE
# A word from Jake ...

On our very first date back in the summer of 2020, Jess told me how close she was to her nan. We spoke for hours and hours on that date and by the end of it, I knew all about Norma.

But I didn't truly understand the strength of their bond until I saw them together in person.

What they have is unique. They are everything to each other and are the best of friends – even more than that – and I've never known a relationship like it.

So I've been fully aware of the family dynamic from the beginning and I'm absolutely fine playing second fiddle to Norma. Actually, these days, in terms of the pecking order I'd say I'm even below Joey, the dog!

We could be on the most luxurious holiday somewhere, but after three or four days Jess is itching to get back to Norma. She never likes to leave her for long because she misses her too much.

I knew I'd fallen for Jess on that first date. She was so down to earth and didn't mince her words, which I loved – she gets that from Norma. It was like she wanted to know exactly who I was, there and then, to cut out any of the nonsense so that we both knew where we stood from the get-go.

It all felt so easy and light. It's still like that now and has been all the way through.

It was a few months after me and Jess started seeing each other before I met Norma for the first time. I don't generally get nervous about anything ... but this? This was different. I was SO anxious because I had built it up so much in my head.

By this time, Jess had told me all about her past and I knew that from losing her grandad and through all the challenges she'd

# INTERLUDE

overcome as a teenager, Norma was her backstop. She was the one Jess relied on and shared everything with.

So I knew if there was anybody in Jess's life I had to impress, it was definitely Norma, and I couldn't screw this up.

I needn't have worried. Norma lived up to all the hype and all my expectations – she was exactly as Jess had said she'd be: kind, funny and sharp as a tack. She asked me lots of questions about my life, but it wasn't like a grilling. She was just genuinely interested and a great talker.

She's phenomenally quick. I come from a sporting background where there's a lot of banter and walking the line with what you say to each other and that's how Norma is. Especially with Jess. She's blunt and has no filter; good, bad or ugly, she'll say it, which cracks me up.

I remember we were all playing Articulate! at Christmas – the game where you have to describe different categorised words from a card. Jess's mum and brother were on a team together and Kate was trying to explain the action word 'falling'.

'What happens if you go over the end of a cliff?' she said to Cadan. 'What are you doing?'

Cadan had no idea.

Without flinching, Norma, who had been quietly listening in the background, piped up, 'You're dead.'

It was quick as a flash and we all collapsed laughing. We often say we need CCTV set up everywhere because the funniest moments are always the ones we don't manage to catch on camera.

But it doesn't half wind Jess up when her nan asks, 'Have you made that lad a cup of coffee yet?' or 'You'd best get home and get Jake's tea on the table'. It's just the era she comes from – I know Norma sides with me and it's become a running joke now.

As well as providing the humour, she's also a very calming influence. She instinctively knows when there's something to be said and when she needs to sit back and listen instead.

Jess has so many of her nan's traits and mannerisms. Sometimes she'll do something small, like push her glasses up on her nose a certain way, and I'll go, 'Oh my God, I'm dating Norma!'

## A WORD FROM JAKE ...

Most of all, though, it's their caring natures that make them like two peas in a pod, and the fact that they struggle to put themselves before anyone else. I've never met anybody as selfless and as caring as Jess.

Not just with Norma, she's the same with everybody. She's always thinking of other people and makes a hell of a lot of sacrifices.

Jess was constantly capturing moments with her nan way before @JessandNorma and the social media stuff started. I'd seen the bits and pieces about their relationship that Jess was putting on her private Snapchat and always thought it was funny. I remember in the early days of us dating, we compared how many pictures we had on our phones and hers was about ten times the number of mine – all of her nan.

The first time I ever twigged that they were taking off, we were in H&M. I jumped on the escalator, chatting away to Jess, only to realise halfway up that she wasn't standing behind me. She was still at the bottom, talking to a girl who I assumed she must know. But then I saw the girl get her phone and take a selfie of them together, which I thought was really weird.

When Jess eventually joined me at the top of the escalator and I asked her who the girl was, she said it was someone who followed her and Norma on TikTok and had asked for a photo. That was mad to me.

These days it's pretty normal for us to get stopped when we're out and about but it's still just as surreal.

As me and Jess got more serious as a couple and I spent more time with the family, I started to appear in more of the videos. Sometimes I'd be in the background helping out, other times I'd be part of the conversation between Jess and Norma. Soon people started asking about me and our relationship.

And so we created our joint page @jessandjakeofficial. Over time, we shared bits about ourselves and gradually it became a career for me too. It wasn't ever expected or planned for, but Jess was needing an extra pair of hands to ease her workload, so I stepped in.

In April 2024 I quit work as an electrician, saying to my employer

## INTERLUDE

that I could still be available for ad hoc work here and there. But within a month and a half, things had taken off in the most amazing, unbelievable way. I've never returned to my old job.

We are financially comfortable, but it's not about the money for either of us. It's much more the freedom it's given us and the ability to manage our own time and spend it doing the things that are important to us. For Jess, that means time with Norma.

We all get so many messages from people telling us how the two of them are a reminder of what they have or had with their own grandparents. People also say that watching Jess and Norma has inspired them to see more of and speak more to their older relatives.

Funnily enough, they've done that for me, too. I moved out and away from home when I was 16 for football, which meant that I drifted from my own family. Seeing Jess with her nan has had a huge impact on me and encouraged me to forge closer ties with them, which I'm really happy about.

I wish I'd got to meet Norma's husband, Michael. I feel like I know him, though, through memories Jess and Norma have shared and from seeing all his things that are still in the house. Some of his stuff in the garage or the shed hasn't been touched since he passed away, and I'm a bit like a kid in a toy shop looking at all his tools. I think we'd have got on well.

I also think, from what I've been told, that Michael would have had a lot in common with my own grandad ... He was a very hands-on and outdoorsy kind of person and people have always said how similar I am to him.

We lost him in a car crash about 30 years ago when I was just a baby. I was in the car too although obviously I have no memory of it. My nan's mum and the family dog were also killed – me and my nan survived.

The tragedy was obviously life-changing for my whole family and it took a lot of resilience to get everyone through. It was also a lesson in just how cruel life can be.

Jess and Norma understand that too, which means we all appreciate what we have and hold on to it that little bit tighter.

## A WORD FROM JAKE ...

*People always bang on about wanting to retire and slow down and live a quiet life, but I think Norma has shown everyone that you can carry on learning and continue to have a purpose, no matter what your age. Pushing yourself and keeping the mind busy can have huge benefits and add years to your life, so you're not just sitting wasting away with nothing to do.*

*Since starting their online platform, I've seen such a big change in Norma. She's still the witty, super-aware woman she always was, but it's almost like she's got younger. It seems to have taken years off her. I genuinely believe that this has prolonged Norma's good health.*

*Jess is careful about how much content they film, mindful not to push her nan or tire her out. It's Norma who will say, 'Come on, we need to go and speak to TikTok!'*

*We don't think too far into the future, but Jess is who she is because of Norma and she will never change. And so, whenever the time comes that Norma is no longer with us, she will live on through Jess and our kids and our grandkids after them.*

*The generations to come are going to experience Norma through Jess.*

*There is so much Jess does behind the scenes that goes unseen by most people, but I see it. I know how amazing she is every day.*

*I'm so proud of her and to be part of this incredible journey.*

CHAPTER FOUR

# Family and Friends

**Norma**  The feeling you have when you're with your family is one that can't be replicated anywhere else. It's a unique sort of comfort, a connection and a sense of belonging.

**Jess**  Families aren't always easy to navigate, though. They come in all different shapes and sizes, especially these days, and they can often be difficult and fragile. We're a prime example of that, aren't we? Our family isn't conventional and a lot of our relationships are quite complicated and messy.

**Norma**  That's true – and families don't come with a handbook either, unfortunately. Ours is a bit of a tangled web. But family has always been the most important part of my life and I have tried my best to be here for all of you whenever you've needed me.

**Jess**  You always tell us that if we ever have a problem, we have to come to you. And we generally do!

**Norma**  That's my job, Jess. I wouldn't like any of my family to deal with a sadness in their life that I haven't known about.

**Jess**  Our family has held it together through some pretty stormy times because Nan has been at the core. Her values and integrity are the very essence of all of us. She is our role model, our moral compass and our rock.

She's taught us to be polite and kind, to be grateful for the simple things in life, and that spending time with family and making memories together is what counts the most.

# CHAPTER FOUR

**Norma**  Family is the basis of living and I'm never happier than when I have all of mine around me. When any of them goes away, even if it's just for a few days' holiday, I do nothing but fret until they're home. I get that from my mum, who was exactly the same.

**Jess**  You like all your chicks in the nest. The last time my mum went away, I didn't hear the end of it with you sitting here planning and scheming in your head. 'Well, her flight was at nine, so she'll have just got to the airport … '

Five minutes later: 'I expect she'll be going through security now … what time do you think they'll be boarding?' It was constant!

**Norma**  Well, families aren't just for Christmas, are they? And even if they're a bit tiresome, you have to grit your teeth and put up with it.

**Jess**  Er, is that a reference to me?

**Norma**  Not specifically. You're all capable of being a bit tiresome now and again, believe me, but I still love you the same. And you're right when you say families can often be challenging and keeping them together sometimes requires patience and understanding, but I do feel exceedingly lucky with my lot. Some of my friends only receive someone every fortnight and I think that must be so hard.

**Jess**  We're lucky to have you too. The love and affection you've given all of us is at the heart of everything.

**Norma**  That's because I have loved being your grandmother. I always loved being a mum, too, there's absolutely nothing like it. I don't think there's a sweeter smell than when you nuzzle your nose in a baby's neck. As long as they haven't done a doo-dah in their nappy, that is.

I'm not saying motherhood was a breeze. It could be hard

| | |
|---|---|
| | – especially with your mum because she was a colicky baby who never stopped screaming. |
| Jess | I think my mum still has colic now! |
| Norma | She has her moments. Your mum was a very bright little girl, though. |
| Jess | Er, what happened in the years since?! |
| Norma | You'll be in trouble when she reads this! What I mean is she could make a game out of anything and was just as happy playing on her own as she was with her friends. |
| | When she started going out on the town, your grandad and I had to be really alert because she'd alter her clothes to make them shorter and tighter. She'd take a perfectly good skirt, cut it up the side, take a section out and then sew it back together again. I don't know how she could walk. |
| Jess | I'd have liked to have seen you try and stop her from going out. |
| Norma | I chose my battles. I tried to keep as much from your grandad as I could in order to maintain the peace! |
| | I was 29 when I fell pregnant the first time and 33 the second, which was quite old at the time. Although some of these fashionable people like film stars now have babies in their forties and fifties, don't they? It's a funny world, isn't it? |
| Jess | How did you find out you were pregnant? Because back in the sixties there weren't the tests you can buy over the counter like we have today. |
| Norma | No – and there weren't any scans either; you had to have an internal examination to confirm it. I think the first indication was that I was sick all the time. I remember once saying to your grandad that I really fancied some fish and chips and he |

# CHAPTER FOUR

replied, 'I'll go and get you some, Norma, but it'll be a waste of money if you bring them straight back up again!'

It really wasn't the easiest of pregnancies. As well as the illness, I also spent the last three weeks of it in hospital on bed rest with high blood pressure. Added to the time I was kept in following the birth, it was a four-week stay in total.

**Jess** Was Grandad in the delivery room with you when you gave birth?

**Norma** Absolutely not. Men weren't allowed there, Jess, even if they'd wanted to be. I believe there was a worry they wouldn't be able to cope with it and that perhaps they might faint. No, no, your grandad stayed at home, the hospital rang him to say he had a son and then he drove over to see us.

**Jess** It's so interesting how things change because today it's the norm for dads to be there, supporting the mother. We'd think it was weird if they weren't. I'll tell you something for nothing, when I give birth, I'm not only going to have Jake with me, I'm going to make him watch every inch of the action down at the business end!

**Norma** That poor lad.

**Jess** I'll need him there with me; I'm not sure I could get through it on my own. Didn't you feel alone giving birth without anyone you knew there with you?

**Norma** No, I was too busy, Jessica! I never made a big thing of it, although I do remember the nurse telling me I'd done very well, which I was pleased about.

Giving birth was painful but even worse was when they used a knife *down there* to cut me and help it on. Afterwards, I was told by the nurse to get into a salt bath twice a day to heal it. Think of that.

# FAMILY AND FRIENDS

**Jess**  Ouch! I'm crossing my legs.

**Norma**  When I got home my doctor was very cross I'd been advised to do that. He said you wouldn't put a cut finger in salt water, let alone … well, you know. Say no more.

I do agree it's much better that fathers now have the option to attend because, dare I say, some of them might even be useful. And I've no doubt many of them would be thrilled to be there. Others might not want to picture it. I don't think your grandad would have wanted to be there in a month of Sundays.

**Jess**  A bit too gory for him, probably.

**Norma**  I had your mother at home four years later and he didn't come into the room for that either. I was in the bedroom with the midwife while your grandad sat waiting outside on the landing with my sister Betty. They held onto each other until the baby was out and it was all over.

Your grandad was a lovely dad, though. I was the softie while he was more firm – he never shouted, but he stood by his word. I couldn't say he was 'hands on' because the men back then simply didn't take part in the day-to-day practicalities of looking after a baby. He never changed a nappy or fed them even though both of them were bottle-fed with formula because I wasn't keen on the idea of breastfeeding.

I know it's all changed now and I do think it's right that the men help out more. Especially because we women have already done so much of the hard work.

**Jess**  That's one thing I'm not worried about at all. I know that when we have our own family, Jake will be 50-50 with everything.

**Norma**  Jess, I would so love to hold your baby. I really would.

## CHAPTER FOUR

Jess     You see, that makes me feel really emotional because that would be the ultimate for me.

Me and Jake are both keen to start a family, but I feel really strongly that it needs to be the right time and at the moment I can't see how it would work. Making sure you're happy, comfortable and safe is my sole priority right now, Nan. Can you imagine me trying to get you washed with a newborn latched on to my nipple?

People say, 'Oh, you'll adapt ... ' but I love my life as it is and I don't want anything to change just yet. If it *were* to happen, we'd be pleased and we'd find a way to make it work. Something somewhere would have to give and we'd cut back on the amount of work we're doing.

Norma     When you do become a mum, will you make sure you do one thing for me? When you wipe their little face with a flannel, don't do it like you do mine, else they'll fall over.

Jess     Are you saying I'm aggressive with my flannel?

Norma     Just a bit. Mind you, your mum's worse.

Jess     Nan, you're going to get us accused of elder abuse! My mum's always in a hurry and sometimes she can be a bit slapdash. I'd love for her to be able to take her foot off the gas once in a while. Maybe that'll happen when I have a baby.

Norma     She'd like you two to get a move on so she can be a grandmother.

Jess     Crikey, no pressure. I am quite happy with my dog Joey for now. You had a family dog too, didn't you?

Norma     Oh yes, your Grandad had always loved dogs. He had a spaniel called Brandy before he met me, so he didn't take much convincing when your mum turned 10 and started asking for a dog.

## FAMILY AND FRIENDS

We went to Grimsby to pick up our cocker spaniel, Jamie, in 1978. I still remember his little scrunched up face on the day we got him. He was only six weeks old, which was usual for the time but seems so early to be bringing a dog home now. The poor little thing didn't know where he was or where he was going when we got him home, but he was so lovely.

Your mother adored Jamie and spent ages grooming him, but she'd promised she'd take him for walks and she didn't do it for long…

| | |
|---|---|
| Jess | I heard you spoiled that dog something rotten. |
| Norma | Well, I baked him a chocolate cake every week. |
| Jess | I'm not sure you're supposed to give dogs chocolate… |
| Norma | He managed to live until he was 17 so it clearly didn't do him any harm! And I went to the butchers to get him bits of offal. I'd boil him bits of lung in a pressure cooker that I didn't use for anything else. |
| Jess | Thank God for that. |
| Norma | And I cleaned and changed his bedding every week. When I'd finished, I'd shout, 'Jamie your beddie is on!' and he'd come tearing around the corner to get in it. Mind you, that was about the only thing he did when I told him to. He'd sit when Michael told him to sit, but he'd never stay there for me. |
| Jess | That sounds like the early days of having Joey. Jake has trained him so amazingly now, but he was quite a handful when we brought him home. |
| Norma | Do you remember when he latched onto your top? |
| Jess | Oh my god. He jumped up and wouldn't let go of my sleeve. I was despairing. I didn't tell you I was hoping to get a dog as I knew you'd say they're a lot of hard work and a lot of responsibility. We only meant to go and have a look at Joey, |

## CHAPTER FOUR

who's a working cocker spaniel, but we fell in love with him as soon as we saw him.

We were going to call him Jamie after your dog, but then I remembered those wallabies we saw on your birthday at Yorkshire Wildlife Park – there was a little joey in his mama's pouch, and I loved the name. I still remember your reaction when we first brought him to see you.

**Norma**    When Jake walked through my front door holding him in his arms, I didn't know what to do with myself. I still feel the same now. Whenever Joey walks in, I just feel happy.

**Jess**    He's very in tune with you. Whenever you feel poorly he likes to keep you company while staying at a distance.

**Norma**    Sometimes he'll pop his head on my knee, but he's always so gentle. Such a lovely boy.

**Jess**    You have a special bond with him. It was the same with Bob cat.

**Norma**    I don't know why you call that lovely little thing Bob cat.

**Jess**    Sorry, Bobby. He was my cat, you know, I'm allowed to call him what I want.

My mum, Cadan and I had had Bobby from being a kitten. When I was about sixteen and Bobby was about four, the four of us were between homes and had to move in with Nan for a short time. After a time me, Mum and Cadan left Nan's house as we were supposed to, but Bob cat wouldn't come back to us. He'd just keep walking back to Nan's.

I personally think he knew where his bread was buttered. Didn't you feed him six sachets of cat food a day?

**Norma**    He had a healthy appetite.

**Jess**    He didn't have as healthy an appetite when he was at home with us!

Norma   He was such a lovely thing, I couldn't stop myself. And besides, if I didn't give him it, he'd have taken it. He brought me in a whole row of sausages one day. And one day I lost an entire joint of beef.

Jess   We found it in the dining room, didn't we, all mauled. He'd stolen it from the counter.

Norma   He'd always be sitting on my knee downstairs, and when I used the stairlift to go to bed he'd come up with me on my feet. But we did end up having a problem when we went back down the stairs. He'd come on my stairlift and put his paws on my leg and would end up scratching me. After many years and multiple infections, the doctor said he had to move on. I was so sad. Your mother spent six weeks finding him a suitable home.

Jess   He lives on a farm now.

Norma   And my word does he reign supreme there. We've been to see him, haven't we, Jess. I really had hoped he'd run towards me with his arms stretched out wide, but he didn't.

Jess   He's a cat, Nan.

Norma   That might be the case, but he does talk. When he came in the living room ... now don't laugh at me, Jessica ... I swear he used to say 'aye up'.

Jess   People are going to think you've lost the plot.

Norma   Maybe I have.

Jess   We were grateful you gave him such a good home for all the time you did. You've always been such an amazing support to us. Was your mum a good support to you when you had your two as well?

Norma   She was such a big help. The only thing she wouldn't muck in with was the laundry because she refused to go near my

# CHAPTER FOUR

washer. She'd never had one before and I'd tell her, 'Look, Mum, it's so simple!'

It was a Hotpoint Countess but she did not want to know. She'd only ever washed by hand and she didn't trust the machine an inch!

'I'll do anything for you, Norma,' she'd say, 'but don't ask me to look at the washer.'

But just her presence there was reassuring for me and she loved my kids.

**Jess** Obviously your mum knew all about this, having gone through it three times herself with you and your sisters.

**Norma** She did. I remember she came round once to find me ironing nappies. We didn't have the disposable ones you get today – instead we had the cloth kind which I'd soak in a bucket with Milton sterilising fluid before wringing them out and putting them in the washer. What a carry on. Goodness knows why I was ironing them as well.

'You'll not iron those nappies long,' she told me.

And she was quite right, of course. I gave up after a few weeks.

**Jess** You've told me before that your middle sister Betty was great with your kids as well.

**Norma** She loved being round my two and was always very much involved. You see, she couldn't have children of her own and my goodness, she longed for a baby. She went to a clinic in Sheffield to have her fallopian tubes flushed out and she did fall pregnant after that, only to suffer a miscarriage. She went on to lose another baby and then she had an ectopic pregnancy. Poor, poor Betty. It was dreadful for her and she was very pained by it. She used to say that her arms ached to hold a child.

## FAMILY AND FRIENDS

**Jess**  When I was younger, Betty would tell me that she'd always wanted a baby girl. She'd often move my hair out of my face and say I was gorgeous and shouldn't hide behind my hair. It used to really annoy me, but now I look back and think how lovely for her to tell me I was beautiful every time I saw her.

**Norma**  She adored both you and Cadan.

**Jess**  It's so sad, isn't it? We know a lot more about infertility now and she might have been able to explore other options like IVF. Or they may have been able to identify whatever was causing the problem and treat it.

**Norma**  Medicine has moved on so much and that's a wonderful thing.

I was always very careful with Betty. I was conscious not to rub her nose in it, for want of a better phrase, and I tempered my joy about being a mother a little bit.

Gosh, she had some really low points. I'd say she was probably clinically depressed at times.

When they'd married, Betty's husband, Bert, was a widow with a 17-year-old son from his first wife and while I think he would have liked another child, he wasn't quite so desperate.

**Jess**  So Betty also married a man who was much older than her, just like her parents, Jessie and Tom.

**Norma**  That's right. There were 18 years between them and Betty was only 59 when he died. Bert was a lovely man. He used to be a fireman and then he went to work at the power station. We did have some laughs together because he was absolutely hopeless at DIY. He once tried to make a bird table, but there were so many nails sticking out of it that he had to cover the ends of them in Blu Tack so the little birdies didn't hurt their feet.

**Jess**  You were very close to Betty, weren't you?

# CHAPTER FOUR

**Norma**  Yes, because Betty and I were on the same wavelength, more so than my eldest sister Joan. Joan was strong-minded and never wrong. She was a very intelligent, hard-working woman and if you were in trouble, she'd be there. But she could be …

**Jess**  … A bit stubborn?

**Norma**  Yes, I think that's probably fair to say. But she was sensible and practical, with a good head on her shoulders. When your mother was very badly sunburnt as a little girl, within 15 minutes, Joan was at the door with ointment. If you needed her, she'd be there.

We were just more carefree, Betty and I. I could have more fun with her. We were so silly together and she'd make me laugh at inappropriate moments. She only needed to look at me.

I remember when home perms came out – it must have been sometime in the forties. Betty was doing Joan's for her when one of the wind-up rollers fell off. Joan thought all her hair was falling out and she was in such a panic. Well, Betty and I couldn't stop laughing. We actually laughed about that for years. I'm not sure Joan ever saw the funny side. She had a different sense of humour to us.

**Jess**  You and Betty were like two peas in a pod.

**Norma**  I don't think we could have been any closer. We spoke twice a day, morning and night, until she passed away on New Year's Day in 2014.

**Jess**  I remember. I was 17 when Betty went and that was a big hit. We all felt it.

**Norma**  She'd suffered a lot of health issues – diabetes, breast cancer, gallstones – but she died of angina in the end. She had so much to contend with in her life, she used to say to me, 'Norma, I think I must have killed a robin.'

More than ten years on and I still miss her every day. I'm sure I'm now the last of my grandmother's grandchildren.

Jess   Remind me again of your aunts and uncles. There was a small army of them.

Norma   Let me think about this to be accurate. Mum's eldest brother was William – shortened to Billy – then there was Joe and Tom and her sisters were Elizabeth – whom we called Ciss – Dora, Mae, Hilda, Ethel and Connie. I think that's all of them.

Jess   With all Jessie's siblings – all those aunts and uncles – you must have had so many cousins, Nan.

Norma   Auntie Ciss had two, Mae had nine …

Jess   … OK, I've run out of fingers already.

Norma   Ethel had two, Dora had one, Connie had one, Billy had three and Hilda, Tom and Joe didn't have any. Hilda had a hysterectomy when she was quite young and so wasn't able to have children.

Jess   Then there was you, Joan and Betty as well. So I make that 21 cousins just on your mum's side.

Norma   And we did quite well at keeping in touch with each other. One of our relatives started researching the family tree and managed to make contact with someone in America who knew about me because my dad's brother had emigrated to Oregon as a young man and got married there. It sends a tingle down your spine, doesn't it?

Jess   You got goosepimples recently when we got to use Ancestry through a paid partnership, didn't you?

# CHAPTER FOUR

**Norma**  Oh Jessica, it was lovely. We were able to find the 1921 census. My dad's handwriting was on it, and recorded him as the head of the household and my mum as carrying out 'home duties'. A different time.

**Jess**  And we had another full circle moment when you celebrated your 90th birthday in Headon, which is where your mum's family roots are. You've always spoken so positively about the times spent there as a child visiting the aunties and uncles and so for the birthday party, we hired out the village hall, which had once been the school your mum and siblings attended, wasn't it?

On the walls there were photos from years gone by and we spotted one picture of some local schoolgirls being awarded medals for 100 per cent attendance in the early 1900s. One of those girls was nan's aunt Connie – or Auntie Con as she called her.

**Norma**  How lovely it was to see that! She couldn't have been older than 11 in the picture. Of all the siblings, Auntie Con was probably closest to my mum, possibly because she had also lost her husband. She was married to a merchant seaman called Bert and he'd become unwell with a goitre – a swelling around his neck. He was booked to go into hospital in Sheffield for what should have been a routine procedure and he said to my mum, 'Now, Jessie, have I to book a single ticket to the hospital or a return?'

'Don't talk so daft, Bert,' said Mum. 'You get yourself a return ticket.'

Well, he died. Auntie Con ended up getting a little job as manager in a shoe shop and later went to work as a live-in housekeeper for a businessman in Retford.

**Jess**  She sounds like a strong, determined woman. We've a few of them in this family.

| | |
|---|---|
| Norma | She was. She had to be, given what happened. Now, you'll giggle at this, but Auntie Con had a couple of little health rituals which she swore by. The first was eating an onion every day in some form or other. And the second was keeping a potato in her stockings, which she claimed guarded against arthritis. |
| Jess | I've heard it all now. And did she ever suffer from arthritis? |
| Norma | She occasionally complained about her knees but apart from that she was fine so it might have worked. |
| Jess | Careful, you'll start a TikTok trend at this rate. |
| Norma | She was a gem, my Auntie Con. And I felt so close, both to her and my mum, being in that village hall on my 90th, knowing that they'd once sat there as schoolgirls. I wouldn't want people to think I was going mad or sounding silly, but I could feel my mum's presence. |
| Jess | It's not silly at all. I'm not embarrassed to say that I believe in ghosts. I went to see a clairvoyant once because I was hoping he'd give me some reassurance during a difficult time in my life. And he did. He told me he saw an elderly female relative who was chucking psychology and sociology books my way. I had literally just decided that I wanted to go to uni and do social work and, in my eyes, that was my nanny Margaret (my dad's mum) saying it was the right decision. |
| Norma | That was good of her to take the time to do that. |
| Jess | She also told me that my tyre pressure was low. |
| Norma | Helpful, too. Did she give you that week's lottery numbers? |
| Jess | Sadly not. |
| Norma | Wasn't that clairvoyant the one you phoned to make a second appointment with, only to find out that he'd died? |

## CHAPTER FOUR

**Jess**     Correct.

**Norma**   Didn't see that one coming, did he?

**Jess**     Very good, Nan.

**Norma**   My sister Betty used to think she had a little man smoking a pipe upstairs. She could smell the tobacco and sometimes it felt like she was walking through him. And my mum used to tell me how the frontline soldiers would have an angel appear and spread her wings over them as they came up and out of the trenches. That could have been just a war story, but I really do feel there is something there.

Saying that, I've never seen anything myself so the ghosts obviously don't want to talk to me.

**Jess**     Or me.

**Norma**   Little wonder. They wouldn't get a word in edgeways.

**Jess**     Says she!

**Norma**   Whether they exist or not, I did feel an atmosphere that day on my 90th and I like to think it was Mum. Her heart was always in Headon.

**Jess**     When did Jessie pass?

**Norma**   Gosh, it was 1969. I was 35 and your mum was only one, so they never had the chance to form memories of her, which is something I've always been saddened by. She had cancer of the oesophagus and the day before she went into hospital for surgery, I sat with her on the settee, putting my arm through hers and resting my head on her shoulder. She went in very early in the morning, having emptied her little teapot in the kitchen, turning it upside down so it could drain – she hadn't let anything be left other than the way she liked it.

She never came home from the hospital. They operated, but couldn't do anything else.

## FAMILY AND FRIENDS

**Jess**   Do you think she knew she might not make it?

**Norma**   She must have done, bless her. I loved my mother more than anything and I still miss her desperately. Even now, all these years later. Does that sound daft?

**Jess**   Not at all. The relationship you had with her was irreplaceable.

**Norma**   You're never too old to want your mum.

**Jess**   Too right. I often just want my mum.

Our family today is really just me, you, my mum, Cadan and Jake. I would love to have massive get-togethers at Christmas, but we don't have the numbers.

**Norma**   We're small but perfectly formed.

**Jess**   Imperfectly formed might be a better description.

**Norma**   I don't think I've ever met a family who haven't got their problems somewhere. You've had an awful lot to deal with over the years and I just hope the stability and love you've had from me and your grandad has helped you through it.

**Jess**   Without a doubt. And I have family on my dad's side who mean a lot to me, too. Both his parents (my nanny Margaret and grandad Brian) have passed, but my auntie Sue, who is Dad's oldest sister, has been my rock and my biggest supporter. Whenever I call her, no matter what time it is, she answers. Whenever I've needed her, she's provided a shoulder to cry on. She has listened and given really good advice throughout my life, and I am so fortunate to have her.

I'm also close to my cousin Georgia, the daughter of my dad's brother, my uncle Neil, who sadly passed away at the start of 2025. I've been supporting her through the loss of her dad – it's been devastating and the whole family will miss him forever. There are only five months between me and Georgia

# CHAPTER FOUR

and she's like a best friend and a sister all rolled into one. We've followed quite similar paths, heading off to uni in the same year, me going into social work and her becoming a mental health nurse. We've gained together and we've lost together and she's absolutely hilarious. She also introduced me to Ellie, who is one of my other incredible best friends. I'll always be grateful for that. Ellie is truly amazing and we have a very special bond.

Nan, Mum, Sue and Georgia are proof of the importance of family ties and why we should nurture and cherish the ones that enrich our lives.

**Norma**   I also think friends can become your family, can't they? And can be just as important.

**Jess**   Totally.

**Norma**   I feel very blessed to have had some wonderful friendships in my lifetime. I still meet up for lunch once a month with the girls I worked with at the telephone exchange in the fifties and early sixties. There used to be 12 of us but now it's just myself, Stephanie, Freda, Cheryl, Joan and Valerie. We lost lovely Jean last year. She was 92.

We've always got on so well; there's never been any arguing or nastiness. Such a lovely group of girls.

**Jess**   I love that you still call them the girls. Getting out to meet them can be difficult for you mobility-wise, but we always prioritise that lunch.

**Norma**   I enjoy our meet-ups so much. And we're never short of things to talk about.

**Jess**   You're not wrong there … You lot never shut up.

**Norma**   Just recently I received a letter from an old exchange friend called Pauline whom I haven't seen for about 50 years after

# FAMILY AND FRIENDS

she moved away. She wrote that she'd seen us online and it had made her very proud. Isn't that wonderful?

One of my good friends over several decades was Niff Burton who worked in the post office. She's the one I met your grandad through. Her real name was Cecily but everyone called her Niff – I've no idea why and she's passed away now so we can't ask her. Niff and I took a trip to Paris together when we were about 21, catching the ferry from Newhaven to Dieppe and then the train from there.

**Jess**  Tell us what happened on the boat …

**Norma**  Ah, thank you for bringing that up, little monkey. That was the second time I went to Paris, with my good friend Pat Oakes. Let's just say I don't have sea legs. I managed to get to the side in time, but then the wind was blowing it right back at me. Hideous.

**Jess**  I think the travel sickness is an unfortunate trait you've passed down to me because I used to be awful in the car. Grandad would get really annoyed with me having to stop every ten minutes to spew my guts up.

**Norma**  Both those times I went to Paris, I didn't know a word of French except for 'une bière'.

**Jess**  That's handy enough.

**Norma**  It was useful, yes! As Niff and I were walking down the Champs-Élysées, we believed we saw Ingrid Bergman, who was a world-famous Swedish actress and one of the leading Hollywood stars from the Golden Age of the forties and fifties. She made her name in *Casablanca* and she was wonderful. Anyway, Niff was adamant it was her and so she quickly got her camera out to take a picture.

Unfortunately, she only managed to get the back of this very

## CHAPTER FOUR

|   |   |
|---|---|
| | tall lady's head so there was never any hard evidence. We did have a giggle. |
| Jess | And you created lifelong memories which are priceless. What you say about friends becoming family is so true. I met my best friend Hannah in year seven at school, so that's coming up to 20 years of friendship. You know when you meet someone and just click? We have the same sense of humour – the things that me and Hannah will be in fits of hysterics at, everybody else will think is ridiculous and not in the slightest bit funny. |
| Norma | That's what friendship is all about and when you find someone like that, you treasure them. Sadly, when you've lived as long as me, you have to say a lot of goodbyes to those friends. |
| Jess | We do go to a fair amount of funerals these days. But what's incredible is that you're still making new friends, even now in your nineties. |
| Norma | I've a lovely friendship with Kay who comes to clean for me. And a new-ish friendship with Mandy – who comes to help me sometimes – she does make me laugh. I know her daughter Harlee means a lot to you too, Jessica. It's the companionship that keeps me going. |
| Jess | I'd hate to think of you sitting here with no one to talk to. |
| Norma | Some days I can enjoy my own company and I rather like the peace! But I can be quite fidgety and restless if I've not had a chat in a while. We should always have room in our lives for new friends. |
| Jess | That's like me and Alia. I was at a point a few years ago where I thought I had my people and didn't need anyone else. But in early 2021 I trained in doing eyelash extensions just to earn a little bit of extra money while me and Jake were in the |

## FAMILY AND FRIENDS

process of buying our house. Alia booked in to get her lashes done and from that appointment this lovely friendship has blossomed which has been life-changing.

She's so calm and collected; she gives the best advice and she really helps to ease my anxieties when I need it. She's a caring, supportive influence and I'm so grateful to have her in my world.

**Norma**  Friends are the family we choose, Jess. And you can never have too many of them.

**Jess**  Amen to that.

INTERLUDE
# Norma's secrets to a long life

**In no particular order, here are
my secrets to a long and happy life:**

Laughter. There's been plenty of that in my life.
We've always been able to put a fun spin
on anything and keep smiling.

*

Home-cooked meals. That's what keeps my strength up.

*

Family time. If you can't be together,
keep connections up with phone calls.

*

Keeping the brain active. You've got to carry on
taking an interest in things, being curious and learning.
If you switch off, you fade away.

*

Socialising. I can be quite the social butterfly
and love being with friends.

*

## INTERLUDE

A good cuppa. Or rather, several each day.

\*

Butter. We've all been brought up to think it's bad for us but it's not. I slather Lurpak on my toast and I swear it's kept me going.

\*

Fresh air. I make sure I fill my lungs with it as much as I can, it's no good being cooped up inside.

\*

Werther's Originals. They have got me through many a tough time.

\*

Treats. A little bit of what you fancy does you good. It's miserable to deny yourself what you love.

\*

A hot drink before bed. Worth its weight in gold.

CHAPTER FIVE
# Work

**Norma**    The world has changed so much for women since I was growing up. Mostly for the better. Women and girls have such very different opportunities now – they can be whoever or whatever they want to be. Do you know, I almost feel as if I've missed out.

**Jess**    When you were younger, I guess it was more normal for women to go into a vocation, such as teaching or – like you – to work as a telephonist. They generally weren't career women or 'boss ladies' or CEOs.

**Norma**    Not at all. And once we had children, we stayed in the home.

**Jess**    Was it always the expectation that you would grow up, get married, have kids and look after the home as your full-time job?

**Norma**    It was. Women were there to clean and cook and have the children. But it wasn't thought of negatively, Jess. It was just the way things were and everybody abided by those traditions. You had your husband's meal ready on the table for when he came home. None of this 'it'll be ready shortly' carry-on. I hate to break it to you, love … but you would have been quite lost.

**Jess**    Haha! You're always saying to me, 'What are you feeding that lad tonight?' and I know we laugh, but deep down it does irritate me a little bit. If 'that lad' has arrived home a couple of hours earlier than me, he should be the one getting the tea on.

## CHAPTER FIVE

**Norma**   In that case, I think you're a very lucky lady.

**Jess**   I don't see that as luck. That's what should be normal. A relationship is a two-way thing. Just the same as running a house is a two-way thing.

**Norma**   I was just brought up in a different time. But I do think men should take their fair share of the load, especially if the woman has been out to work as well. It's all changed and women have, rightly in my opinion, demanded more. Why should a woman be tied to the kitchen sink when she's got a good brain in her head and could do a great job somewhere? If women have the ability, they should be able to put it to use.

**Jess**   High fives to that. We shouldn't be held back. We should have exactly the same opportunities as men. What would you have chosen as a job or career if you'd had the opportunities of my generation, Nan?

**Norma**   Probably something to do with helping people. Maybe a social worker, like you were before you started making videos for TikTok.

**Jess**   I'd always wanted to be a teacher, I think because my experience at primary school had been so positive.

**Norma**   You'd have made a fabulous teacher, Jess.

**Jess**   Whatever I did, I wanted to feel like I was making a difference somehow. Not like changing the world kind of stuff – I'm not deluded or anything! But enough to have a positive influence and to make a contribution to my little patch of the planet.

**Norma**   I know exactly what you mean. It's about having a purpose. You can have a great work ethic – as you always have done, Jess – but purpose is what makes that hard work mean something.

## WORK

**Jess**  And what's your purpose now?

**Norma**  Annoying you.

**Jess**  You're very good at that. You probably deserve a promotion.

**Norma**  And a pay rise.

**Jess**  I'll speak to HR.

**Norma**  Doing something you enjoy is probably the most important thing of all. They do say that if you find a job that you love, you'll never work a day in your life. And some of the happiest years of my life were spent working at the General Post Office telephone exchange in Retford.

**Jess**  You still have a telephone voice from those days.

**Norma**  'Number, please … Can you hold the line? … Trying to connect you … I'm still trying to connect you … I'm sorry, there's no reply.' I've still got it, haven't I?

**Jess**  Never lost it, Nan.

**Norma**  I loved that job. And I got on like a house on fire with the girls I worked with – 70 years later and we're still friends. We all say if only we could go back, even just for one day, we'd jump at the chance. Jean, God rest her soul, once said she'd like to have a switchboard installed at home, just to play around with!

**Jess**  If you went back for a day on the telephone exchange, that would mean I wasn't born yet.

**Norma**  Yes, so I'd get some peace and quiet, too. That's what I'd call a win-win.

**Jess**  You absolutely made friends for life there. Hearing your stories and seeing you all when you get together and knowing how much those friendships have meant to you through the years is one thing that makes me question whether the new

## CHAPTER FIVE

working-from-home culture is really for the best. Those work relationships can be special and long-lasting.

**Norma**    I know everything changed with Covid and lots of people got used to working at home, and I can understand the appeal of having that flexibility as opposed to travelling to the office every day. But going to work is important socially – we need to mix with our colleagues, to help and support each other and to swap our little stories.

**Jess**    On the whole, I love the shift to working from home. It massively helps out people with care responsibilities. You can also put a load of washing on during the day and be in for any deliveries. Plus, I can do my meetings dressed only from the waist up and no one is any the wiser.

**Norma**    They are now.

**Jess**    But I do think you're right, Nan. By not going into the office, we miss out on all those everyday conversations – and people don't go for drinks after work on a Friday, which is often how you get to know your colleagues better and friendships are formed. That's a shame.

**Norma**    A nice chat over a tea break might seem like nothing, but it's good for the soul. It can help make your day and put a spring in your step without you even noticing.

I'd often go to the pictures with my friends from the exchange, taking a teacake with some cheese in as a snack.

**Jess**    A teacake with cheese?! Who would settle for that at the cinema now? If there's not a Tango Ice Blast, some Ben and Jerry's ice cream and a packet of Maltesers on the menu then I don't want to know.

**Norma**    Well, people soon won't have anyone to share their Tango Ice wotsits with if they don't have work colleagues. It must be lonely.

# WORK

**Jess** There's also been a blurring of boundaries which isn't always healthy, because when your home is also your place of work, it can be difficult to switch off. If you have an actual journey to and from work, there's a clear separation between your personal life and your professional one. I've always used the commute back to unwind and reflect on my day, even now when I'm heading home after being at yours.

**Norma** I often tell you that you need to take it a bit easier.

**Jess** I know and I'm trying to learn how to achieve some balance between Jess at home and Jess at work. Especially as I'm still quite new to being self-employed as a social media content creator, which was never part of the plan. I'm often editing, responding to comments and answering emails long into the evening.

**Norma** It was a lot more straightforward when people went to work and clocked in and clocked out again. We all knew where we stood.

**Jess** How did you end up working at the telephone exchange?

**Norma** After leaving college with my secretarial qualification, I'd taken an office job, which I did for about a year, but it wasn't where I wanted to be. I wasn't comfortable and I knew I couldn't stay. Going to work there used to give me anxiety. One day I dropped a typewriter, breaking it, and my boss told me my mother would have to pay for it even though it had been a complete accident. I was worried sick because I knew she wouldn't be able to afford it and it gave me sleepless nights, Jess.

In the end, thank goodness, my mum didn't get the bill so all my distress had been for nothing.

**Jess** You have the same anxiety as me. It runs in the genes.

**Norma** You've got the family madness, love. We're all over-thinkers.

# CHAPTER FIVE

It was my sister Betty who told me they were doing interviews at the exchange. She was a supervisor there and she thought I'd be good at it. So, I applied and I got it and then spent a month in board and lodgings over in Lincoln where we did our training. That was a big thing for me because I wasn't a 'go away from home' type of person. But my landlady, Mrs Eastmead, was a lovely woman, a fabulous cook and she made me feel settled.

Number five, Lakeview Road. That was the address. I shared a bedroom with another girl called Pat who was on the same course – she would later emigrate to Australia so we lost touch.

Here's something that'll tickle you. After three weeks at Mrs Eastmead's, she needed the room back so Pat and I were sent to another lodging house round the corner on Rookery Lane. Oh, we weren't happy there one bit. We went back to Lakeview Road and begged Mrs Eastmead to take us back. We were on our hands and knees.

Jess    But wasn't the room you'd been in now occupied by other people?

Norma    Yes, but she did have another smaller room available. Problem was, there was only room for a single bed in it and Pat and I would have to share it.

Jess    Poor Pat!

Norma    Why poor Pat?

Jess    Sharing a single bed must have been a struggle, what with you being, you know, quite plump!

Norma    Both of us were more than prepared to put up with it and there was only a week left of the course. I don't remember if we slept top to tail or side by side – what I do remember is there was barely room to breathe!

# WORK

And once we'd finished our training, we came back to the exchange in Retford, where we were all tested to see how quick we were on the switchboard and how pleasant our phone manners were.

**Jess** This was obviously before people had landlines and could call each other directly house to house. I don't know much about how the exchanges worked but they were all over the country, weren't they? And the women like you who worked there were nicknamed the 'Hello Girls'. So cute!

**Norma** We were. And it was a majority female workforce, which gave women a level of financial independence we'd perhaps not had before.

I couldn't tell you what my salary was because I honestly can't remember, however we all suspected that the men were paid more than the women. But it was hush-hush in those days and you certainly wouldn't dare ask. Heaven forbid!

**Jess** Tell me what the job at the exchange involved.

**Norma** Back then all telephone calls were connected manually by us operators. We all sat in lines at our stations, where we had a headset attached to a cord which we used to plug ourselves into the switchboard. When the caller – or 'subscriber' as they were known because people rented their telephones from the GPO – picked up their handset, it sent a signal to us via a light on the switchboard. We'd ask which number they wanted to call and then we'd connect them to the appropriate line by plugging in one jack to another.

**Jess** That actually makes my brain hurt. It sounds really complicated.

**Norma** It required a certain level of concentration, but it was fine when you knew what you were doing. There were one or two subscribers we didn't like answering, though, because some

# CHAPTER FIVE

of them could be quite rude. And we hadn't to be rude back, of course.

There was one telephonist, Mary, who was a good friend of Betty's. She had lovely, natural red hair and she'd get just as red in the face trying to stay polite on the line to the most unpleasant subscribers. She'd be so mad and we'd say, 'Mary's on the warpath again!' but we had to remain deadpan.

**Jess**    Maybe that's why you've always been so calm with me. It might stem from your telephonist days.

**Norma**    I've never thought about it like that.

**Jess**    You were well trained!

**Norma**    Rudeness we had to put up with. But if it went beyond that, we could act. There was one time after I'd been promoted to a supervisor, one of the telephonists asked me to help her because she had a man on the line who was being abusive. You could tell where the person was calling from and we identified this fella as being in a phone box that was just outside Retford next to a sub-post office.

I said to the telephonist, 'I know it's not nice, but can you try to keep him on the line?' and, very bravely, she did that while I quickly rang the sub-postmistress, who went out and took down his van number.

**Jess**    I love this!

**Norma**    We called the police and they came to the exchange to take a statement, which meant I had to tell them what he'd said. I really didn't like to repeat it, so I asked for a pen and paper and I wrote it down for them instead.

**Jess**    What was he saying that was so awful?

**Norma**    Jessica, I can't recall and I wouldn't want to upset you anyway. What I do know is that he ended up going to court, where he pleaded guilty and was fined £5, which was a lot of money back then. And the post office awarded me with two large bath towels for my good service.

**Jess**  You got him, Miss Marple!

**Norma**  I did.

**Jess**  And I think you deserved more than a measly couple of bath towels for your detective skills.

**Norma**  Do you? I was utterly thrilled with them! Those towels lasted me years.

**Jess**  We've actually been back to the old exchange building for a visit, just to have a look at it, haven't we?

**Norma**  It's been closed for many years now.

**Jess**  It was turned into a restaurant for a time, which has since shut again. It brought back some great memories seeing it. You recognised the door you used to come and go through for your lunch break.

**Norma**  Yes, I'd often bike home for my lunch and Mum would always have something ready for me. Sometimes I'd stay and have lunch with the girls. Whoever had their lunch hour first would go and fetch fish and chips for everyone and they'd be kept warm in the oven in the restroom until we each had our break.

There was also a little café – it's a hairdresser's now and where your mum started out, funnily enough – called the Robin Hood, and their apple pies and cheese puffs were fabulous. We often had a stack of those brought in, but you had to eat it in your relief time.

The shifts were 9am until either 4pm or 7pm and, as well as your lunch hour, you had a morning break of quarter of an hour, which was just enough time to go upstairs, make yourself a drink and get back to your station.

# CHAPTER FIVE

We didn't work nights; those shifts were done mostly by men who also had daytime jobs. When the lads came in for the changeover, one of them always went and flung the window right up because he said he felt stifled. I remember one of the other chaps once said to him, 'Tell you one thing, Gordon, I wouldn't like to be on a submarine with you!'

**Jess** How long did you work there for?

**Norma** I started in 1952 when I was about 18 and I became a supervisor three years later. We had wonderful parties at Christmastime where all the workers could bring their children along. I didn't have any kiddies back then so I used to take Joan's daughters Lucia and Julia, dressed in their nice party dresses. Gosh, they're both in their seventies now. They live away from the area these days, but we keep in touch by phone, which is lovely.

The exchange closed in 1963 because telephones went automatic and callers were able to dial numbers directly themselves. It was a strange feeling when it shut. A very sad one. There was a lot of publicity around the closure because the exchange had employed a huge number of people in the Retford area.

They offered us all a move to the exchange in Doncaster (the closures across the country were staggered over a number of years), but because I was newly married by then, I didn't particularly want to do that, so I left and took a job in the tax office instead, doing general admin and helping direct the customers as they came through the door.

I'd only been there about nine months when I realised I was pregnant.

**Jess** So you'd been a busy lady in between your tax office shifts …

**Norma** You could say that. And back then women didn't return to work after having children, not like they do now.

# WORK

**Jess**     There was no maternity pay, I assume?

**Norma**     Oh no. That didn't come in until much later and there were none of the legal protections you have today for pregnant women in the workplace. In my case I chose to leave but your grandad didn't have any paternity leave either.

**Jess**     Workers' rights are much stronger now, thankfully. Did you know that these days if you take a week off with illness, you don't even have to provide a doctor's note? They call it self-certified sickness.

**Norma**     Is that right? Well, I never.

**Jess**     I might take seven days of self-certified sickness myself after you complained this morning about how I made your toast. I'll sign myself off with chronic stress.

**Norma**     Be my guest, love. I shall treat it as a holiday.

**Jess**     It's actually so interesting how the world of work has changed over the decades. It used to be the norm for people to find a job or a career and stick with it for life. People chop and change a lot more now.

**Norma**     That's right, it was more about stable, long-term employment and loyalty, and people would often work for the same company until retirement. Your grandad worked for several years in a responsible job at Clark's Dyeworks and later got a job at a power station, where he worked until he retired.

**Jess**     And that probably meant people were more likely to stay in jobs they didn't like or find fulfilling. So many of us career hop or pivot now without so much as a blink. I read recently that it wouldn't be unusual for Gen Z …

**Norma**     … That's your lot, isn't it?

**Jess**     Yes, my lot. Apparently it's not going to be out of the ordinary for us to have as many as 16 jobs across our working lives.

# CHAPTER FIVE

**Norma**  That's unbelievable to me. But I suppose it's a positive thing that people have more options and can move around should they wish to. And it's never too late to try something new.

**Jess**  Look at you and your glittering social media career!

**Norma**  You know, after all her years at home my mother started working part-time at the age of 70, serving in the refreshment room at Retford train station. She used to bike up there to start her shift at 7am and she loved it because she was mixing with people and having interesting conversations – it was more about that than the money.

**Jess**  That was amazing of her, doing that at 70.

**Norma**  She was so happy in that little job. One day a lady came in and asked for a cup of tea. And my mum said to her, 'You're Lady Barnett, aren't you?'

**Jess**  Who's that?

**Norma**  Lady Isobel Barnett was very famous back in the fifties and sixties for being on the panel of a game they played on the telly called *What's My Line*?

And Lady Barnett said, 'Yes, I am.' Mum came back all elated because she'd spoken to her.

**Jess**  And that's how people feel about you now. You're a modern-day Lady Barnett.

**Norma**  There's not much modern about me, love.

**Jess**  We took a little trip to the station a while back, didn't we? You couldn't remember the last time you'd been on a train, so we bought a ticket from Retford to Worksop and while we were waiting, we popped into the refreshment room where your mum used to work and had a cuppa.

**Norma**  It's now a trendy coffee shop and completely changed from

## WORK

|  |  |
|---|---|
| | when my mum worked there, but it felt very soothing to be there. |
| Jess | Good for Jessie, getting out there and finding a new outlet for herself. Working can be about so much more than just a pay packet. Life is too short to spend it doing a job you don't like or trapped in one that grinds you down. |
| Norma | It's taken you a few attempts to find the right path, Jess. |
| Jess | Yes, and I might change direction again at some point! I've always had a real interest in health, social care and psychology – ever since I studied them at A level. I knew they were all connected, but wasn't sure how they could lead me to a career. After I finished school in 2015, I worked in the village store, where I'd already had a Saturday job while I tried to figure out what I could do with the rest of my life.

I later got a job in admin at an opticians and I hated it. It was dull and beyond boring. |
| Norma | You were living back at your mum's by this time so we were only a few minutes away from each other. You started helping me out with things like putting the bins out, accompanying me to appointments and getting the shopping in. |
| Jess | You had started needing a bit of extra help, so I was glad to be around for that. I was job searching and applying for loads of different roles when one came up for a 'reablement support worker' in the community, helping vulnerable people live safely at home, and I thought, 'Hmm, that's interesting …'

Because I'd already been helping you, I was able to put that down as experience. I applied for this job and before I knew it, I was heading off to Spalding for a week-long training course. |
| Norma | You thrived during that training. The change in you was something to behold. |

## CHAPTER FIVE

**Jess**    That's because I knew this was what I wanted to do and I felt confident that this was where my future was – helping people get back on their feet and regain their independence after setbacks. The more I learned, the more I wanted to make a difference. By this time, it was January 2017 and so I applied to Sheffield Hallam University to do a degree in social work and really start on the career ladder.

**Norma**    We were thrilled for you. University, Jess! What an achievement – you were the first in the family to go away to uni. Sheffield seemed perfect because although we were going to miss you, it wasn't too far away from home. You'd be able to come back when you wanted.

**Jess**    This felt like my time to shine. As I prepared to leave, you and I would go shopping and each week you'd buy me something for my new life in Sheffield – a potato peeler here, a saucepan there – and I had this big pile of stuff to get me started. I was so looking forward to finding some independence and experiencing the student life.

**Norma**    Ahem.

**Jess**    And I lasted three weeks.

**Norma**    Not even a month.

**Jess**    I got homesick, didn't I?

**Norma**    You used to call me, saying, 'Nan, I want to come home,' crying on the phone. You didn't like the flat you shared with the other students and you missed all of us back home.

**Jess**    I didn't particularly gel with many of my flatmates, possibly because they were a bit younger than me; they were 18 and fresh out of school, and I was 21, having taken some extra time to finish my A levels and then some more time to decide what I wanted to do. And the dimly lit university halls felt dark and unwelcoming to me. It wasn't home.

# WORK

I wasn't settled, I wasn't happy. In fact, I hated it with my whole being. But I didn't want to quit so I made the decision to come back home and then commuted the 40 miles to Sheffield whenever I needed to be there for lectures. I drove back and forth for the whole three years of my degree course and ended up graduating in 2020 with a First. Part of me wondered if I'd missed out, not being involved in the drinking and partying of uni life. But maybe I wouldn't have managed a First if I'd thrown myself into the social side of things.

Norma   That picture of you with your graduation hat takes pride of place in my living room. That was such a proud day for the whole family.

Jess   In the end, getting my degree was the most important thing to me – more so than the university experience – and I worked hard to get it. It involved doing a couple of placements and the first one happened to be back at my old secondary school. That was interesting because I was now working on a professional level with the same teachers who had been disciplining my bad behaviour just a few years previously!

Norma   I'll bet it was quite a shock to them to see the change in you.

Jess   It was. I was a completely different person to the angry, troubled teenager they remembered. I was happy and confident and working towards a career I felt passionate about.

I was also learning so much about myself. In my final year, my placement was at a hospital where I had to assess people being discharged who had social care needs, looking at how they were going to manage at home and what sort of support we could offer to help them stay safe.

That work was good for me because it confirmed that I wanted to be based in the community, not a hospital where it

## CHAPTER FIVE

was so fast paced that there was never a chance to build up a relationship with the clients. And once they were discharged, I didn't ever know how they were getting on unless they were readmitted.

I wanted conversation; I wanted to learn about who these people were – their backgrounds, hobbies and interests, what their family was like.

**Norma**   That's what you've always been good at, Jess. You're a people person and you care so much. Too much, sometimes.

**Jess**   That's what had led me to social work in the first place. I was very eager to start working and successfully applied for a full-time agency position in an older adults team, which I was able to do alongside completing my degree. I started there in March 2020.

**Norma**   And we all know what happened in March 2020 …

**Jess**   Covid.

**Norma**   What a time.

**Jess**   Within days of starting this new job, we were all sent home for lockdown and I had to work virtually, which, like many people around the country, I found really hard. Everything had to be done over the phone or via Zoom; we were making decisions as important as whether someone could live in their own home with carers or if they needed to move into residential care. And we were doing that without ever seeing the person face to face.

Even when the lockdown restrictions were eased, we still had to justify why we needed to go and physically see people. It was so frustrating, even more so when we found out that the Prime Minister had been eating cheese and drinking wine with his pals.

## WORK

**Norma**  Don't get me started on that. During lockdown, my family could only come to my window and speak to me on the phone. We did everything we could to stick to the rules and not be near each other, didn't we? When I think of the sacrifices everyone made and those poor people in care homes who had no visitors and our wonderful Queen having to attend Prince Philip's funeral alone, it makes me so angry that the politicians in charge were breaking the rules. Unspeakably cruel and heartbreaking.

**Jess**  It was a massive kick in the face, wasn't it? All those loved ones passing away in hospital on their own.

**Norma**  Even now I get upset when I think about it.

**Jess**  When they permitted support bubbles in June 2020, me and Nan formed one together and I stopped seeing my friends. Remembering that first hug we had after all those weeks apart makes me so emotional. It made me realise how powerful the human touch is and I basically broke down as I held her.

**Norma**  That was the best hug ever.

**Jess**  It was around this time that Nan finally agreed to have WiFi installed, which meant I could work from her house in the upstairs bedroom. But I was disillusioned with the job. I'd gone into social work wanting to make a difference to people's lives, but I just felt like part of a conveyor-belt process.

I'd moved from working with the over-65s to the over-18s and had an incredible team who really cared, but we were all so stretched. From the difficult time I had during high school I knew how important it was to be able to offload to somebody – I wanted to be the person who could listen, not just for the people I was working with, but for their family too. And I couldn't do that in this job.

# CHAPTER FIVE

Away from work, I was looking after Nan more and more and also providing care for my grandfather on my dad's side. When he died suddenly in December 2022, I took some compassionate leave, which ended up becoming an opportunity to sort my life out.

It was like an epiphany moment – I knew I wanted to give my time and energy to Nan. So I handed my notice in and left in February 2023.

**Norma**  I was so worried for you, Jess. Not having a conventional job in this day and age and with a mortgage to pay.

**Jess**  It was a risk, but thankfully it's worked out so far because of how the social media side of things took off in a very unexpected and amazing way. It's been a big career change for me and I couldn't be happier.

**Norma**  And you'll always have your degree as a cushion. No one can take that away from you. It goes back to what we were saying before about trying new things and finding something you really enjoy.

**Jess**  This might sound weird, but I feel like I'm making more of a difference now than I ever did as a social worker. The number of people we're connected with, who enjoy what we do and take comfort from it makes creating content the most fulfilling job I've ever had. I'd say to anyone out there who's thinking about making a career switch, just to go for it. Take the leap.

**Norma**  Even before all this TikTok business, I had a bit of a second career myself.

**Jess**  Didn't you go back to work as a school dinner lady when my mum was a bit older?

**Norma**  Yes, I did that for nearly 20 years from the early seventies. The kids were both at school by then and I wanted something to fill my time now they were no longer around during the day. It was a lovely little job because you know how much I love children, and they were all delightful. Some of them you couldn't take your eyes off, they were so sweet. And honestly, the things they'd come out with … I must tell you this because it's funny, although I was a little upset at the time. I had a little mole on my face which I had to pluck the whiskers out of.

One day I must have forgotten to pluck and one of the kiddies came up to me and said, 'Miss, you've got a spider on your face.'

Jess   Oof! That's brilliant. When I did my social work placement at the school one of the kids said, 'Miss, your face is always covered in spots.' That was a great day for me.

Norma   They just say what they think, don't they? Unfiltered.

Jess   Not unlike yourself.

Norma   I did Monday to Friday at the school and my job was to go around and try to tempt the children into eating a bit more from their plate. I used to say to them, 'Will you promise me you'll have a bite the size of a fly?'

Once they'd done that, they often had a little more and then more again. It was a tactic that worked. My friend Jean was the school cook and her gravy was delicious.

Jess   You've told me all about Jean's gravy. It's been 30-odd years but you still rave about it so it must have been quite something.

Norma   Sometimes she'd have some left over which she'd put in a big jug and go round the children asking if they wanted a bit more poured. The headmaster didn't like her doing that for some reason, but she'd say to him, 'That gravy is goodness,' and she'd get rid of it all.

# CHAPTER FIVE

To encourage the kiddies to eat parsnips, she would fry them like chips. And with her cabbage, she'd add a spoonful of mint sauce. Things like that can make all the difference and she was an excellent cook.

I loved the job but I had to retire earlier than I would have liked to because I had tinnitus, which had become very difficult to cope with in a noisy dinner hall. My deafness was also worsening. When I left, they gave me three little pieces of Aynsley pottery and some wonderful pictures that the children had drawn for me. I've kept them all.

**Jess** How did you plan to spend your retirement?

**Norma** Grandad and I did a lot of day trips to places like Boston and Scarborough. We went all over! There was a company in Retford called Kettlewells who would arrange the coach and off we'd go. Retirement was nice … while it lasted.

**Jess** Which wasn't very long, really. Because then I arrived to shatter the peace!

**Norma** That's a very good description of what happened. And as soon as you were old enough to not need me quite so much, I started all over again with Cadan. I pretty quickly moved from one job to another. Only I have to say this one – looking after you both – came without holidays or a pension and it paid considerably less. In other words, nothing at all.

**Jess** But the job satisfaction was unbeatable, right?

**Norma** I'll get back to you on that one.

## INTERLUDE
# Getting to know you ...

### First heartthrob?

Norma    I used to love James Mason. His voice would make me melt.

Jess    Probably someone from Busted, the first boy band I got into. If you pushed me I'd say Charlie Simpson, the one with the eyebrows.

### Any phobias?

Norma    I've never been on an aeroplane. I wouldn't say it's because I'm too frightened, but it's just never happened and it's definitely not going to now.

Jess    Water, specifically the sea. I'm scared of sharks and as a child I used to convince myself they were going to appear in the pool when I was swimming or up through the plug in the bath.

### Where would you time travel to?

Norma    Back to the Edwardian or the Victorian times. I find them fascinating and always enjoy going around a big old stately home and learning about the families who lived there. My sister Betty was the historian so I get it from her. She was another big reader as well.

Jess    I would go back to Nan's childhood so I could see all the stories she's told me through my own eyes.

INTERLUDE

### Where is your happy place?

Norma  Home, especially when I get up to go to bed and I feel all safe and secure. I do have to give a special mention to the café at Morrisons though, because I used to go there a lot with my husband Michael.

Jess  Nan's house. As soon as I walk through the door, I get a feeling that I don't think I'll ever be able to describe other than 'home'. Me and Nan are both home birds. Whenever we're coming back from a day out, as soon as we start to notice the familiar sign that says 'Welcome to the market town of Retford,' we both get that same lovely feeling.

### Most treasured possession?

Norma  My wedding ring.

Jess  My dog Joey.

### Do you have a secret talent?

Norma  I used to be able to waltz and foxtrot. But my biggest talent has been keeping the peace in this family!

Jess  My Yorkshire puddings. They are insane, even if I do say so myself.

### Who do you most admire?

Norma  The late Queen Elizabeth II. She took on a hard job and handled it beautifully.

Jess  Nan.

**GETTING TO KNOW YOU ...**

### Describe each other in three words.

Norma   Jess is loving, caring, always right.

Jess   That's four words but we'll let you off. Nan is caring, funny and wholesome.

CHAPTER SIX
# Grief

**Norma**    Grief is the price we pay for love. Queen Elizabeth II once said that and it's so true. And while I am immensely grateful for my long life – it is a genuine privilege to reach this age – one of the drawbacks of getting older is having to lose so many people along the way.

**Jess**    That must be so hard, Nan. Grieving is part of life, isn't it? We live and we die and we know it's coming for all of us one day, but death leaves damage behind every time it hits.

**Norma**    We all have to find our own way of coping with loss. I met a lady recently who had lost her husband, and the only place she could get any comfort at nighttime was on the stairs. So she'd just sit there on her own in the dark. You do what you have to do to get through it.

I didn't think it was possible to grieve as badly as I grieved for your grandad. It was all-consuming and physically painful.

**Jess**    But does grief get easier, or is it just something you learn to live with?

**Norma**    It gets a little easier over time, but the sadness is always there and I still think about your grandad every day. More than 20 years on and he's never out of my mind. It's lovely to have the memories, but they can also be bittersweet.

**Jess**    We've always tried to keep Grandad's memory alive. We say he might not be here in person but he's always here in our hearts. We speak about him all the time, even though it sometimes hurts to do so.

## CHAPTER SIX

**Norma**    There's another quote I rather like because it makes a lot of sense to me: 'Grief is a place none of us know until we get there.' It's saying we're not all the same and so what helps one person won't necessarily work for the next. Grief affects everyone differently.

With your grandad, I just felt numb. It was like there was a fog all around me – I wanted to push it away, but I couldn't and it was as if I'd been wiped out mentally and physically. Some days I felt that I was just dragging myself around.

I'd experienced grief before losing Michael, of course. Big losses. My dad when I was so young, my mum in 1969 and my sister Joan in 2002 after she suffered a stroke in the garden.

But it's different when you lose a partner. It's a very unique sort of love that you have for your husband.

**Jess**    I think you did a lot of your grieving for Grandad in private.

**Norma**    That's probably right. I don't believe I got through it very well at all, but I did it in a controlled way. I didn't want to make other people feel uncomfortable.

You and your brother were a huge comfort for me, Jess, but when I got back home from your mum's on my own and I locked that front door … well, it was dreadful.

**Jess**    I've often said to you how strong you are and you'll say, 'You don't know what happens when I'm here on my own … '

**Norma**    I remember saying to your mum one night, 'Kate, I think I'm going to lose my reason.'

'No, you're not,' she said. 'Because we won't let you.'

Having the support from everyone in my family was vital. Grief and loss are things that everybody has to experience at various points and I just hope anyone who is suffering has the love of a good family to help them.

# GRIEF

**Jess**    You were lost for so long. But I know you wanted to stay strong for us.

**Norma**    I was on autopilot a lot of the time. I'd make two coffees, forgetting that he wasn't here any more.

**Jess**    All of us were having to adapt to a different life. Getting used to coming into the living room and only one of you being there was horrible.

**Norma**    It's a bit like having a limb chopped off, isn't it? Some days I'm not sure how I got through it. It was the shock, Jess. The suddenness of it. We'd only just had lunch together. Your grandad got up to go in the garden, I went to collect you from school and Cadan from the childminder and by the time I came back, it was all over. He was whipped away.

**Jess**    It's a very traumatic experience to remember for me, not just because it was so unexpected. But also because I was the one to find him.

**Norma**    And you were only seven, bless your heart.

**Jess**    It was 18 March 2004. Nan had picked me up from school and brought me back to their house, same as she did every day.

**Norma**    As we came through the door, I said, 'Grandad's in the garden,' and you tore off to see him.

**Jess**    That was what I'd always do. As soon as I got back from school, I'd go and find my grandad and, without fail, he'd be working away in the garden or the garage. I remember I shouted for him but didn't get a reply and that wasn't normal. Usually he'd call back.

I went outside to the shed and he was there … slumped on the floor, unconscious. That image of him is something I've never been able to erase. It's etched on my brain.

# CHAPTER SIX

I screamed.

'There's something wrong with Grandad!'

You came running through, but I don't think you realised how serious it was.

**Norma**  Not until I got out there, no. Michael was lying there with this vague look on his face, as if he was a perfect stranger. I can't explain it better than that. I knew then that this was very bad. I had to leave him to come back into the house to phone on the landline for an ambulance.

**Jess**  I remember you put a blanket over him, didn't you?

**Norma**  Yes, but I was all fingers and thumbs. Mr Perkins from next door came to help me while we waited for the ambulance, and I sat down next to your grandad and I spoke to him – 'I'm here now, don't worry,' that sort of thing – hoping that he could hear me. He did look at me briefly and I think there was a flicker. But I couldn't say if he knew me.

When the ambulance arrived, I had to let him go on his own while I got you and Cadan, who was only a baby, sorted out.

**Jess**  You took us round to the childminder Louise's until Mum could get back from work. I was too young to fully understand what was happening, but I remember being very frightened.

**Norma**  By the time I got to the hospital, they were able to tell me that he'd had a massive bleed to the brain. I went to his bedside, but he was unconscious. It was horrible to see him like that.

After several hours, the nurse suggested I go home to get some sleep as I was completely exhausted, so I told them I'd be back first thing in the morning. But at about 11.30pm, I received a call from the hospital to say that Michael had deteriorated and I ought to get there as quickly as I could.

# GRIEF

I arrived just after midnight, which was about five minutes too late.

**Jess**  Oh, Nan …

**Norma**  They took me through to see him. All I wanted to do was drink loads of water, because every part of me was boiling hot. Strange, isn't it?

I wish I'd never left him, but perhaps he wouldn't have known either way if I was there. I just don't know. You go through everything over and over. Could I have done this or that differently? It's torture.

**Jess**  You've said that looking back and reflecting, you'd noticed some tiny changes in him in the weeks beforehand, as if he was getting tired.

**Norma**  Your mum and I had both noticed that. He wasn't getting anywhere with the jobs he was doing and that wasn't like him at all. He used to keep a lot of scrap wood in the spare bedroom and he'd said he was going to tidy and sort it all out, but when I went up there he wasn't making any progress. He was usually a very fast worker who could tackle anything, so it was out of character.

But I console myself with the thought that at least he didn't suffer. I'm not sure I could have coped with it if he'd suffered.

**Jess**  I don't know if there's a 'good' way to go. If you know it's coming, you dread it. And if you don't know, it's a complete shock. To lose him like that out of the blue totally rocked the family. We never got to say goodbye. My mum was absolutely devastated and seeing Nan in so much pain was horrible.

**Norma**  He'd been our constant and then to take that away so suddenly was horribly difficult. Gosh, it's amazing what one day can do, isn't it? How it can change everything.

## CHAPTER SIX

Jess    I was too young to go to the funeral service, but I was there afterwards at the wake. My mum got me ready in a brightly coloured outfit, not wanting it to be all dark and gloomy.

Norma    We had a lot of classical music at the funeral because that's what Michael enjoyed. I chose Handel's Largo from Xerxes and Vivaldi's Four Seasons and for the hymn we sang 'The Day Thou Gavest, Lord, Is Ended'.

Our neighbour Mr Perkins did the eulogy and he finished it by saying, 'He was a quiet man. He was my friend.' I thought that was very nice.

Jess    And me, Mum and Cadan all moved in with you for quite a while afterwards, didn't we?

Norma    Yes, you stayed with me for several weeks and it was a wonderful comfort, but I knew at some point you needed to get back to your lives at home.

'I really think you ought to carry on as normal now and sleep in your own beds,' I said to you.

And I remember you started to cry. 'But you're going to be on your own, Nan.'

I told you, 'If I need anything, I will ring you.'

Jess    I just didn't like the thought of you going to bed on your own and waking up on your own.

But Betty would come over for little sleepovers, wouldn't she?

Norma    Yes, she'd come and stay with me for a few nights every now and again. When she visited just after Michael had passed, she put her arms around me.

'Oh my poor baby,' she said. She was already a widow herself by then.

## GRIEF

I remember one day she went into that spare room with all the wood that your grandad hadn't managed to clear away and she said, 'Would you like me to hoover in here for you?'

It was the first time I'd smiled. Because there really wasn't anywhere to stand, let alone hoover.

**Jess** While Nan was trying to come to terms with what she'd lost, she also had to learn how to do everything Grandad had always taken care of. They'd had quite a traditional marriage where he had been 'the man of the house' and the one who made sure all the bills were paid. Everything was in his name and Nan had to take over sorting everything herself.

**Norma** I felt like I was wading through treacle a lot of the time, but I was determined. I have to admit, I'd never so much as changed a lightbulb in my life. But I told myself I was going to do this. I got all the bills and contracts moved into my name and over the next few months I taught myself how to manage it all and budget in the same way Michael had been so good at.

**Jess** He was a master at budgeting. Grandad was the kind of man who would walk from one end of town to the other to save seven pence on a tin of beans!

**Norma** He was very careful – that's not a bad thing. If we ever had anything left over at the end of the month, we'd have a day out in Worksop as a treat. But you know, we were comfortable and I never went without.

There were some things of course I couldn't quite manage on my own. Your Grandad had taken so much pride in his garden, and I knew maintaining it was going to be too big a task for me. Fortunately, our lovely neighbour Keith, who has sadly passed now, stepped in to help me for many years, and now I have my gardener Oliver. I've been so lucky to get

## CHAPTER SIX

such wonderful support from so many people. I wouldn't have been able to continue living here on my own without it.

Jess   I think Grandad would have been really proud of you.

Norma   I hope so.

Jess   And you've kept yourself busy, too.

Norma   I think you've got to, otherwise you'd curl up in a ball and be done with it.

Jess   After he passed you made sure you were out and about in the local community, seeing people and doing things to stay active.

Norma   I joined the flower club in the village – it was one night a week and we did flower arranging together. I enjoyed that a great deal. It took my mind off everything and what could be nicer than working with flowers?

We once had a little competition between us where we had to do an arrangement in the theme of a book. I chose my favourite, *Rebecca* by Daphne du Maurier, and I featured driftwood and a handkerchief embroidered with the letter R. And I won!

Jess   And there you were saying earlier you'd not got a creative bone in your body.

Norma   I also used to go to whist drives.

Jess   What's that?

Norma   Whist is a card game and we'd all meet up, divide into fours and play. Whoever won on one table would then move to the next so that you weren't playing with the same people.

Jess   A bit like speed dating, then?

Norma   No one was looking to click, Jessica. But it all helped. Just mixing with people and keeping your mind occupied takes you away from that feeling of loss, at least for a while.

The grief would sometimes hit out of nowhere, though. It was often little things that caught me. I'd receive post addressed to him, which always threw me. Or I'd see the couple who lived opposite coming home from doing the shopping together, opening the boot and taking the bags in. And I'd think, 'That's what Michael did … '

On my 71st birthday, which was the first year without Michael, we went out for a meal, and a close family member handed me a package to open when I got home. I unwrapped it on my own later and it was a beautiful framed photograph of your grandad at Nostell Priory. I broke down and I sobbed and sobbed.

**Jess** Had you and Grandad ever talked about death or what would happen when one of you went?

**Norma** No, he didn't like to. He'd get uncomfortable with things like that. I think having lost his father when he was just 19, death wasn't an easy subject for him.

As the eldest child he'd taken on a fatherly role with his younger sisters and he'd been a total rock to them. As he was to all of us. I know you took it very hard, love.

**Jess** After Grandad died, I developed this anxiety where I became really scared of death and dying and losing people, and it would keep me up at night. I used to call it my 'worry worms' because it felt like I had things moving around in my stomach and it often made me feel quite sick. It was definitely all stress related.

I didn't know what it was until I started having therapy fairly recently, but it was this overpowering fear of loss. I'd creep into my mum's bedroom to check if she was still breathing,

# CHAPTER SIX

|  | |
|---|---|
| | because I was terrified that everyone was going to go. If I could see her chest moving, I'd know she was still alive. |
| Norma | I'm so sorry you had to suffer like that, Jess. No child should see what you saw that day. |
| Jess | I'm grateful for the lovely memories I have of him and the three of us together. We had so much special time and Grandad really made the most of that. I just can't help but feel that he was robbed of time with Cadan, who was just a baby when he died. |
| Norma | I've always been sorry about that, too. Cadan was exactly nine months old on the day Michael died. He'd actually just taught him to stick his tongue out, which we all thought was very funny. |
| Jess | Ah, that's adorable. Cadan was such a sweet little boy and Grandad would have loved him, wouldn't he? |
| Norma | Yes, he would. He'd have waited patiently while Cadan looked around in the garden for stones and twigs, as he did when he got a little older, and we'd have both told him which ones we thought were the best. And he always liked to have a project on the go, like your Grandad, didn't he? |
| Jess | He used to come around and say, 'I want to invent something.' |
| Norma | That's right, he'd say, 'Nan, you've got to have some idea!' But often I didn't. I remember helping him come up with some sort of heating for the heel of a shoe one time. I mean… why we ever thought that was important beats me. I'm sure your Grandad, with how practical he was, would have been able to come up with much better. |
| | I think when anyone dies, young or old, though, you're going to feel sad that they're missing out on everything that happens afterwards. I wish he was here to do so-and-so or to see this and that. You could keep on saying that forever. |

| | |
|---|---|
| Jess | It's never-ending. I wish that he could have seen my graduation. |
| Norma | He would have liked that very much. |
| Jess | I wish he could have met Jake. Jake is actually really similar to him in that he can turn his hand to anything. And he would have loved spending time with Grandad in the garage, learning new skills. Even now it's hard not to feel a sense of injustice that we lost him when we did because he was so fit and he looked after himself. |
| Norma | He was 73 when he died, so he wasn't an old person. He didn't drink or smoke. |
| | And I think I was a bit angry at one point, especially when I thought about the lifestyles of other people who were still here. Why did Michael have to go when he wasn't any trouble to anybody? But anger doesn't do anyone any good, Jess. |
| Jess | No, it's a wasted emotion. It doesn't change the fact he is gone and we can't bring him back. |
| Norma | We had 41 happy years together – I wish we'd been able to have longer but you can't arrange that. We never have enough time with the people we love. Whether someone dies young or lives to 100, there's never enough. |
| | I have to say, sometimes I think that because he was such an active man, it would have driven him mad to be stuck in a chair not able to do anything for himself. So I'm thankful for that. |
| Jess | He wouldn't have been happy being dependent on other people. |
| Norma | He was always a terrible patient. He once got neurodermatitis and had to have bandages changed twice a day for 11 weeks. Oh, he wasn't fit to live with. He couldn't do anything for himself and that was a nightmare for him. For me and all! |

# CHAPTER SIX

**Jess**   I can still feel him in the house. He's still here. His jacket is still hung up in the downstairs toilet along with his hat.

**Norma**   That's been there for more than 20 years. I won't take that down. You know, I used to go to bed with his pyjama jacket at the side of me.

**Jess**   And you still have his hankie, don't you?

**Norma**   Yes, it's made of lawn, which is a lovely, soft fabric. If he ever got a bit of a cold, he always said that one was gentle on his nose.

I know I'd be better off in a bungalow, but I could never move from this house, because I couldn't leave Michael. He made this house and he's everywhere in it. He was excellent at DIY and because of that we never had a bill apart from the MOT on the car. He built our front porch, the extension at the back, he fitted our kitchen on his own – he'd not quite finished laying the floor when he died. He put the archway in our front room as well.

**Jess**   That arch is in the background of all of our videos.

**Norma**   We had a caravan way back when and he built a carport by the side of the house to shield it from the bad weather. That's still there.

**Jess**   It's got a few holes in it, mind.

**Norma**   It's disintegrating like me … But the shed he built in the back is still standing strong.

What's lovely about that is the door on it is actually my mum's old back door. Your grandad adjusted it to fit and so I feel like I've got a piece of my mum there as well.

**Jess**   When I first met Jake, the roof on the shed was broken and there was water coming through. Jake and his dad repaired it because you couldn't part with it, could you?

**Norma**    I would have been devastated to take it down. Your grandad was so clever and skillful.

**Jess**    And anything he didn't know how to do, he'd go and get a book on.

**Norma**    That pile of books, bless him. All of them about mechanical engineering. I wonder how many there were. Hundreds! Every so often, perhaps on a rainy day, he'd bring them all downstairs and sit and look through every one of them again.

**Jess**    Me and Jake have just decorated the spare bedroom at Nan's house and I suggested to her that she might want to move into this newly done-up room. But she wanted to stay in the bedroom she shared with Grandad.

**Norma**    I miss his presence, his company. I miss having a man about the house.

**Jess**    Steady on, Nan!

**Norma**    I mean I miss having a gent opening the car door for me, that kind of thing. When I had that I don't think I appreciated it enough. And we did make each other laugh. He liked to pull my leg now and again. There was one evening he'd arrived home a bit late from his shift at the power station.

'You're a little late,' I said.

He replied, 'Yes, you see I have to climb up the top of the chimneys to put all the lights off.'

'Well,' I said, 'I think that's disgusting – that shouldn't be your job!'

He broke into this huge grin. He'd been joking of course and afterwards I couldn't believe he'd managed to kid me.

**Jess**    I remember him with his cup of tea and a Wagon Wheel; the ones in the blue packet with the jam were his favourites. But I struggle to remember what his voice sounded like … One

## CHAPTER SIX

|||
|---|---|
| | of the beauties of life today is having videos of everyone. We don't have that for Grandad. |
| Norma | It's amazing what your mind can store, though. |
| Jess | I hope you don't mind me mentioning this, Nan, but when you've lost your husband and seen so many of your friends pass away and attended so many funerals, it must make you think about your own mortality. |
| Norma | Yes, especially when the night closes in and my brain does overtime. But what can you do? You can't sit back and give up. You've got to have an objective, something to make you happy, and I do have such fun days with my lot. |
| Jess | We always make sure to go to the funerals. I come with you because unfortunately you can't self-propel in that wheelchair. I find them uncomfortable and sad to sit through, but it's important to be there, isn't it? |
| Norma | It's showing your respects and saying goodbye. Funerals are part of the grieving process. |
| Jess | You're very good at reflecting on what's important and seeing loss as a way to appreciate life that little bit more. |
| Norma | Absolutely. You have to be kind to yourself, take it day by day and talk about the person you've lost. And value and treasure the people you still have in your life. They will get you through your worst days and help you see the light again. |

## INTERLUDE
# It's good to talk ...

**Jess**  As you will know by now, one of the things me and Nan are most passionate about is encouraging people to have good conversations. It sounds like such a simple concept, but we understand many of you struggle to know where to start.

**Norma**  People get frightened of saying the wrong thing, don't they? Especially when it comes to sensitive topics like bereavement and loss. When my sister Betty lost her husband, Bert, she would walk into town and people she knew would cross over the road to avoid talking to her. I think it's the same sort of awkwardness that stops people asking older people questions about their past.

**Jess**  We shouldn't be afraid. We should be keen to ask these questions and have these talks. We should be making time for them because they are valuable and rewarding for both sides.

**Norma**  I'd imagine most people would be delighted to be asked about their childhoods and experiences and be more than happy to share all their memories.

**Jess**  And grief, too?

**Norma**  Yes, because talking can help with the process. It also means our lost loved ones aren't forgotten about.

**Jess**  For anybody who feels a bit unsure about how to get going, me and Nan have come up with a list of suggested conversation starters and ice breakers. Asking gentle, open questions and allowing people the space to answer should

## INTERLUDE

lead to a rewarding chat. If you have any old family photos, these can be useful to get the ball rolling and jog memories.

We hope these pointers are helpful. Take the plunge and happy chatting!

What was the street you grew up on like?
What is your earliest memory?
When were you happiest?
Can you describe your house?
How did you find school?
Who was your favourite teacher and why?
Who was your least favourite teacher?
Did you ever get into trouble? What for?
What games did you play as a child?
Who was your best friend?
What was your favourite outfit as a child?
What did you want to do when you grew up?
What was better about life years ago?
And what is better now?
What were your parents like?
How did you get on with your siblings?
Where did you go on holiday?
What were your grandparents like?
Who were the big characters in the family?

## IT'S GOOD TO TALK ...

How did you celebrate Christmas?

What were you like as a little boy/girl?

What was your first job?

Who did you work with?

How did you meet your husband/wife?

Where did you go on your first date?

What are the big world events you
remember most vividly?

Tell me about your wedding day.

What do you remember about becoming a parent?

Is there anything you wish you'd asked your parents?

When did you first experience grief?

What are your favourite memories of the
loved ones you've lost?

What advice would you give to
the younger generation?

# NORMA

*Above:* This is my mum, Jessie, and dad, Tom. They were hard up, but you'd never be able to tell from these photos. Don't they look amazing.

*Above and right:* I'm three months old in the photograph above, being held by Mum. In the middle, I'm with my sister Joan. I'm four and Joan is twenty. To the right, I'm six years old, having fun in the sand at Skegness.

*Above:* This is my class at infant school. We'd just knitted the blanket at the bottom together. I'm in the middle row, furthest to the left.

*Left:* I'm thirteen here; my glasses had finally been upgraded from the wire ones I found so painful.

*Below:* Goodness, I must have been tired. I'm on a family holiday near Mablethorpe, age eighteen.

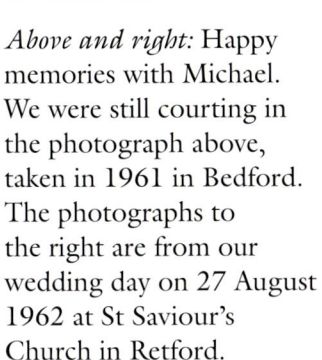

*Above and right:* Happy memories with Michael. We were still courting in the photograph above, taken in 1961 in Bedford. The photographs to the right are from our wedding day on 27 August 1962 at St Saviour's Church in Retford.

*Below:* Michael and me on our honeymoon in 1962.

*Left:* Here I am, sitting at my station at the General Post Office telephone exchange. A subscriber would call us and we'd connect them to the appropriate line by plugging in one jack to another. I made friends for life there.

*Above:* With my mum, Jessie, in Sutton on Sea.

*Left:* Me and my sisters, Betty on the left and Joan in the middle, in the early 1990s.

*Left:* This was the first time Michael and I met our troublesome little monkey Jessica, in June 1996.

*Below:* Me helping Jess to walk in 1998. This was before she learned to start running away …

*Right:* Jessica always loved seeing the things her grandad was growing in his garden.

# JESS

*Left:* Nan's house has always been my favourite place. This is me, age three, in the same lounge we film content in now.

*Below:* Nan sitting with me as I opened presents on my seventh birthday.

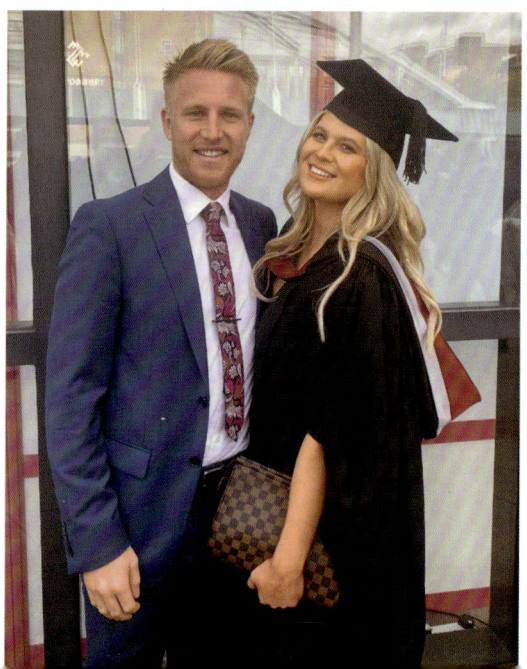

*Left:* I worked so hard to graduate with a first-class degree in social work in 2020. Jake and I had recently started dating. He told me he loved me for the first time while we were celebrating.

*Above:* On the left is a picture of my mum, Kate, and the spaniel Jamie that Nan spoiled so much. I didn't tell anyone that I wanted to get a dog. As soon as I saw Joey, I knew we had to take him home. Nan loves him too.

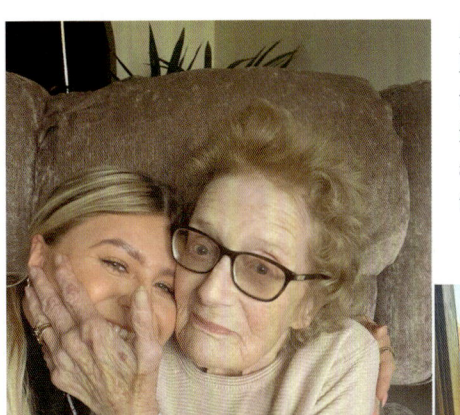

*Left:* My bond with Nan has only got stronger over the years. I started caring for her full time in 2023 and wouldn't want the job to fall to anyone else.

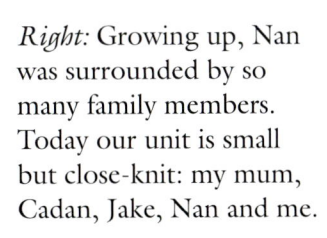

*Right:* Growing up, Nan was surrounded by so many family members. Today our unit is small but close-knit: my mum, Cadan, Jake, Nan and me.

*Above:* Social media has had us doing all sorts of unbelievable things together, from filming fun content on the left, to turning on our local Christmas lights on the right.

*Left:* We were lucky enough to be invited to the *Emmerdale* set for their summer fête in 2024 to celebrate 10,000 episodes of the soap. Nan loved it.

I'm so proud of our journey and grateful we've been able to do all this together. © Nicky Johnston

CHAPTER SEVEN

# Fame and Social Media

**Norma**  I still can't get my head around what's happened over the last couple of years, I really can't. It is absolutely beyond me but it's been such a joy.

**Jess**  We get stopped in the street wherever we go. Who'd have thought making a few silly videos would lead to this?

**Norma**  Certainly not me, Jess. Everyone is always so lovely and polite. They'll approach us and say, 'I'm so sorry to disturb you, but are you the lady from TikTok? We love your videos!'

**Jess**  We've not had one bad encounter in person with anybody.

**Norma**  Apart from that one lady ... The one who asked me, 'Does she make you do it?' while pointing to you. She was rather direct, wasn't she?

**Jess**  I think she was just curious, but she had made an assumption that I must be forcing Nan into doing the videos. Trust me, there's no way in this world anyone could make this woman do anything she didn't want to do.

**Norma**  Absolutely not. I have had the time of my life with this social media business. We were in town just the other day and as we were getting into the car, a lady came up to us with her husband. 'I love you,' she said. 'Keep doing what you're doing.'

# CHAPTER SEVEN

**Jess**  We're very comfortable with that sort of attention now that we're used to it.

**Norma**  It is a sheer pleasure to meet people and they're all so appreciative. It's a range of ages, too, from small children all the way up to my generation. A young girl came up to me outside the Edinburgh Woollen Mill in Retford wanting a photo and I don't mind admitting that I felt like the Queen.

**Jess**  We've met people in the midst of grieving who have said we've helped them. One lady spotted us in a supermarket – she'd lost her partner that same week and was doing her first food shop since he passed away.

**Norma**  She said she didn't know how to shop for one person instead of two and my gosh, our hearts went out to her, didn't they?

**Jess**  We scurried off and bought a bouquet of flowers which we gave to her before we left the store and that was a lovely moment. We often talk about her and hope she's doing OK.

**Norma**  There was the young girl Bracken who we met in Rotherham.

**Jess**  That was quite early on. This girl came to us crying, saying how our videos had helped her through her chemotherapy. She was only in her twenties and was being treated for blood cancer – we've kept in touch with her ever since. And Jake and Cadan ran the London Marathon in April 2025 to raise money for Blood Cancer UK.

**Norma**  With my sister Betty's husband Bert having passed away from the same form of cancer, it felt like a good fit, didn't it?

**Jess**  It did and we were all so moved by Bracken's story. We both feel very connected to our followers.

**Norma**  I've had people burst into tears when they see me, they're so overcome. Sometimes they look as if they're going to have a heart attack from the shock.

## FAME AND SOCIAL MEDIA

**Jess**    We love meeting people when we're out and about, but I'm also very aware of the need to get the balance right. Nan isn't a spring chicken any more and she has a limit of how much time she can spend out of the house without being tired and in pain. I've got to be conscious of that. But we always want to give something back to the people who have taken the time to follow our story and we'd never want to come across as rude or that we think we're better than anyone else.

**Norma**    We've met some famous people as well, haven't we?

**Jess**    Haven't we just. I know who you're thinking of.

**Norma**    Alfie Boe. The most charming of men.

**Jess**    Nan loves Alfie Boe. Loves him. She listens to his music all the time. But when we met him the first time, she didn't recognise him.

**Norma**    It was my cataracts, Jess!

**Jess**    You blame the cataracts for everything.

**Norma**    He was dressed down in a leather jacket and jeans whereas I'm used to seeing him all suited and booted. I thought he was just a friendly chap who had come over to say hello. I was mortified when you told me afterwards who he was.

**Jess**    Your face when you realised! I'll never forget it. I practically had to scrape your jaw off the floor.

**Norma**    You wheeled me back over so I could apologise to him. Thankfully he took it well and wasn't offended in the slightest. He's such a lovely fella. We had a thoroughly nice chat and then he serenaded me with my favourite song, 'You Raise Me Up'. I felt like the luckiest woman on earth. He has the most beautiful voice.

**Jess**    Nan has since developed this really lovely friendship with

## CHAPTER SEVEN

|||
|---|---|
| | Alfie. He even came to see her at home in November 2024 as a surprise. |
| Norma | He drove all the way up from London just to see me. I couldn't believe it. |
| Jess | You knew I was up to something that day, didn't you? |
| Norma | I could hear you rustling about in the kitchen and then Jake drew the curtains so I couldn't see out the front window. So, I had detected there was something fishy going on and I think I even joked that Alfie Boe must be coming. Either him or Peter Levy from the *Look North* local news. I didn't think for a second that it would actually be true. |
| Jess | He stayed for two hours. This internationally successful singer sitting in Nan's front room eating sandwiches and crisps. |
| Norma | You think that celebrities are going to be a bit high and mighty, but Alfie is so genuine and down to earth. When he serenaded me in my living room with 'Have Yourself a Merry Little Christmas,' I was transfixed. I think it's a miracle that someone can have a voice like that. If anybody else had sat there and sang to me like that, I might have felt a bit embarrassed. But this was so natural and I didn't want it to end. |
| Jess | I should have asked him to do a duet with me. |
| Norma | Thank goodness you didn't, Jess. You have many talents, but singing is not one of them. |
| Jess | Thanks a bunch. |
| Norma | Just leave the singing to Mr Boe and save all our ears, I beg of you. |
| Jess | After Alfie left, Nan was on quite a high for the rest of the day. |

## FAME AND SOCIAL MEDIA

**Norma**  I was on cloud nine. Even the next day I was still feeling funny and sort of fluttery.

**Jess**  In a good way?

**Norma**  Oh yes. It was a lovely feeling.

**Jess**  We've also done set visits to *Emmerdale* and *Coronation Street*. *Corrie* was fun for me, rumbling you over the cobbles in that wheelchair.

**Norma**  I have loved *Coronation Street* since the days of Ena Sharples back in the sixties. I used to go round to my friend Pat's house so we could watch it together.

And I've been an avid viewer of *Emmerdale* for 25 years, ever since Kim Tate bumped off her husband Frank when she refused to give him his pills. She was such a villain, that one, but she was ever so good at it.

**Jess**  It's such an honour getting invited along to these places. We have to pinch ourselves, don't we?

**Norma**  It's fascinating being there where they film – the sets are tiny compared to how they appear on the TV. I got to go behind the bar at the Rovers Return, the home of so many iconic landladies. Not that I could reach the pump to pull a pint.

**Jess**  When we went to *Corrie* for the second time to celebrate your 90th, they all greeted you like an old friend.

**Norma**  Tina O'Brien, who plays Sarah, gave me such a warm hug. She's wonderful. She told me she has three children in real life and I couldn't believe it because she still looks so young herself. She's not aged at all.

**Jess**  From what she's told us, Tina had a very close relationship with her own grandma and she loves watching our videos.

**Norma**  She got in touch with you the day after and said, 'Look after

# CHAPTER SEVEN

|||
|---|---|
| | your nan,' which I thought was very sweet of her. I also got a nice cuddle from Andy Whyment, who plays Kirk Sutherland. He sounds exactly like he does on the show. |
| Jess | Who else would he sound like? |
| Norma | He has a very distinctive voice and I thought he might have put it on for the role. But apparently not. |
| Jess | What we've realised from the time we've spent with people in the public eye is that most of them are just completely normal. And they've gone out of their way to make sure Nan has a special day. |
| Norma | When we were introduced to Mark Charnock, who plays Marlon Dingle in *Emmerdale*, he pretty much swallowed me up in a cuddle. |
| Jess | And the guy who plays Eric Pollard – Chris Chittell – was hilarious as well. He'd just had a hip replacement and he was walking about the *Emmerdale* village, chatting away. It was brilliant. |
| | It's all quite surreal when I think about it. |
| Norma | I received a 90th birthday card from Dawn French! And a letter from that member of parliament who wrote to us, too. |
| Jess | That's right – Matt Vickers, who's the MP for Stockton West. |
| | He wrote, 'I just wanted to take the opportunity to wish you a very happy 90th birthday. I hope you're being spoiled with treats and a celebratory bag of mints. Thank you to you and Jessica for bringing a bit of daily cheer to so many people. Your videos are a must watch and for those of us who no longer have our grandparents with us, they remind us of those precious memories. Happy birthday to you and here's to many more years of laughs.' |
| Norma | I mean, it's so overwhelming. When we first started doing all |

## FAME AND SOCIAL MEDIA

|||
|---|---|
| | this, I remember saying to you, 'Who is going to watch this daft nonsense?' But for reasons I will never fathom, it has worked out. |
| Jess | Shall we rewind a little bit and tell everyone how all this 'daft nonsense' started? |
| Norma | I think that would be a good idea. Because I'm still not sure how we've ended up here myself. |
| Jess | Like most people my age, I'd always dabbled a bit in social media. I would upload short clips to TikTok of me and Jake on my public page which was available for everyone to see. |

Alongside that, I'd make little videos of me and Nan, but always kept those as private Snapchat stories. Only people I actually knew were able to view them, but all my friends would reply and say how funny they thought me and Nan were together and how much they loved it when I posted with her. A few said I should think about posting the Nan videos to TikTok because they'd probably do really well on there.

I wasn't so sure. Personally, I thought TikTok was for kids filming themselves dancing to Jason Derulo, but I was intrigued to see what would happen.

So, in what was only ever supposed to be a 'testing the waters' experiment, in March 2022 I uploaded a rough and unedited 20-second clip to my TikTok account of Nan trying to give me some money – an everyday scenario in this house and has been since I was a kid.

|||
|---|---|
| Norma | That has always been my privilege, Jessica. I know you try to refuse it, but it's something I like to do. |
| Jess | Even now, Nan will say, 'Take that for your petrol, love,' while forcing a note into my hand. 'Just be quiet, take it and don't upset me, Jessica. I'll hear no more about it.' |

# CHAPTER SEVEN

The day it went up, I was out somewhere with Jake and I remember checking my phone and not being able to believe what I was seeing. The views and comments on this video were off the scale. Still to this day I have no idea how it took off in the way it did. I hadn't used hashtags or done anything in particular to promote it, but somehow it had picked up momentum and flown.

The next day I went to Meadowhall shopping centre with Nan and this lady came up to us and said, 'I've just been watching the video of you with the money!', which knocked my socks off.

**Norma** This meant nothing to me because you – little madam – hadn't yet informed me that you'd put me on the internet.

**Jess** That's because I hadn't expected it to do anything. I felt a bit bad as I told you, 'Um, I've posted a video of you on TikTok and it's gone viral.'

**Norma** I know now that 'viral' means it went wild, but at the time you might as well have been talking to me in a foreign language. I wasn't in any way au fait with this sort of thing.

**Jess** The video carried on gaining traction and within the space of a week, we had hundreds of thousands of views. Everyone seemed really taken with it and we were getting so many positive comments. But while I was blown away by the attention and all the love we were receiving, I was also at a loss about what to do with it. Loads of people have these one-off, randomly viral videos, but they're mostly only ever a fleeting moment. I was fully aware that this might be the same for us, but also excited and I wanted to see if we could possibly build on it. I don't know why, but I had a gut feeling that this could somehow lead to something.

I said to Nan that it was totally up to her how we moved forward. We could leave it with that one video and disappear

## FAME AND SOCIAL MEDIA

off into the sunset, or we could post another and see how it went.

**Norma** And I said that we might as well give it a go. We had nothing to lose, did we? I didn't know a thing about social media or how it worked apart from when Peter Levy would ask people on *Look North* to get in touch via this TikTok. I'd heard of it, but I had no idea what TikTok was.

**Jess** You thought it was a clock.

**Norma** Oh, you do exaggerate, Jessica. I'm not that simple.

**Jess** If I was to put Facebook, Instagram and TikTok in front of Nan, she wouldn't be able to tell me which was which. I don't think she's ever actually seen the apps themselves.

**Norma** I wouldn't even know what an app was if it came up and bopped me on the nose.

**Jess** I rest my case. I once showed you some photos on my phone to swipe through and you licked your finger as if to turn the page.

**Norma** I knew about Facebook, but I'd never used it in any way. Still haven't. It's all so technical and beyond my brain – I've never seen anybody go faster on a phone than you with your electric fingertips, Jess. It's like wizardry.

**Jess** We made an agreement from the off that Nan called the shots. If at any point she wanted to call it a day, we'd say no more about it, and that decision still stands. She's the one in control of this thing and she can pull the plug at any time.

The next video I posted was of Nan reacting in horror to Cadan's new tattoos.

**Norma** Please don't remind me, Jessica. It was a big spider's web on his knee. He already had a flippin' great snake going up his arm. I know it's his money and his body and he can do what

## CHAPTER SEVEN

|       | |
|-------|--|
| | he likes, but I thought he could have gone for something a bit more … |
| Jess  | Subtle? |
| Norma | Exactly. I don't approve, I'm afraid. I just look forward to winter when he covers them all up with long sleeves and trousers. |
| | I once saw a man on *The Jeremy Kyle Show* who didn't have any spare space on his body because it was covered in tattoos. He even had his *eyeballs* done. Imagine not treasuring your eyesight! I really hope your brother never goes for his face like that. What are we going to do with him with his great big snake up his arm and the cobweb on his leg? |
| Jess  | As long as he likes it, Nan. |
| Norma | I said to Cadan, 'Love, it's your money, you've earned it and if you can afford it then it's up to you. But I don't like it.' And then he went and got another one. |
| Jess  | You're never going to come round to Cadan's tattoos … Weirdly, when Cadan was very little, he became anaemic and ended up needing an eight-hour blood transfusion. After that, there were many trips back and forth to Sheffield Children's Hospital and he developed a fear of needles. |
| Norma | I think we can safely say he's over that phobia now. |
| Jess  | I've not got any tattoos yet, but I'd love to get something timeless and personal. Maybe something meaningful about you, Nan. |
| Norma | Not in my name, please. |
| Jess  | Would you never get a tattoo? You could get 'Jess' across your knuckles. |
| Norma | Really, Jessica. I do worry about you sometimes. |

## FAME AND SOCIAL MEDIA

**Jess**   Do you feel the same about Jake's tattoos?

**Norma**   Well, I can't say I've noticed them, unless he's got one somewhere I don't know about. They're subtle.

**Jess**   Of course you like golden boy Jake's. Anyway, people enjoyed that tattoo video as much as the first one. It snowballed from there.

**Norma**   Even though I don't understand it, I can appreciate how wonderful it is that social media keeps people so closely connected. Some of the people we've been in touch with live such long distances away and that is extraordinary to me.

**Jess**   How does it make you feel when someone reaches out and says they're from Canada? Or Buffalo, USA?

**Norma**   Buffalo, goodness gracious me. I wasn't even too sure where it was, but it made my day, that did. It's a sensation I struggle to describe. We've had people get in touch from Nova Scotia, the Netherlands, Australia, Sweden …

**Jess**   In the early days when people were saying they were watching us all the way from the Australian Gold Coast or the United States, Nan would get goosebumps as I read those comments out to her.

We get messages all the time from people saying our videos have put a smile on their face or cheered them up on a rough day. Sometimes they'll tell us they've been going through a loss and watching us has helped them through, which is always incredible to hear.

**Norma**   Do you remember the lady who got in touch asking us to send a message of support to her mother who was very ill? I was so happy to do that and she was delighted to receive it. I'm not an oracle, I don't have all the answers, but I do like to give people a little something if I can.

## CHAPTER SEVEN

**Jess**     The more videos we put out, the more our audience grew. We started receiving handwritten cards and gifts of appreciation from all over the world. Everything from hand warmers to scarves to brooches.

**Norma**     Someone sent me a toaster and a tea maker.

**Jess**     You were sent an inappropriate 'toy' as well! Come to think of it, I don't know where that went … Can you shed any light on that one?

**Norma**     Whatever are you insinuating, Jessica?

**Jess**     Nothing, nothing. We've also had toiletries, perfume, a soap on a rope …

**Norma**     I was over the moon with that soap on a rope.

**Jess**     It got a bit out of hand so we asked people wanting to send us something to make a donation to charity instead.

**Norma**     And we had some lovely messages from people saying they'd donated to their local food bank or children's hospital on our behalf.

**Jess**     There's a restaurant called The Foresters Arms in Huddersfield where me and Jake went on a date night meal once. I loved the steak pie there so much I ordered a second one to take home to Nan and she devoured it. She said she'd not tasted gravy like that since her mother used to make it.

We did this video on the pie, which went viral and the restaurant got in touch and asked if they could add a stamp 'approved by Norma' to the pie on their menu. For every one they sell, they donate £1 to a local charity that works to combat loneliness.

**Norma**     It's things like that which make me think I must be dreaming.

**Jess**     We have so many examples like that. Special surprises we could never have predicted.

## FAME AND SOCIAL MEDIA

It was a good friend of mine called Scott who, in May 2022, suggested we brought what we were doing on TikTok over to Instagram. Initially I was a bit reluctant, but I'm so glad that we did it as we quickly built up the most amazing community.

People who have been with us from the beginning might remember that at this point I was still just a voice behind the camera, talking to Nan. I'd not shown my face in the Norma videos. But I was receiving emails from people praising our relationship and saying how it reminded them of their grandparents, so I set us up with a @JessandNorma account on Instagram.

**Norma**   You made it all official.

**Jess**   And by June, when we'd been posting for about three months, we started getting approached by brands wanting to work with us. I was so surprised; to me this was just a bit of fun on the side – a hobby – it wasn't how I was planning on generating an income.

The first advert we did was for a meal delivery service, one that me and Jake had used ourselves in the past, and it felt like a nice fit for our account.

**Norma**   There were fish and chips on the menu so that was perfect. You know how I like my 'one of each'.

**Jess**   I've witnessed you hoovering up the pensioners' special in Morrisons often enough.

**Norma**   I think the next advert we did was for the shampoo, wasn't it? I had Claudia Winkleman speak to me on FaceTime. She called me her 'hair icon', which was very kind of her.

**Jess**   It was for Head & Shoulders, a brand Nan has used for years …

**Norma**   Decades, Jess.

# CHAPTER SEVEN

**Jess** … So again, it was perfect for us. The tagline was, 'I didn't know you had dandruff, Nan.'

**Norma** I don't.

**Jess** Get you, remembering your line. Such a pro!

**Norma** We've since seen Claudia advertising a scalp serum for the same brand and I'm a bit affronted because I think she's stolen my job.

**Jess** Will you be having words?

**Norma** She should watch her back.

**Jess** Seriously though, we love working with brands that have always been staples in our home.

I'm very careful about who we choose to team up with – sometimes it might be a product that doesn't feel right for us both and I'll negotiate doing an ad on the page I share with Jake, @jessandjakeofficial, instead.

The most important thing is remaining authentic and making sure that the ads don't take the place of our normal, non-branded content, which people love. Believe me, there are way more offers we've turned down than accepted.

**Norma** Like what?

**Jess** I said a polite 'thanks but no thanks' to Lovehoney.

**Norma** They sound like a nice company. Do they make honey?

**Jess** Try again.

**Norma** Jam?

**Jess** Adult toys.

**Norma** Oh. Probably best you said no that one, love.

**Jess** After we'd done a few paid posts, a management team

## FAME AND SOCIAL MEDIA

contacted me and said that we could earn an income from Facebook if we wanted to give that a whirl as well. My first thought was that my mum wasn't on TikTok or Instagram but she did have Facebook and this would be a way for her to watch us.

We put our first Facebook video out in September 2022 and started getting paid shortly after that. We earn money via adverts that are embedded in our ordinary content.

All three platforms are different and I had to learn very quickly how to create and edit for each one.

**Norma**  I think you are ever so clever with it, Jessica. You have so much to do – my job is to sit there and look pretty.

**Jess**  You do a lot more than that, Nan!

The videos that do well are the natural, wholesome moments between the two of us. I read all the comments. For instance, I once noticed that a few people were asking what Nan had done as a job and so we filmed a quick video of her talking about that.

Besides being led by our community, and by Nan, there was no strategy. But it had started to blossom into this beautiful thing.

Following the death of my dad's dad in December 2022, I had a bit of an epiphany moment. I decided I wanted to take some time out to care for Nan who was needing more help. I also wanted to see whether social media could be a viable career for us if I had more time to dedicate to it. So, I left my job as a social worker in February 2023. I had enough in savings to support myself for four months while I figured it all out.

**Norma**  I know you still had your degree in social work and could have gone back to it at any time, but it still scared the living daylights out of me.

## CHAPTER SEVEN

**Jess**    I'll admit it was touch and go at times, with us experiencing a bit of a lull in brand deals when I first left my job. But I had this feeling that everything would be OK. Our views and follower numbers were going up all the time. I believed in us and had faith that if you put your time into something, it would pay off.

Once we hit a million followers on TikTok, it was like everything had fallen into place.

**Norma**    I remember very clearly getting to the million milestone because we'd been to the safari park for my 89th birthday the day before. So, on 7 March 2023, a whole year after you had put that first video on the internet, we made it to one million followers and I just couldn't comprehend it.

**Jess**    There was no stopping us after that and by Christmas we had two million. But because Nan's so humble, she still can't understand why people want to watch us. And obviously she doesn't come from a smartphone generation so it's even harder for her to grasp.

**Norma**    They tell me when I go out that I'm funny.

**Jess**    You are funny, Nan!

**Norma**    We've always had our own banter, you and me, but I never thought it would appeal to anyone else. There are a lot of quite heavy things happening in the world in this day and age and if we can have a little bit of fun and put a smile on a few faces, then that's a good thing.

**Jess**    I always aim to keep our content light-hearted and relatable. Basically, it's real family life.

We hope you feel like you're sitting in Nan's living room with us while you're watching. It's not highly edited, it's not glossy or professionally lit. It's just genuine and it reflects the same connections people either have themselves or did have in the past and perhaps wish they had again.

**Norma** We didn't really know what we were doing to start with and it took us a while to learn what people wanted. But we've done it, the two of us, haven't we?

**Jess** We used to sit here and ask each other what we could do for our next video.

**Norma** Never for long, though. It's not often that we're stuck for an idea.

**Jess** Nan is actually brilliant at finding out about local events from the paper and suggesting that we go along and film.

**Norma** And I do love our beauty salon skits.

**Jess** That's when I play the part of a gossipy manicurist asking Nan whether she's been on any dates lately.

**Norma** It's where 'Leonard', 'Cheating Charlie' and 'Wild Wilma' came from.

**Jess** They've all become running jokes.

I'm so happy that the world can see what I've always known. To me, my nan is the most amazing, loving, funny, witty woman and now everyone else loves her as well. She's a natural on the camera because she is just herself. In fact, I'd say the camera doesn't do her justice.

**Norma** I don't really notice the camera, not any more. That phone is always in your hand anyway so it's hard to tell the difference, love.

**Jess** Remember that day we had the proper TV cameras in?

**Norma** Heavens. Somehow we found ourselves being interviewed live on ITV's *This Morning*.

## CHAPTER SEVEN

**Jess**     That was the single most nerve-wracking thing we've ever done. We'd been invited on the show to talk about our social media journey and a crew came round to film us from Nan's living room. It was Josie Gibson and Craig Doyle hosting that day and all morning I was pacing the room, thinking, 'Are we doing the right thing here? We're just a normal family and this is crazy.'

**Norma**     I was absolutely fine, by the way.

**Jess**     I know! You were cool as a cucumber; it was me who was like a rabbit in the headlights.

**Norma**     It started to go a bit downhill when they gave us those earpieces.

**Jess**     We were both given these earpieces to wear so we could hear the audio from Josie and Craig in the *This Morning* studio. Just before we went on air, the producer asked me to take Nan's hearing aid out so she could wear a second earpiece. They thought it would give her a better chance of hearing what was being said from the studio. As soon as Josie and Craig began speaking with us, Nan's landline started ringing.

**Norma**     You'd unplugged the phone from the wall, so goodness knows how it managed to ring.

**Jess**     We were live on national television. I was thinking it was a sign from my grandad. Could it have been his way of telling us he was with us? Was there something really deep and profound happening here? Um, no.

**Norma**     It was my friend Mary.

**Jess**     She left a voicemail saying, 'Hi Norma, it's Mary! Call me back when you can.' She hadn't realised we were on the telly.

And then once the interview started, I quickly realised that without her hearing aids, Nan couldn't hear anything.

## FAME AND SOCIAL MEDIA

I had two options. I could either deal with all the questions on my own, which would look like Nan was mute, or I could flag up live on air that we needed to get this hearing aid back in. I chose the second option, which was super-awkward but we got it back in as quickly as we could.

I think they cut our segment short in the end; they were probably terrified about what we would do next. After that whole disaster I felt truly awful, thinking, *What on earth have I just done to my poor nan in front of the entire nation?*

**Norma** Did you, love? Why would you think that? I thoroughly enjoyed myself.

**Jess** And that's the funny thing. While I was agonising over everything and vowing never to do live television ever again, she was happily flicking through her Damart catalogue, not a care in the world.

It was a good reminder to me to be really careful about what we say yes to. We get invited to a lot of things and there are so many that would be great experiences, but as a general rule if it's over an hour away we turn it down. If it's something super-special like *Emmerdale* or *Coronation Street* then Nan makes the decision as to whether or not she feels up to it.

**Norma** People think because I'm sitting down, I must be resting. But my body gets very tired and even more so when I'm travelling in a car. Life is getting that little bit harder, unfortunately.

**Jess** It's the hustle and bustle of it that exhausts her. We were invited to go and meet Rishi Sunak at 10 Downing Street when he was Prime Minister and we did look at how we could make that work.

**Norma** We were going to get a tour around parliament and Westminster, which would have been a dream come true for me. But we have to be sensible and realistic about what I can do.

Jess   The Prime Minister should be coming to you, anyway!

Norma   We'd make him a nice Ringtons tea, wouldn't we?

Jess   I'm sure we could stretch to that.

It's all about being mindful of you, Nan, and what you can manage. We've gradually reduced the number of videos we record. In the earlier days we were doing around ten a week but we've significantly reduced that now – I know everything will have to keep slowing and tapering down. Unless we buy you a pair of roller-skates.

Norma   Or a skateboard. I can see myself on one of them.

Jess   Everything is led by Nan. If I get here in the morning and she's not up to filming, we don't film. And on the days she's got more energy, we make the most of it. The most important thing is that it's always fun.

Norma   I'm delighted that it's bringing some money in. I know a lot of people think social media isn't really a 'proper' job, but I see how hard you work behind the scenes.

Jess   Maybe it's not a 'proper job' in the traditional sense and I'm not saying I'm down the mines, but it can be intensive and it's often around the clock. There's filming, editing, making sure the videos are right before they go out, engaging with the comments, the multiple meetings behind every brand deal … there's a heck of a lot to navigate.

On the flip side of that, we're financially more comfortable than we could have imagined. We've been able to treat the people we love – buying Cadan a pair of designer trainers he'd wanted for his 21st birthday felt special, we have plans to redecorate my mum's bedroom, and we make a significant charity donation once a month to give back, too.

## FAME AND SOCIAL MEDIA

**Norma**  You manage everything, and I'm so proud of you. You're a real businesswoman. Who would have thought that my tiresome little monkey would go on to do this?

**Jess**  Our income has not only allowed me to be with Nan every day; it's also meant we can make her as comfortable as we can in her home. We've just had air conditioning fitted to keep her cool in the summer months. And Jake is always listening to the issues we experience in the house and coming up with solutions to make it all feel better.

I'm so pleased to be able to do this for Nan, and hope the financial security we have now will also mean I can be more present with my children in the future (when I have them) and I'm not going to have to penny-pinch, which is how it was when I was growing up.

At the centre of this, as ever, is Nan. She's the reason I managed to get the grades to go to university by providing me with encouragement and a safe haven when everything else around me was falling apart. She's the one who helped me with my petrol money as I travelled to and from lectures. And here she is again, building this career with me.

Our income is generated from advertising and brand deals. We get the odd moan from followers about the paid partnerships we do, but the truth is, without the incredible opportunities offered to us by brands, I would not be in a position to care for Nan in the way I do. The income from those deals allows me to be here full time and I know most of our followers appreciate that.

**Norma**  I don't even dare think what we would do if you weren't able to be here with me.

**Jess**  At the very minimum we would have a care package of people coming into the house on a daily basis. Social media has enabled me to do this for you.

## CHAPTER SEVEN

**Norma**  It's mind-blowing, Jess.

**Jess**  Did you know that someone offered to buy Jake's underpants the other day?

**Norma**  They never did!

**Jess**  This is absolutely true. Two grand for a pair of his boxers.

**Norma**  They do say that there's nowt so queer as folk. What's Jake spent the money on?

**Jess**  He didn't accept the offer, obviously! We've got a reputation to maintain. And we're doing OK without having to resort to that.

Despite the odd dodgy request like that, the support we receive from our followers is amazing and the vast majority of reactions are positive. However, like most other content creators out there, we do get some negative comments. They tend to be loudest on Facebook for some reason, but I manage that side of things on my own.

**Norma**  I don't read those comments; I wouldn't know how to. You protect me from all that, which I'm very grateful for because I understand that some people can be rather rude and I've no interest in seeing it.

**Jess**  The trolling is something I've deliberately sheltered Nan from. We actually sailed along quite happily for some time without any negativity, which I think was down to the nature of our videos. But when the odd comments here and there did start to trickle in, I took them personally and I'd get upset. There have been some awful ones, but they are only ever about me. They are never about Nan.

**Norma**  Other than the one who thought I'd had a stroke.

**Jess**  OMG, that was the day your speech was a bit slurred because you'd got some new teeth you were adjusting to.

## FAME AND SOCIAL MEDIA

We had people telling me to get you to the doctor ASAP.

I don't mind people voicing a difference of opinion or offering friendly advice. That's fine. What does bother me is when people start coming for my character. I get comments questioning my motives, like the time I was decorating your porch and someone said I was only doing that because I wanted the house to be left to me in the will.

**Norma** Give over!

**Jess** Or they'll say Nan isn't capable of consenting to be filmed and I'm taking advantage.

**Norma** I'd like to put it on the record again that I have never been and will never be pushed into anything.

**Jess** Anyone who genuinely watches our videos would realise that this 'sweet little old lady' says it exactly how it is. I would never allow anyone to take advantage of her and she'd be the first person to say, 'I'm not doing that!' if she didn't want to do it.

**Norma** Which I do say from time to time.

**Jess** Sometimes people will comment on my appearance, which is difficult for someone like me who struggles with low self-esteem. They'll criticise my house, my clothes, the way Jake looks. People have even suggested that Jake is controlling – they just find a narrative and run with it. One person said, 'I don't like Jess. I can't trust her. It's her jaw.'

I mean, that's wild, isn't it? I know ignoring it is the best policy, but if I'm in a bad mental health period, it plays on my mind and I can spiral.

**Norma** Some of them say your voice is annoying ...

**Jess** And you love that, don't you! We have a giggle at those ones.

# CHAPTER SEVEN

People are obsessed with you needing a more comfortable chair, a lap tray and to raise your legs for circulation.

Norma — I'm happy with my chair, I've tried a lap tray and didn't like it and I do raise my legs. Does that clear everything up?

Jess — And there we go. Every now and then, we'll do a little video to make it publicly known that Nan is an adult with a voice and just because she's in her nineties doesn't mean she can't make her own decisions. It doesn't mean she's lost her sense of humour either, so the odd very gentle prank is a bit of fun. That's all.

Sometimes I'll respond, like the time I was accused of speaking to her like a baby and so for a joke we dressed her up as a giant baby. But I tend to block, move on and try to forget.

I've turned all my messages off so no one can DM me calling me horrible names. I shouldn't have to expose myself to that sort of abuse. My skin's getting thicker.

Norma — What I don't understand is why people don't just use the off button. No one is forcing anyone to watch. If you don't like it, don't watch it. There's no need to be mean.

Jess — I've been seeing a therapist since 2020 and it's something we've explored quite a lot in our sessions. What I've noticed is that it's all proportional and that's helping me rationalise it. When you have millions of followers, it feels as if the negativity is getting louder but it's actually just a reflection of the size of our audience.

And the people writing these comments, I've got no idea what their upbringing was like, what their values are, whereabouts in the world they live, if they've got health problems or other things troubling them. So I try not to dwell on it.

## FAME AND SOCIAL MEDIA

**Norma**  The good that's come out of this adventure far outweighs the bad.

**Jess**  It does. Nan has always been my person, my very best friend. But the opportunities we've experienced together, and the amount of time that we now get to spend with each other, has brought so much light to what could have been quite a difficult time.

Having said that, if one more person messages me saying Norma doesn't look comfortable in that chair …

**Norma**  If I wasn't comfortable, you'd be the first person to know about it.

**Jess**  Ain't that the truth!

INTERLUDE

# Going viral

There are so many to choose from, but these are a few of our favourite videos we've made. They don't necessarily have the most views, but they are the ones that have made us laugh the most. We hope you love them too.

### The £10,000 prank competition

**Jess**  This was a little prank I played on Nan where I told her TikTok were giving away ten grand to whoever deserved it the most.

**Norma**  You had me going with this one, you wicked child.

**Jess**  I told a real sob story about how we were living in poverty and had been so desperate for money that my mum had been forced to sell drugs. That's where the name Mafia Kate comes from. People still stop her in the street to call her that wherever she goes.

**Norma**  Your mum's tickled pink by that. She loves it. I think that nickname suits her down to the ground.

**Jess**  I also said you'd been forced to sell your body on the streets, Nan.

**Norma**  Oh, Jessica!

**Jess**  And you said you had a body 'like a crinkle cut chip', which made me howl. That video still makes me laugh because the whole time I'm telling the story, you're sitting behind me

# INTERLUDE

looking more and more outraged. It's those facial expressions again, Nan.

**Norma** I knew you were teasing me by then and I eventually told you to pack it in – you were doing my head in.

**Jess** I'm constantly doing your head in. That's part of my job description.

## Nan meets Alfie Boe

**Jess** I think this one has a little bit of everything. It's got humour because at first Nan doesn't recognise Alfie and she's mortified when she realises it's him. And it has a lot of emotion because when Alfie later serenades her with 'You Raise Me Up', it was such a special moment and we both became tearful.

**Norma** That song really does 'raise me up' whenever I hear it and if I ever have a bad day, I pop it on the Alexa and it brightens everything up.

**Jess** To have the actual Alfie Boe singing it to us was magical.

**Norma** It was gorgeous. And he was so kind, a memory to treasure.

## Fake Miss World competition

**Jess** I told Nan I was entering a beauty competition and gushed to the camera about how I didn't eat processed food, abstained from chocolate and spent hours each day working out.

**Norma** What a load of hogwash. You said you'd only drink water from puddles.

**Jess** It was your face-pulling that made that video.

**Norma** I couldn't believe the rubbish you were coming out with.

Jess   A few people moaned about it and said I shouldn't be pranking Nan. But I'm the centre of the joke and Nan is the one revealing all with her eye rolls and sighs.

Norma   It's just a bit of fun.

### Nan goes to Dunkin' Donuts

Jess   OK, this was proof that you can learn something new every day. We were sitting in the car with a takeaway cup of coffee and a box of Dunkin' Donuts. Nan kept on dunking her strawberry donut into her coffee, which I'd literally never seen anybody do.

Norma   You were laughing at me but what else are you supposed to do with a dunkin' donut?

Jess   Nan couldn't see what I found so funny about it, so I Googled and, to my surprise, I found that dunking your Dunkin' Donut is actually a thing.

Norma   The clue's in the name, isn't it? Dunkin' Donuts. You dunk them.

Jess   It was when you said to me, 'That took a long time for the penny to drop.' You had me creased.

Norma   Sometimes I wonder what goes on in that brain of yours, love.

Jess   I think that was also the video where you asked for eight sugars in your coffee. The same coffee you were dunking your sugar-laden donut into.

Norma   I admit that did get a little bit too sweet for me.

Jess   Hallelujah! Finally something that's *too* sweet' for you. Shall I contact *BBC News*?

INTERLUDE

## Flying fish and chips in the car

**Jess** We've posted a few of these 'take the money' videos because people relate to them so well, but this one is probably my favourite. It's where Nan is trying to get me to accept a £10 note and she won't hear it when I say I don't need it.

**Norma** Is that the one where I'm eating fish and chips?

**Jess** Yes! And when you say, 'Jessica, *please*,' a piece of fish shoots out of your mouth. Everyone was leaving fish emojis in the comments, which really made me laugh.

**Norma** You're easily pleased, Jessica.

CHAPTER EIGHT

# Technology

**Jess**  Nan, if I was to ask what an old fogey like you made of modern technology, what would you say?

**Norma**  First of all, I'd say, 'Less of the "old fogey", madam.'

**Jess**  Old fart, then.

**Norma**  Dearie me. Whatever are we going to do with you, Jessica?

**Jess**  OK, what do you, as a senior lady, reckon to all the technological progress which is supposed to have improved our lives?

**Norma**  Well, I sort of feel whatever will they think of next? I like to think that I'm quite intelligent, but anything involving a computer is beyond me.

**Jess**  You are intelligent, Nan! It's nothing to do with intelligence. Even as someone who spends a massive amount of time online, I can struggle to keep up with pace of change. I totally understand why people of your generation find it all too much.

**Norma**  It's a young person's world, that's for sure. I appreciate all the wonderful things we're able to do now but it is very daunting. The only piece of technology we had in the house when I was growing up was the wireless. My mum kept it quite high up on a shelf and I had to stand on a little stool to reach it.

I'd listen to *Dick Barton – Special Agent*, which was a thriller serial on the BBC every weekday evening about an

# CHAPTER EIGHT

ex-commando turned criminal investigator. He was aided by his two assistants Jock and Snowey and together they solved all sorts of cases. Each episode was just 15 minutes long, but I wouldn't allow anyone to come near me or talk to me while I listened. I *loved* it.

Jess   It's strange to think that the radio was the most high-tech bit of kit in the house!

Norma   Yes, but it was a vital 'bit of kit'. Especially during the war when we needed information and news. My mum would always have the BBC on. I remember listening to King George VI, who reigned until 1952. He had a stutter, and my mum and I felt so sorry for him. Whenever he made an address, she'd say, 'Come on, Elizabeth' – who was his wife and our future Queen Mother – 'get to his side and help him out!'

There was a film made about him, *The King's Speech*.

Jess   When did you first splash out on a telly?

Norma   I bought a black and white television set for me and mum when I was in my early twenties and we both enjoyed watching Laurel and Hardy and Charlie Chaplin. Oh, they were funny, Jess. Beautiful stuff.

I offered to leave the TV behind for Mum when Michael and I got married but she wouldn't hear of it. She said she wasn't too bothered and would be happy enough with her radio.

Sometimes I think it would be nice if we could go back to a simpler time when the wireless and television were considered mod cons.

Jess   I think you've embraced a lot of tech changes really well.

Norma   I've never sent an email in my life.

Jess   But the things you have taken to have genuinely enhanced

# TECHNOLOGY

your life. We got you an Alexa a couple of years ago and she's been a fab little addition, hasn't she?

**Norma**    When she behaves herself.

**Jess**    Occasionally we ask her a question and she'll blatantly ignore us.

**Norma**    She can be a rude little so-and-so sometimes.

**Jess**    I once pranked Nan by programming Alexa to say, 'Jessica is a fat, annoying granddaughter.' She thought it was playing through every person's speakers in the whole of the UK.

**Norma**    That's because I have no clue how she works. But I tell Alexa to turn off my lamps and she does that, which is very impressive.

**Jess**    Before Alexa came along, Nan was relying on someone else turning the lamps off before bed because she struggles to find the switch. So it's given her some extra independence.

**Norma**    She lets me listen to music, too. I tell her what I fancy and she puts it on for me.

**Jess**    Sometimes I'll be out and about and I'll check Spotify on my phone and see that Nan is listening to Alfie Boe. I think, 'How lovely that she's sitting in her chair having an afternoon with Alfie.'

**Norma**    I make sure to say goodnight to Alexa every night and she'll often reply, 'Goodnight, sleep well.' I like that.

It's so many years since your grandad passed and obviously the changes in that time have been astronomical. But I'm sure there's a lot he'd have found very interesting. Mind, I don't know what he would have made of TikTok. He'd have probably said, 'I'll just leave you girls to it.'

**Jess**    What do you think he would have said about a self-service

# CHAPTER EIGHT

|   |   |
|---|---|
|  | checkout? Because they can't have been around when he was here. |
| Norma | He'd have refused to shop wherever they were, I should think. |
| Jess | I get that. There are a lot of new technologies that end up excluding older people and self-service checkouts in supermarkets are a perfect example. |
| Norma | If I go to the supermarket, I like to have a chat with the shop assistant. For some people, that might be the only person they see all day. If you take away that one bit of human contact and replace it with a computer, what is that doing to people? |
| Jess | I know, those little interactions can make such a difference. Not only that, the self-service systems are tricky for older people to manage. There's no way you'd be able to use it without me there to help, is there? |
| Norma | If you weren't with me, Jess, I wouldn't have a clue what to do. |
| Jess | And they're such wind-up merchants with all that 'unexpected item in the bagging area' nonsense. They drive me crackers and I know what I'm doing! |
|  | It's not just the checkouts that have switched over to self-service. Things have drastically changed at the café we enjoy going to. There used to be a hatch where you gave your order to a waitress then you found a table and they brought everything to you. Now you do everything on a screen and you have to get your coffee and tea yourself from the machine. |
| Norma | When we went recently there was an elderly gentleman on his own and he'd got himself into all sorts of bother before you spotted him and went to help. |
| Jess | The tea and coffee machine has two spouts – one for hot |

## TECHNOLOGY

water and one for coffee. This poor fella was trying to fill a teapot with hot water but he'd placed it underneath the wrong spout. So when he pressed for hot water on the screen, it came gushing out everywhere and could have caused a nasty burn. It made me really sad and I just thought, 'What are we coming to?'

**Norma** And of course everything is paid for with a card tap now.

**Jess** Yes, contactless. We're moving towards a cashless society, which is weird because cash was always king, wasn't it? And the best way to support local businesses used to be to pay by cold hard cash. You're proper old school, Nan, because you still love a cheque!

**Norma** Not many businesses accept one of those any more.

**Jess** Because cheques are practically prehistoric.

**Norma** A bit like me.

**Jess** I think you might have one of the last remaining chequebooks in the whole of Britain. We should put it in a museum. I suppose they became unfashionable because it used to be a bit of a hassle to bank them, but your gardener accepts a cheque. He takes a photo of it, sends it to his banking app and it goes straight into his account.

**Norma** I'm flabbergasted by that every time. How clever.

**Jess** But the shift to online banking is another aspect of modern tech that puts up barriers for older people. You don't use online banking, do you?

**Norma** Goodness no. I need to speak to a human being but it's virtually impossible to do that now. All the banks have automated phone systems where they ask you to press two for one thing and then three for another and I often can't hear what the instructions are because of my deafness. I end up in a right old tizzy.

# CHAPTER EIGHT

**Jess**  And they've closed a lot of the branches so it's not like you can pop in to see anyone in person.

**Norma**  Round here, you've got to travel miles to access a branch, which, for a lot of people, isn't an option. It makes your head spin because the changes have come at us all of a sudden. When I see what you lot do on your phones, it's crazy.

**Jess**  When you were still able to go out of the house independently, you had an old Nokia. Do you remember? It looked like a brick, had the game Snake on it and the battery would last for 3,000 weeks. I think you only ever used it to call yourself a taxi.

**Norma**  That was my limit. I couldn't text anybody, I wouldn't have known how to. While I find it quite astonishing the things you can do on your mobile, Jess, I do think you've got phone fever. The three of you – you, Jake and Cadan – are addicted to those things. It's a bit of a morbid thought, but it often makes me wonder if it can cause health issues.

**Jess**  The amount of screen time has got to have some negative impact on the brain. Smartphones definitely have their positives and they make life so much easier, but it is really concerning how much time people are spending on them, especially children.

**Norma**  You do see a lot of children with their heads buried in screens. It can't be good.

**Jess**  I'm grateful for the fact that Snapchat, TikTok and Instagram weren't a thing when I was at school. The bullying that goes on via these apps is unreal.

Me and my friends used MSN Messenger to chat to each other after school and I'd log in on our massive PC which ran off Windows 95. God, that seems ancient! But MSN was the OG of all the social platforms. You used to be able to 'nudge'

## TECHNOLOGY

people if they hadn't replied (I was *always* nudging and must have been so annoying) and you could also send a 'knock' where a giant hand would appear on the screen. Cringing!

I had a Bebo account as well, which was a really early version of social media where you could change your 'skin' on your profile page to represent how you were feeling and you'd ask people at school to be your 'other half on Bebo'.

I've lost you again, haven't I, Nan?

**Norma** To be quite honest, I'm completely bamboozled. What was the point of it?

**Jess** It was just a way of communicating with your mates (or the lad you fancied). You could have music on your page, so when someone visited your profile they'd hear your choice of track. I can remember having 'No Air' by Jordin Sparks and Chris Brown on mine. And you'd write messages on there as well. It was very strange, looking back.

**Norma** Sounds it.

**Jess** It all seems so silly now. And innocent. I've had Facebook since 2008 so I would have been about 12 when I got it and I'd update my status three or four times a day. Every time I had something to eat I'd post about it, like anyone would be remotely interested.

The way we use social media has totally changed. I do fear for the world my future children will be living in.

**Norma** I should imagine a lot of kids take harmful information from the internet and are influenced by it.

**Jess** We hear of children filming themselves doing things they shouldn't be doing and then those videos ending up getting shared around the school. It just shatters the innocence of childhood.

# CHAPTER EIGHT

The worst I ever had at primary school was someone at school telling me Santa wasn't real. That was as harsh as it got. It's just really sad.

**Norma** I'm not saying I can't see the benefits of mobile phones. When I was about 19, my mum was taken ill in the night and the only telephone I could reach was a kiosk several roads away and there was deep snow on the ground. Thank goodness that's not still the case, but we do seem to have all sorts of trouble now that never existed before these fancy phones were invented.

**Jess** I admit that I'm on my phone a lot, but it's mostly work-related. And it's a double-edged sword for me, because without my phone, I wouldn't have a livelihood.

**Norma** I do try my best to learn about all the new-fangled things we have, but just when I get used to something, everything seems to change again. My mum would have said, 'I can't do this. Don't even tell me about it.' She hated anything new.

**Jess** Do you remember we tried you with a Kindle as a Christmas present? That went down like a sack of spuds.

**Norma** It wasn't the same as reading a book, which is something I've always loved to do. I can lose myself in a good whodunnit – my mum used to say, 'You've got your head buried in a book again, Norma. You're not much good company.'

**Jess** I think you were just being awkward with the Kindle.

**Norma** But books have a feel and a smell like nothing else. I like being able to pass books on to other people when I've read them. Ian Rankin, Lynda La Plante, Jeffrey Deaver, James Patterson and Val McDermid are just a few of my favourite authors.

**Jess** You do like your crime thrillers. Maybe you're an undercover criminal.

# TECHNOLOGY

**Norma**   Jessica, you lot have no idea what goes on here after dark …

**Jess**   Maybe we're onto something here because you like your crime telly shows as well.

**Norma**   I do, but there are far too many channels.

**Jess**   There's another massive change – streaming has transformed the way we watch TV but you still only watch One, Two and Three.

**Norma**   Occasionally I push the boat out and venture over to Channel 4. And I like 5USA because it has *Law and Order*.

**Jess**   I really can't imagine thinking of Channel 4 as adventurous. When I was in primary school, my mum and her partner got Sky TV for the first time and it was like the best thing that had ever happened to me!

The package meant we had the Disney Channel and so I was finally able to join in with conversations at school about *The Suite Life of Zack and Cody* and *That's So Raven*. Life-changing for an eight-year-old!

**Norma**   I don't think I know any of those shows, Jessica. I go through the TV magazine each week and decide what I'm going to watch. It's always the soaps first and foremost and I get vexed when they get interrupted by a football match put on in their place.

**Jess**   Nan has a little telly upstairs in the bedroom and sometimes she'll watch something on a plus one, but that's as far as she'll stray from the traditional terrestrial channels.

She has access to Netflix via my account and we watched *The Crown* on that together and the Harlan Coben drama *Fool Me Once* because she's a big fan of his books. But she needs me here to get her logged on; there's no chance she'd manage it on her own.

# CHAPTER EIGHT

**Norma**    I've tried to locate Netflix myself but to no avail.

**Jess**    I've written down foolproof instructions for you in the past but without success. And it definitely isn't because you're not clever enough. I think it comes from a fundamental lack of interest. It was exactly the same with the DVD player. Not interested.

**Norma**    It's more about the difficulty of having to take something else in. It sounds like I'm giving up, but these are all things that are out of my comfort zone and I don't have the capacity for that any more.

**Jess**    It's just what you're comfortable with and happy with and that's fine. At least you've had WiFi put in now so we can use the internet when we're here. Although that took a lot of convincing. You'd been saying no for years because you didn't want it or have any use for it.

**Norma**    I didn't need it, Jess.

**Jess**    No, but we did! You were worried it would interfere with your landline and it was a fear of having something new in the house you were unfamiliar with.

But it has been useful for you. You like a little browse online and sometimes if you're not feeling up to going out shopping, it's easier to do it on my iPad together.

**Norma**    I think online shopping can be good, but I feel sorry that some of these young ones aren't having days out together going round the stores like we used to. My shopping trips up to Sheffield with my sister were so precious.

You've got to have contact with people and we're losing all of that. We've even got robots delivering parcels now. I can appreciate that the brains that have gone into inventing all this are amazing, but is it going too far? It feels a bit dangerous.

# TECHNOLOGY

**Jess**    The robots are everywhere, Nan. University students are using artificial intelligence to write their essays for them. There are even driverless taxis in some parts of the world – there's no human in there, the cab drives itself.

**Norma**    You wouldn't catch me in one of those. I'll tell you that for nothing.

**Jess**    Have you seen those robots in restaurants? They work as waiting staff, take your orders and deliver your food.

**Norma**    You're making that up.

**Jess**    I'm not, it's real. They whizz around the floor with your plates on and take them all to the right tables.

**Norma**    Where do you find them, then?

**Jess**    I don't think they've made it to Retford yet, but they have them in the bigger cities.

**Norma**    Oh, that's awful. Part of going out is having a little bit of laughter and talking to the waitress and asking questions about the menu. And I can't eat cinnamon. How would I tell a robot about that? It sends my mind all over the place. Where will we be in ten years' time?

**Jess**    Ruled by robots. It'll get to the point where no one has a job any more.

**Norma**    You nearly lost one this morning. I hate to tell you this, Jessica, but Jake made my toast while you were on your call and he made a lovely job of it so I'm not sure your services are required any longer.

**Jess**    That's shocking, Nan.

**Norma**    I might replace you with a robot. It would probably give me less cheek.

INTERLUDE
# Norma's best one-liners

**Jess** 'Can I get you anything else, Nan?'

**Norma** 'Maybe a nice fella?'

\*

**Jess** 'How did you sleep last night?'

**Norma** 'With my eyes shut.'

\*

To a garden-centre assistant when Norma and Jess had temporarily lost Kate: 'Can you say on the tannoy that there's a woman with dreadful hair gone missing?'

\*

**Jess** 'Stay there a minute.'

**Norma** 'Where do you think I'm going?'

\*

To Jess after she'd lost some weight: 'Lose any more and you'll slip down a drain.'

\*

Handing over a water sample to Jess to take to the doctor: 'You could sell that and be a millionaire.'

# CHAPTER NINE
# Holidays

**Jess**    Now here's a fun fact for everyone. We've never been away together, have we?

**Norma**    Good gracious no, I couldn't face that!

**Jess**    Am I too much trouble for you?

**Norma**    We've always had day trips out, ever since you were little. But you're right, Jess, we've not been on a holiday.

**Jess**    If I could have taken you anywhere, it would have been to Italy to look out onto the Bay of Naples.

**Norma**    Ah, that would have been a dream.

**Jess**    When me and Jake were in Italy for his 30th birthday in 2023, I could see the Bay of Naples from where we were staying. Do you remember I gave you a ring to tell you what I was looking at and to say that I wished you were there?

**Norma**    Yes, and I was green with envy! It always looks absolutely out of this world from the pictures.

**Jess**    You've not really strayed too far away from home, have you?

**Norma**    No, I've never been on a plane. I've never even stayed in a hotel since my honeymoon in 1962. I've always been a homebody and my sister Betty was even worse than me! My eldest sister Joan, on the other hand, was the polar opposite and couldn't wait to get away. She went everywhere – camping, caravanning, abroad – and she never liked coming back.

## CHAPTER NINE

**Jess**   I think that must be part of our makeup, Nan, because it's exactly the same with me. That trip to Rome and the Amalfi coast with Jake was the holiday of a lifetime, literally breathtaking. But after a couple of days I wanted to come home. I was walking around the Colosseum thinking, 'This is lovely, but it's not as nice as my front room!'

  I do really want to go back to Italy – Lake Como is on the bucket list. I'd also love to go to Paris. Jake is always saying that we need to get a holiday booked. I do love going away ... but I like being at home even more.

**Norma**   Paris is magical; you must go, Jessica.

**Jess**   Do you remember there was a school trip to Paris one year that my mum paid for in full, non-refundable? As the date we were leaving drew nearer, I started feeling increasingly uneasy and at the last minute I decided I didn't have the guts to go ... I still feel bad about that to this day.

**Norma**   You missed out. I visited Paris twice in my early twenties with my friends, before I met Michael. Notre Dame, the Sacré-Coeur, and the most beautiful pastries. I can see them now in the patisserie window.

**Jess**   Well, I do love a good croissant.

**Norma**   Yes, I can tell that.

**Jess**   Food hits different when you're eating abroad. Me and Jake both love Italian food. We thought we'd eaten great pizzas and pasta dishes here ... until we went to Rome. That was next level. Everything we'd had before just paled in comparison.

**Norma**   When my children were small, we used to go to Sutton-on-Sea in Lincolnshire where we'd stay in a little flat – it was a holiday let run by a lovely lady. Not even the fact that it was above a funeral director's parlour put me off! Your grandad

## HOLIDAYS

|||
|---|---|
| | and I eventually bought a caravan and started to venture further afield. |
| Jess | Did that caravan live outside the house? |
| Norma | No, I kept it in the bedroom, Jess. |
| Jess | All right! I meant was it a static or touring caravan? |
| Norma | It was a little touring one and we'd take it up to Northumberland where I fell in love with Bamburgh and Holy Island. Oh, it was so beautiful and full of history, with a magnificent castle overlooking the beach. It really got to me. |
| Jess | I bet that caravan was dead old-fashioned inside. |
| Norma | Of course it was, we didn't have new-fashioned money! It had everything we needed: a kitchen at one end, a bunk bed, a table and chairs in the middle that turned into a double bed and, thank God, it had a toilet. |
| Jess | No need for a potty! |
| Norma | The kids loved it, so that was the main thing. We had such fun days with that caravan, spending most of the time on the beach. We went to Filey and your mother lost one of her new sandals on the Brigg, a rocky peninsular up from the beach. Your grandad searched the length and breadth of that place looking for the missing shoe but he never found it. We had to buy her a new pair. |
| Jess | I bet Grandad was fer-yooming! |
| Norma | He was but he hid it well. |
| | Another holiday took us to Edinburgh. I still remember walking up to the front door of a museum and a man saying to your mum, who must have been about eight, 'I can't let you in, sonny, you're eating an apple.' Your mother was absolutely livid that he'd thought she was a boy! |

# CHAPTER NINE

**Jess**     That was probably because of the godawful haircut you gave her. I've seen the photographic evidence of that bowl cut and it's bordering on child abuse.

**Norma**     It wasn't a bowl cut! I prided myself on your mother's hair; it was healthy and it shone. And Edinburgh was such a wonderful place. It's got its own feel and smell.

**Jess**     I've never been there and I know I should because it's pretty easy to reach on the train from where we are. I need to pull my finger out and start exploring a bit more. You forget that we have so many beautiful places to visit right here in the UK.

**Norma**     Years ago, people tended to holiday in the UK much more. When I was growing up, my mum would take me and my sisters to Scarborough and Skegness where Joan would disappear, making a beeline for the cockles and mussels stalls. We'd be looking all over for her and that's where she always was!

When I was a bit older, me and my mum would go to Sutton-on-Sea and I used to have to sneak off into the dunes to have a cigarette. A couple of times she caught me and if looks could kill … She couldn't tolerate me smoking.

I don't know if they actually were, but I remember the summers being longer and warmer back then. Flying was so expensive that you kind of accepted going anywhere by aeroplane was out of your league, which is the mindset I've been stuck in. That might explain why I never did it – that and the fact that the very idea of getting on a plane is terrifying to me.

**Jess**     Nan, you've got more chance of being in a car accident than a plane crash.

**Norma**     Maybe with your driving, yes.

**Jess**     Haha, very funny.

I didn't really have any family holidays when I was a kid, as we didn't have much money spare. I remember my mum saving up all her tips in this little tin we had at home to take us to Italy. I was only small, about six or seven, but I remember counting the change with her and us both jumping up and down with excitement when we'd gathered enough to go to Florence. I don't remember much about the trip besides visiting the shops and feeling a bit hot and bothered, but I know my mum worked so hard to take us there. We'd occasionally go to Cornwall, which I really did love, but apart from that I didn't go away again until my late teens and early twenties.

**Norma**     Your grandad always wanted to go to America. And he often said he'd like to take me to Ireland because he'd had a good holiday there before he met me. But we never did.

Sometimes I do see these beautiful places on TV travel shows – programmes like *A Place in the Sun* – and I find myself thinking, 'Oh, I'd love to go there … ' But deep down I know I wouldn't.

Even when we were away as a family, I'd enjoy it for a while and loved being with my husband and children, but there was always something making me yearn for home. I don't know what it was.

But do you know what? It didn't happen when I was in Paris as a young woman. I was very happy to be there and didn't get that little voice in my head.

**Jess**     That was before you met Grandad, though. I think being happy and settled down at home might have a part to play.

**Norma**     I didn't get homesick on my honeymoon.

**Jess**     Probably too busy, eh?

## CHAPTER NINE

**Norma**  Jessica, I can't take you anywhere. No, not because of that! It was a lovely three days away and I'm so grateful to have such clear memories of that time. I haven't lost my upper drawer yet, which is something to be thankful for.

**Jess**  I went on girls' holidays before I met Jake, which I loved. Tenerife and Malia in Crete – seven days of drinking and partying all day and night and I couldn't get enough! I had the time of my life in Benidorm one summer, home of the infamous Sticky Vicky.

**Norma**  Vicky who?

**Jess**  If you know, you know.

**Norma**  Well, I don't know.

**Jess**  She's an 'entertainer', Nan. The act basically consists of her pulling items out of her you-know-what. Flags, bottles, links of sausages …

**Norma**  You what?

**Jess**  Oh yeah, she's a Benidorm legend.

**Norma**  I see. Shall we go?

**Jess**  You don't mean that! My point was that now I'm settled and happy, I feel differently about going away. There's also the thought of leaving you behind, which I struggle with.

Jake and I first went on holiday together for a fortnight in Cyprus in September 2020 to see his mum, who lives there. It felt like such a grown-up thing to do, going away with a boyfriend, and it was very romantic – although holidaying with a partner is a big step and staying with their family on holiday is even bigger! We had the best time, but two weeks was too long to be away from you and I knew I wouldn't do it again. I missed you too much.

## HOLIDAYS

**Norma**  I don't want to hold you back, Jess.

**Jess**  OK, well, do you want me to go now?

**Norma**  No.

**Jess**  Thought not! I wouldn't change it, though. Do you have any regrets about never having left your living room?

**Norma**  No, love. I've never felt like I missed out on anything. I've always had more than enough lovely people around me in my life right here.

**Jess**  The best part about going away for me is coming home.

**Norma**  I couldn't have put it better myself, Jess.

**Jess**  It's a big wide world out there, but give me a natter and a custard cream in your living room over sun, sand and sea any day of the week.

# INTERLUDE
# Lingo Bingo

*How well does Norma know her Gen-Z slang?*

### Shade

Norma    Get in out of the sun?

Jess    No, sorry! If someone is throwing shade, they're being mean or sly.

### Salty

Norma    That's when I season my dinner.

Jess    No, it's someone who is angry or grumpy.

Norma    Like you in the mornings.

### Lit

Norma    Maybe someone who is all lit up with happiness?

Jess    Ah, that would be nice. But no, it's someone who looks good.

### YOLO

Norma    You what?

Jess    It's an acronym – the letters stand for something.

INTERLUDE

**Norma**  Hmmm ... I give in.

**Jess**  You only live once. So, if you were debating whether to have a cream cake, I might say, 'Go on, YOLO.'

### Thirst trap

**Norma**  The inside of my mouth.

**Jess**  No, it's when someone posts a sexy picture or video of themselves online.

**Norma**  This is way out of my league, Jess.

### Ick

**Norma**  I beg your pardon?

**Jess**  If I was to say, 'Norma's snotty hanky gives me the ick,' what would I mean?

**Norma**  Well, I assume it means you don't like it much?

**Jess**  Correct!

### Rizz

**Norma**  No idea.

**Jess**  If someone has good rizz, they have charm and great chatting up skills. Apparently it's derived from 'charisma', which I've only just learned.

**Norma**  This is an education.

### Situationship

Norma     Do young folk actually use these made-up words?

Jess     This is more Cadan's language than mine. Go on – situationship?

Norma     Tell me.

Jess     It's the hazy in between stage of a relationship where you're more than dating but not officially girlfriend and boyfriend.

### Delulu

Norma     A house with two toilets.

Jess     Haha! No, it's short for someone who is deluded or delusional. They're delulu.

Norma     I quite like that one.

### Menty B

Norma     Give me a clue.

Jess     If I was stressed, I might say, 'I'm on the verge of a menty b.'

Norma     Oh, a breakdown?

Jess     Yes, it's short for a mental breakdown.

Norma     I think I'm having a menty b right now.

CHAPTER TEN

# Past Versus Present

**Jess** Simple question for you, Nan. Do you think things were better in your day?

**Norma** That's not a simple question at all. That's a toughie, because there are elements that I feel were better, yes. Very much so. But there is also plenty that has improved everyone's standard of living and wellbeing. Indoor toilets, for one.

**Jess** Yes, thank God for indoor plumbing and not having to do number twos in the potty at night. Also for WiFi and the Dyson Airwrap. How did you ever live without either?

**Norma** We just about managed.

**Jess** I guess it's science and medical advances that are the most obvious ways the present trumps the past.

**Norma** They are something to behold. The treatments for cancer, all the vaccines and organ transplants to name a few. I think of Betty as a young woman trying to have children all those years ago and how things might have been different for her if that had been today.

**Jess** People are living much longer now and are more able to have a healthy and fulfilling old age. It's a shame that none of us really have a family doctor any more, though. When I take you to the GP, we never know who we're going to see, so there's not much continuity of care. It's a couple of quick questions about the problem, get a prescription, done.

**Norma** I'm not sure they have the time to delve into what's the

# CHAPTER TEN

matter and get a proper answer to what's causing the bother. And because you see a different person each time, they don't get to know you or your history.

When I was a little girl our family doctor was Dr Want and he was a wonderful man. He would come out to the house and everyone knew and liked him. A few years ago I read an article about him in the local paper by someone who was remembering what a fantastic doctor he was. He had such a lovely way with people. We don't get a service like that any more.

**Jess** The system might be more 'efficient' now, but it's lost some of that human touch, hasn't it? What I always think sounds so gorgeous about the era you grew up in is the community spirit. Everyone knew their neighbours. Fast forward 80-odd years to where we are now and that's probably not the case for most people.

**Norma** I've got lovely neighbours around me now, Jess, but I do know what you mean. Years ago we all mucked in, helped each other out and people spoke to each other with politeness and kindness, which are qualities that are a bit scarce these days. We'd always say good morning to one another, even to strangers we passed on the street.

**Jess** Ah, I really like that. If I'm out, I like to smile and say hello to people, but I'm a bit of a weirdo and that's definitely not the norm. And when you go to places like London, no one looks at each other at all. Heads down, move out the way.

**Norma** Many years ago, a friend of mine lived in London and she said it could be the loneliest place on earth. But yes, I agree that we've lost that community togetherness and common courtesy. The men used to stand up when someone new entered a room as a show of respect. I can remember my dad tipping his hat whenever he passed a lady in the street.

## PAST VERSUS PRESENT

**Jess**  If a man did that now, people would think there was something wrong with him. Imagine if Jake went round raising his cap at random women! I think the police would want a word. He'd be in the local newspaper with a great big 'Wanted Man' headline.

**Norma**  I can't get over the lack of manners now. When we go into a shop with me in the wheelchair and it's one of those doors that opens both ways, some people just let it swing back without a second thought.

**Jess**  The number of places we've struggled with that wheelchair is unreal, even in the doctor's surgery, where you'd think people might be more aware. When we do get the door held open for us, we're so grateful because it's such a rare occurrence.

**Norma**  I just can't see why people have become like that. I don't know what happened but maybe we lost it with the age of the computer.

We did see a glimpse of a return to the old days of community during Covid, though. People rallied round and cooked for their neighbours, checking in on the older ones and fetching them their shopping, and that was lovely. Just like years ago when they would do all of that anyway.

**Jess**  There was a glimmer of it, but I think we've reverted back again and people are reluctant to do anything that so much as mildly inconveniences them.

**Norma**  We should all look out for each other. It would make everyone feel safer.

**Jess**  There was much more of a 'make do and mend' culture as well back in the olden days, wasn't there?

**Norma**  The 'olden' days! Watch your language, Jessica.

**Jess**  You know what I mean. If something was broken, you'd fix

# CHAPTER TEN

it, right? Now people tend to throw things away and order a new one. We're a lot more wasteful – we buy cheap and then replace without a second thought.

Norma   A lot of the mending and fixing skills are gone. We spoke earlier about how needlework and woodwork aren't really taught in schools any more, didn't we? It's a shame. My mum used to knit our socks – she never even followed a pattern. She just knew.

Jess   Today we'd just go to Primark and get a pack of five socks for two quid rather than knitting them from scratch.

Norma   Which is much more practical and less time-consuming, of course.

Jess   In that sense, fast fashion is a blessing and a curse. It's given customers loads more choice but it's also created such a disposable, 'throwaway' culture and I'm guilty of that as much as the next person.

Norma   Clothes used to be built to last. I've got a beautiful winter hat which belonged to my mother and is still in immaculate condition. It must be coming up to 100 years old.

Jess   It's the same with furniture. You've got a cracking chest of Stag drawers upstairs which you've had as long as I can remember.

Norma   I've had it since before your mother was born and it's very sturdy and still in great condition. I used to keep the heated tray for her bottles on it for the nighttime when she was a baby. I've no use for it now, but it's too good to chuck.

Jess   I'd love it for when I eventually move into my forever home. When I get my Mrs Hinch-style farmhouse with my alpacas and chickens, I'll put that chest of drawers in my bedroom and keep my baby's tray on it and think, 'Ah, Nan used this.'

Norma   That would be wonderful, Jess. What a lovely thought.

## PAST VERSUS PRESENT

**Jess**    Having experienced rations as a young girl, do you think we're also more wasteful with food now?

**Norma**    I do. I don't like to see perfectly decent food thrown in the bin. I never have. I try never to leave any food on my plate.

**Jess**    Nan's one of these people who, rather than asking for a takeout box or a doggie bag in a restaurant, will wrap the food up in serviettes and stuff it in her handbag. She never leaves a restaurant without a few slices of beef in her bag.

**Norma**    Only if the dustbins sitting around the table haven't eaten it up for me first.

**Jess**    The meat is usually dripping with gravy, which means the napkin rips and you've got a bag full of wet beef. How pleasant.

**Norma**    I think people have got a bit idle with food. I grew up on homegrown veg, fresh meat and proper home-cooked meals, and what you didn't eat one day went into the next day's dinner.

**Jess**    There's much more choice now and we can try cuisines from all over the world, which is brilliant. But there's also masses of fast food and ultra-processed food, which is having an impact on our health. I've been reading a lot about that recently.

**Norma**    Maybe some of the health issues are to do with a lack of physical activity and not getting outdoors as much. Do families go out for long walks together any more? We'd always go for a long walk on a Sunday after our roast. My mum would clear away the plates and make the kitchen all neat again – she called it 'siding' – and we'd go over to Newtown Fields and walk off what we'd just eaten.

**Jess**    People are probably more likely to stick Netflix on or scroll through their phones after a meal than go for a walk now.

# CHAPTER TEN

**Norma**  But we are all much more aware of health now and understand more about what's good for us and what's not. Look at what we've learned about how harmful cigarettes are – it's rare to see anyone smoking these days, isn't it?

I smoked during my twenties. I only ever had three or four cigarettes a day and I stopped when I met your grandad because he really didn't like it. His father had died of lung cancer and his brother did too when he was only 49, so cigarettes were absolutely a no go.

**Jess**  It's actually disgusting thinking what pubs and restaurants must have been like before the smoking ban came into force.

**Norma**  They were choked full of smoke.

**Jess**  I can't believe that's how we used to live.

**Norma**  The air was always thick with it. It can't have been good for anyone.

**Jess**  Definitely a perfect example of how things are better now.

**Norma**  Yes, that's what you'd call progress.

**Jess**  What about music? Do you long for the old stuff or do you prefer modern songs?

**Norma**  This might shock you, but I prefer music now. I love Gracie Fields and I shall keep Nat King Cole in my heart forever because those songs are evergreen. But I also think Susan Boyle is marvellous.

**Jess**  Er, I wouldn't say Susan Boyle is an example of a modern artist, Nan! What do you think of people like Nicki Minaj or Cardi B?

**Norma**  Who are they?

**Jess**  Cardi B released a song called 'Wet Ass Pussy'.

**Norma**  …

## PAST VERSUS PRESENT

**Jess**   For the first time in your life, I think you're speechless.

**Norma**   I'm too stunned to say anything.

**Jess**   Am I right in assuming that kind of modern music is not your thing?

**Norma**   No, it's certainly not. Some of the lyrics that go with these songs have gone a bit too far, quite honestly.

**Jess**   That might be a symptom of everyone's love of oversharing. We're a lot more open than people used to be.

**Norma**   Aren't we just?

**Jess**   There are certain things about my life that will always remain private. I'm all for a laugh and a joke with my girly mates but I'm not going to plaster everything over social media.

**Norma**   People will put anything on the internet now.

**Jess**   Well, I haven't propped the camera up while I'm getting you showered yet. That'll be for our private subscribers.

**Norma**   We could charge a fiver for everyone and make a fortune.

**Jess**   OK, let's be serious for a minute. Because although some people can be a bit TMI, there are positives to come out of us being more comfortable talking about what was previously taboo.

**Norma**   Awkward subjects were brushed under the carpet when I was younger. It's good that girls are educated about their bodies ...

**Jess**   ... And women are having conversations about things like the menopause. That's taken celebrities such as Davina McCall to break the stigma and shame.

**Norma**   I didn't have any problems with the menopause. I'm not even sure I was aware I'd been through it – everything just kind of petered out. But you hear them today talking about how

# CHAPTER TEN

they're suffering with hot flushes and not knowing what to do with themselves.

I'm pleased they feel able to talk about it now. Sometimes just slowing down a bit and getting plenty of fresh air helps.

**Jess** It's a similar story with mental health, which people are a lot more at ease with discussing than they used to be.

**Norma** My sister Betty used to have these attacks of what I would now call clinical depression. She'd kind of sit there, staring into space. She wasn't mad or insane, just suffering. It's a terrible thing to have.

**Jess** Was it spoken about?

**Norma** It was in our family, but I think we were unusual. People tended to keep that sort of thing under wraps and to themselves. And there wasn't nearly as much known about it and so without treatment people were often written off as having gone mad. Some of the soldiers came back from the war very traumatised and those lads never recovered from that.

**Jess** Nowadays they'd be diagnosed with PTSD and given help. We understand so much more about mental health than we used to.

**Norma** I'm not sure people really spoke about their feelings that much. They probably didn't know where to start. But you've got to talk about your demons, haven't you? Get it out of your system by speaking to somebody who can help.

**Jess** Having therapy has made a huge difference to me since I started it. I go once every two weeks for an hour and I think I'll have it for the rest of my life. It's so valuable to talk to somebody who is a total outsider and who's not afraid to tell me when my thought patterns are unhealthy and help me to turn them around. If I'm wrong, she'll tell me I'm wrong.

## PAST VERSUS PRESENT

**Norma**  She should have a medal, that poor woman.

**Jess**  I'm a totally different person now that I have the coping mechanisms to deal with things.

**Norma**  Have you got any going spare?

**Jess**  You're half-joking but I think you'd benefit from a few sessions with a therapist, Nan. There's no shame in having it and I think it should be more accessible to people. What I pay for a session with her is probably what me and Jake would spend on a takeaway and I will always prioritise therapy above a chicken korma.

Giving up alcohol has also been key for me. I used to be a terrible binge drinker – I'd get blind drunk, black out and the next day would be wiped out by these horrendous hangovers where I'd spend most of my time with my head in the toilet.

**Norma**  I remember, Jess, you used to get yourself into some right messes. I'd worry myself silly when you were heading off on a night out with your friends.

**Jess**  In July 2022, me and Jake went to Parklife festival in Manchester and I got the drunkest I'd ever been. I was so hungover the following day that I had a panic attack and that's when I decided I wasn't doing this any more. It was like self-destruction. I said I was never going to drink again and I never have. Christmases, birthdays, not even a sip.

I don't miss it – I actually get anxiety at the thought of drinking and how it used to make me feel. Sobriety has changed my life and when I look back, I can see I was drinking as a coping mechanism for being unhappy.

**Norma**  You've been amazing. I'm not knocking drink, but it can be so damaging to people. Why would you go out to work and earn money just to throw it down your neck? It makes no sense to me.

# CHAPTER TEN

**Jess** I'm so much happier, less anxious and more productive now I don't drink. As a society, we've made great strides when it comes to talking about mental health, but we need to go much further in terms of what support is available. Many people have to reach a crisis point before they're given any help. Learning about things like adrenaline and your nervous system and how to regulate your emotions is really important and those conversations still aren't happening enough.

**Norma** I think it's more accepted and understood in the younger generations, but there's a big reluctance in older people to admit they have a mental health problem or to recognise there is one.

**Jess** People reach a certain age and think, 'Oh well, I've been this way all my life. I'm not going to change now … ' When Grandad died, you went to the doctors, didn't you? Because you knew you weren't quite yourself.

**Norma** The doctor put me on Sertraline, which we call my 'happy pill', and I've been on it for 20 years now. I'm not ashamed of that whatsoever.

**Jess** Which I think is amazing considering the time you're from and the attitudes to mental health.

**Norma** It is a big help. I'm an overthinker. If someone hasn't come home, my mind has them in a ditch trapped in an upturned car. I've always been a bit of a whittler – a worrier. Just like my mum, although she didn't want anybody to see it. I've been told that my dad used to say to my oldest sister, 'Try and keep worry away from your mother.' He knew she found it difficult.

**Jess** Do you worry about crime more than in the past? People always say there aren't enough police officers on the ground any more.

## PAST VERSUS PRESENT

**Norma**  There were definitely more 'bobbies on the beat' in the past. When Betty was working on the telephone exchange and doing night duty until 6am, there was always a policeman to walk her home safely. How lovely to have that care.

And there does seem to be a lot more crime now. You only have to pick up a paper or watch the news to see that crime is everywhere. Assaults, knifings, robberies, it's terrible. And not just the odd day here and there, it's several times every week.

**Jess**  That's why I don't read the paper or watch the news. It's all so depressing.

**Norma**  But you've got to know what's going on, Jess. It's important to be aware. The hard thing to understand is that a lot of these kiddies involved in crime now are so young. Isn't that dreadful? I'm wondering what could cause it.

I don't think we'd get too many of them queuing up to join a war effort, would we? I know the world is different now, but I did feel sorry that they took away national service, because it used to put a bit of toughness and discipline into youngsters. And I don't think it was such a great hardship to most of them.

**Jess**  When you were younger, would you go out and leave the house unlocked?

**Norma**  My mum would go shopping and leave the key in the little soap box that was just inside the kitchen window. I'd open the window, get the key and let myself in. We wouldn't dare do anything like that now, would we?

But I think another thing that could be playing into the general loss of respect is the fading influence of the church. I'm not saying I loved going there every Sunday and I would never preach about religion, but I do think you've got to have

# CHAPTER TEN

some godliness about you in whatever you do. People don't have that so much now.

**Jess** You see, I don't see the decreasing power of the church as a bad thing. It's better that people are empowered to make their own decisions and don't just go with what their religion tells them to think or believe. We don't even know for certain if there is such a thing as God.

**Norma** There are always niggles or doubts about everything, but I'm not sure how you explain all the beauty in the world without a god. I know you'll say, 'But what about all the killings?' and I concede that it's difficult to come up with a satisfactory answer.

Betty once asked the wife of a late rector she knew, 'How is it that God allows fighting and war and people suffering?'

And the lady replied, 'God gives everybody choices. They do one thing or the other and He doesn't control that.' I've thought about that answer a lot and I'm afraid it doesn't quite cover it for me.

**Jess** It doesn't explain why children get cancer, does it? Or why anyone gets cancer, for that matter. There's no choice in that. I do believe in something – I have a huge fear of loss and believing there is some sort of God makes that a bit easier for me.

**Norma** I say my prayers and it makes me feel better. Do you remember when I had to go and have that procedure done under general anaesthetic, Jess? I was panic, panic, panic.

**Jess** You were terrified for days before.

**Norma** The night before I went in, I saw in my sleep some sort of notice with the words: 'Do not be afraid.' Now I can't say what it was …

**Jess** … Was it a sign? Or just a dream? We don't know.

## PAST VERSUS PRESENT

**Norma**     But I've never had anything like that before or since. Whatever it was, it helped me and people need a little bit of comfort like that in their lives, don't they? For many, religion can provide that and ease their fears. I think it's a shame we've lost it.

**Jess**     I get what you're saying, but there are so many flaws and religions throw up so many contradictions. Some people who are super-religious can have very outdated views such as not believing in same-sex relationships. That's not very 'love thy neighbour', is it? That attitude doesn't make sense to me and I don't think it has much place in today's society.

**Norma**     I agree, Jess. People are people and as long as they're happy and leading a good life, it makes no difference who they fall in love with. We're all human. Everyone has the same fears and worries. What does it matter?

**Jess**     I love that you're totally open-minded and understanding about it, despite having grown up when it was actually illegal to be gay.

**Norma**     I don't fret over it by any manner of means. It doesn't bother me at all.

**Jess**     I tell you what, I'll take you to Manchester and we'll go to a drag show. That'll be an eye-opener for you!

**Norma**     The mind boggles.

**Jess**     Something that has definitely got worse over the years is the traffic.

**Norma**     The roads these days are horrendous. When we drove to Manchester to visit *Coronation Street*, I couldn't believe how many cars were on the motorway. You wouldn't stand a chance if a lorry lost its load, would you?

**Jess**     Everyone is so reliant on their cars now and there probably are too many on the road. You did try to learn how to drive, didn't you?

# CHAPTER TEN

**Norma**    Your grandad attempted to teach me, but he hadn't got one bit of patience with me. You know what men are like with their cars. He used to shout, 'CLUTCH!' And I'd go, 'What's the clutch and what do I do with it?!'

And then once we were married and the children came along, I just never went back to it. He told me I'd be better sticking to pushing prams than driving cars.

**Jess**    Ha! He used to take you wherever you wanted to go though, didn't he?

**Norma**    Yes, I was never short of a ride.

**Jess**    My mum has never driven either. Watching her rely on public transport, taxis and lifts made me determined to pass my test. As soon as I turned 16, I applied for my provisional licence, although it took me about two-and-a-half years to pass my test.

And the first thing I did when I passed was come round to yours to take you out for a spin.

**Norma**    And my heart was beating out of my chest the whole way.

**Jess**    My number plate might as well be 'NORMA 1' because I'm your personal chauffeur service, aren't I?

**Norma**    I must say, you're a very good, careful driver, Jess. You might be hopeless with directions and get us lost a lot, but you don't take risks. I see so much dangerous driving these days.

It was a lot safer for children to play out in the street in my day. They were simpler, quieter times.

**Jess**    I think it would be so interesting for me to just go and have a day back in that era, just to see how different things were.

**Norma**    I'll see if I can get you a ticket. One way.

## INTERLUDE
# Let's play ... Mrs and Miss

### Who is the better cook?

Norma    Jess. She makes meals for me that are delicious and her Yorkshire puddings are the best on the planet.

Jess    I think it's Nan. She's excellent at making traditional hearty meals, just like her mum used to.

### Who is the best at keeping secrets?

Norma    Me. Definitely. If someone has sworn me to secrecy and told me not to say anything then I don't.

Jess    Nan is super-loyal. I would say I'm quite trustworthy, but I'm not anywhere near as good as Nan with secrets. Her lips are sealed shut when she's been told something in confidence.

### Who is the funniest?

Norma    I think we're pretty well matched.

Jess    Nan is by far the funniest. She's hilarious, her comic timing is perfect and her one-line comebacks are the best.

### What is the other one's worst habit?

Norma    Jessica sings all the time and I do find it very difficult to tolerate because she can't hold a tune.

## INTERLUDE

**Jess**  Nan opens packets of food – usually biscuits – without checking if there's already one open. She's terrible for that.

**Norma**  Michael used to say, 'Norma, did you know you've got two packets of cream crackers out at once?'

**Jess**  She drops marmalade on the newspaper as well. And the buttons on her phone get stuck because they're riddled with marmalade.

**Norma**  Just call me Paddington Bear.

### Who's the most stubborn?

**Norma**  Jess, without a doubt.

**Jess**  Yep, it's me. Nan would rather keep her mouth shut to avoid conflict and let things pass whereas I will always stand up.

### Who's the cleverest?

**Norma**  I'd say we're quite equal.

**Jess**  Nan. She is a very intelligent, wise lady.

### Who's the messiest?

**Norma**  I'm afraid I have to claim that one.

**Jess**  Nan, definitely.

### Who is the boss?

**Norma**  Let's face it …

**Jess**  It's Nan. It's always been Nan.

CHAPTER ELEVEN
# Fashion and Beauty

**Norma**  I don't know how you young folk keep up with all the trends of the day. It's exhausting! The fashions change every five minutes and there's so much choice, people must be constantly experimenting.

**Jess**  It is a bit overwhelming – and expensive – if you're easily influenced. Not just with clothes, but with beauty, too. Some people do these time-consuming 30-step routines to get ready to leave the house in the morning.

**Norma**  I'm all for taking pride in your appearance, but it's a wonder they ever get anything else done. They must have to get up at 3am just to make it to work on time.

**Jess**  Not like you, Nan. A dab of Astral and a smidge of powder and you're good to go.

**Norma**  Sometimes a bit of blusher, too.

I've always enjoyed a little makeup, though. I was 17 when I got my very own lipstick for the first time. Pretty Pink by Yardley. My sister Betty bought it for me – it was a dusty pink colour and I just loved it. I wore it all the time and it felt so lovely on.

I like a spritz of perfume as well.

**Jess**  Whenever we go out, you say 'parfum?' to me and I give you a little spray. When I was younger you'd wear Estée Lauder's Beautiful and Yardley's Lily of the Valley and I only

# CHAPTER ELEVEN

need to catch a whiff of either of them and I'm right back to my childhood.

These days you have more expensive tastes because you were very kindly gifted some Opium by Yves Saint Laurent.

**Norma** And it's heavenly.

**Jess** It smells like old ladies.

**Norma** Right, that cheek's been noted.

**Jess** I mean it's got quite heavy floral notes which are popular with the more mature female.

**Norma** I like that Daisy one as well.

**Jess** That's by Marc Jacobs. Jake bought you some Armani Diamonds and you were gifted a Valentino one as well so you've got quite the collection upstairs. You could open a shop!

**Norma** I think it's nice for a woman to have a gentle aroma, that faint smell of perfume. Not like Cadan, who I think sloshes his aftershave on by the gallon.

**Jess** He's dripping in it!

I've recently discovered Carolina Herrera's range, which comes in a shoe-shaped bottle, and that's my new favourite. I grew up wearing Alien by Mugler because that's what my mum always wore.

**Norma** Mothers tend to be who we take our lead from with beauty. Astral has been my base from the day I started wearing makeup, just like my mother before me. She'd rub in the Astral, put some talcum powder on her neck, move it across her face and that would do. Job done.

Occasionally she'd pop a little bit of lippy on, but she didn't do a very good job of that, as I remember.

## FASHION AND BEAUTY

**Jess**  Wasn't Jessie into her makeup?

**Norma**  She was always well presented, but she was never particularly fussed about beauty. Or fashion, for that matter. During rationing, women couldn't get hold of stockings and so instead they'd dye their legs with tea to give the illusion of nylons. I believe some would even use a black pen to draw a thin line up the back as a fake seam. My mum certainly never bothered with anything like that. Perish the thought.

**Jess**  Wow, that's actually a really inventive hack!

**Norma**  It was, until they got caught in the rain … I remember your mum dyeing her legs with coffee during the eighties for a sunkissed look. This was long before all the false tan you see on the shop shelves today.

**Jess**  What did Grandad think about that kind of malarkey from my mum?

**Norma**  Er, not a lot. He could never get over the number of bottles in the bathroom. Lotions and potions everywhere. She could have opened a beauty salon.

**Jess**  My mum has always been like that. She never goes anywhere without makeup on – before she walks the dog, she'll top up her lippy. Even when she was giving birth to me and later my brother, she made sure she had a full face on and her nails freshly done.

I'm not as extreme as her. I'm not afraid to go on a live or do a video fresh-faced, but I do feel like part of getting ready for my day is putting some makeup on. It makes me feel like me.

**Norma**  Your mother used to come downstairs with a great basket full of cosmetics and sit on the floor to get dolled up for the evening, a process that would sometimes take her as long as two hours. She'd say getting herself ready was the best part of going out, which I could never really fathom.

## CHAPTER ELEVEN

Your grandad used to go mad about the amount of hairspray she'd use. She'd spray that can of Shockwaves until we were all nearly choking in the front room and then go out for the night, leaving that flipping basket right there on the floor, which used to irritate your grandad no end.

**Jess**    I can just imagine!

**Norma**    It's not surprising that she grew up to become a hairdresser. She had this hairstyle that stuck out at the side and was backcombed and we used to wonder how she could bring herself to go out in public like that. Then again, everybody else looked like that too. The hair and makeup of the eighties was very different to the fashions I'd grown up with in the forties and fifties.

**Jess**    Who were the big beauty icons of your day? Was there anyone you wished you looked like?

**Norma**    Joan Fontaine, Margaret Lockwood, Phyllis Calvert, Ingrid Bergman, Vivien Leigh. They were all so beautiful. I had a book with all the film stars which I liked to flick through, looking at the pictures. Natural beauties. They don't make them like that any more.

**Jess**    They really don't. These days it's so normal to have filler put in lips, cheeks and jaws, we've almost forgotten how to appreciate our own natural beauty.

**Norma**    I don't know why the girls do that to themselves. There's got to be a certain amount of danger in having it done, like that poor lady on the television who it all went wrong for.

**Jess**    Oh, Leslie Ash and her lip filler? That was more than 20 years ago but it still gets talked about now.

**Norma**    She was so pretty before – she didn't need to do it. You see girls today and they all look like characters out of that animation *Creature Comforts*.

## FASHION AND BEAUTY

**Jess** So we'll not book you in for a facelift? We could pop a little incision on either side and pull you right up.

**Norma** Not today, thank you.

**Jess** Or a Brazilian butt lift?

**Norma** A what?

**Jess** A BBL. It's where they remove fat from various parts of your body and then inject it into your buttocks.

**Norma** That sounds absolutely horrifying.

**Jess** If you think that's bad, get this. For an even more dramatic look, some women have full-on implants put into their bum cheeks. It's all about the big juicy backside.

**Norma** I must say, I've seen some behinds recently that resemble ledges – do you reckon they'll be implants?

**Jess** Probably. It used to be big breasts that were popular and now it's switched to big bums thanks to Kardashian culture. So, trends change all the time and that's one of the reasons why I tell myself I need to be grateful for the way I am. You never know, in 20 years' time it might be fashionable to have a flat bottom and a tummy pouch and then I'd officially be in!

**Norma** You can live in hope, Jess. Some of the women on television have had so much work done on their face, it's as if there's something pulling. It looks painful.

**Jess** It's really sad if people do it out of insecurity and I'd question some of the practitioners performing those procedures.

I'll be completely honest here – back in 2017 when I was about 21, I went to see a lady about getting some filler in my lips and she said she would only give me half a millimetre because I didn't need any more than that. I also asked about having some filler in my jaw to make it more chiselled, but she said no way.

## CHAPTER ELEVEN

'I'm not doing that on you,' she said. 'You're too young and you do not need it.'

She could have had 350 quid from me there and then, but she refused it and I'll always be thankful to her for that. I've never been back for anything else.

**Norma**   I'm so glad you didn't do that, love. You don't need it, you're lovely as you are.

**Jess**   I look back now and can see I was battling with a lot of insecurities around my looks and body image and changing my face was never going to cure me of that. My weight has fluctuated throughout my life and a lot of that has been down to comfort eating and the upheaval during my teens.

**Norma**   You were always on some diet or other.

**Jess**   I tried everything. The 5:2 Diet, WeightWatchers, Slimming World – you name it. I'd say, 'Right, I'm only going to eat apples for a week' – all these ludicrous fads that never worked for long. We've grown up with toxic messages about 'a moment on the lips is a lifetime on the hips' and 'little pickers wear bigger knickers' and how a woman is only attractive if she looks a certain way.

It was only when I hit my late twenties that I finally got into a healthy, happy place with food and a lot of that was with the help of therapy. I also went to see a naturopath who has helped me work on my relationship with food and I now see it as fuel and nourishment rather than the enemy. I've stopped counting the calories and I know whatever size I am, I'm still worthy.

**Norma**   Quite right, Jessica. You know I've had my own struggles with my weight over the years. Your brother Cadan is one of those who can eat what he wants without having to worry about it. I've never been like that.

## FASHION AND BEAUTY

**Jess**  A lot of our followers will be surprised to learn, given that you're so tiny now, that you spent most of your adult life as a plus-size lady.

**Norma**  I was a plump lump.

**Jess**  I was trying to be diplomatic, but if you want to put it like that.

**Norma**  I was never entirely happy being a size 20, but people didn't tend to make the big thing of it they do now. I'd try and diet, swapping bread for Ryvita and what have you. But it wasn't until I was in my late seventies and suffering from painful arthritis in my knees that I did something properly about it.

**Jess**  Nan went to the GP, where it was politely pointed out to her that it would help her knees if she lost some of her bulk. So, she went along to a weight-loss group provided by the doctor and she did really well with it.

**Norma**  I didn't do badly. The group was called Chrysalis and every week we went up to the surgery to be weighed. We were told all the things we should and shouldn't be eating and I found it fascinating learning about how many calories were in certain foods. I managed to lose quite a lot of weight which I've kept off ever since.

**Jess**  I think you got down to a size 16, which is the UK average, and there was a big improvement with your knees because you had been in agony with them.

Changing diets and taking more exercise are positive steps to becoming healthier and more confident. Going under the knife is not the answer. I used to want to get a boob job, but what if I wasn't able to breastfeed my future babies all because social media made me feel like my 'saggy boobs' were unattractive or not good enough?

## CHAPTER ELEVEN

|  | If people in the public eye are having nips and tweaks, I think it's important to be honest about it because they have such a big influence on their followers. That's why now I don't use any filters and all my videos are just raw from my iPhone. |
|---|---|
| Norma | Remind me what a filter is, Jess. |
| Jess | It's a function on your camera that can morph the way you look. People use filters or editing apps to make themselves look more attractive or to give themselves a smaller nose, bigger eyes or higher cheekbones. |
| Norma | Reckon I could do with a bit of that. |
| Jess | But it's not real, Nan. It's a lie. No one looks like their photos or videos any more. Everyone has the same teeth these days, too. It's known as 'Turkey teeth'. |
| Norma | Turkey teeth? |
| Jess | People go to Turkey and they get their teeth shaved down into little pegs and then have veneers put on top. OK, I can see you're shocked. |
| Norma | I am! Have they nothing else to do with their money? |
| Jess | The silly thing is, there's actually nothing more beautiful than a natural smile. I can understand when people have braces or straighteners, but you can spot those bright white fake teeth a mile off. |
| Norma | My teeth come out at night. Like stars. |
| Jess | Your falsies look more realistic than the gnashers they come back from Turkey with! |
| Norma | You make sure to look after the teeth you've been blessed with, Jess. |
| Jess | Overall, when it comes to beauty, I'm fairly low maintenance, like you. I get my nails done every three weeks with builder |

## FASHION AND BEAUTY

|||
|---|---|
| | gel and I've just found a fantastic hairdresser who I go to every three months for highlights and a root drag so it all blends. |
| Norma | Do you think I'd suit one of them? |
| Jess | A root drag? I'm not sure we'd be able to drag your roots very far, Nan. And if you had your hair straight, you'd look like Donald Trump, so you can't really win. |
| Norma | I'll have to stick with what I've got in that case. I keep asking your mother if she can find me a hairstyle that is a bit more glamorous but doesn't take a lot of doing. Unfortunately, she says my hair is very fine and whatever we've tried is just a bit sad. |
| | My hair has often been something of a 'challenge' – I remember once being sent to the local salon and my eldest sister told me to tell the lady that my hair needed sorting out because it was sticking out 'like a duck's bottom'! But you've always had lovely hair, Jess. When you were a tot, you'd wear it in bunches and you looked ever so sweet. |
| Jess | How did your mum do your hair when you were little? |
| Norma | If we were going anywhere nice, she'd put it in rags the night before. That meant taking strips of hair, wrapping it in these long pieces of fabric – anything you could find to tear up – and twisting the hair all the way round. Then I'd go to bed and wake up with ringlets. |
| | But I mostly wore my hair in plaits. It wasn't awfully long, not like some of the women wear it today. |
| Jess | Which will probably be extensions. |
| Norma | Some women wore wigs, but extensions didn't exist. And we didn't have any of the shampoo, conditioner or vast array of products you have today. We used Lifebuoy soap to wash our |

## CHAPTER ELEVEN

hair, which was just the ordinary household stuff. We'd also keep a saucepan in the garden to catch the rainwater, which Mum would then boil up and use for hair washing because it was thought to be healthier for your hair than water from the tap. And I used to put lemon juice in it so it would maintain its colour and keep the grease at bay.

**Jess** My mum washes and sets your hair now and I always think you look so cute in your rollers. I like to give your hair a going over every morning with the brush to try and activate it up a bit.

**Norma** Before your mum took over, I'd always set it myself. I used to buy Lytia setting lotion from Woolworths. It was really claggy stuff, but it made your set – the curls – last that bit longer.

**Jess** How old were you when you started using rollers?

**Norma** I'd say in my late teens. Curls were the height of fashion in the fifties.

**Jess** So you've had the same hairstyle for 70-odd years?

**Norma** Yes, I've not been very adventurous, have I?

**Jess** If you want adventure, how about getting your belly button pierced?

**Norma** I should think not, Jessica. You see some of them with their tongues pierced and if it was me I'd be worried sick about getting an infection. Or worse.

**Jess** Worse in what way?

**Norma** Maybe even cancer. You can't mess with your tongue.

**Jess** I don't think I've ever heard of anyone getting cancer from a pierced tongue, Nan. We could think about doing an alternative part of your anatomy, if you like. Some women get their nether regions pierced. Men, too.

## FASHION AND BEAUTY

**Norma**   Can we get through a chapter of this book without you turning the air blue? The only pierced part of my body are my ears, which I had done after I was married. I'm otherwise intact and that's how I'll remain.

**Jess**   You've got some gorgeous gold earrings, but you never wear them.

**Norma**   I loved earrings and Michael bought me quite a few beautiful pairs. But when I had to go to hearing aids, I felt the earrings were drawing more attention to them. I wasn't ashamed of my hearing aids, I just didn't like the two of them together.

**Jess**   Tell us about some of the jewellery you do wear because you've got a few really lovely pieces which have a lot of sentimental value.

**Norma**   Because your grandad and I were buying the house on Harewood Avenue and all the furniture before we wed, I got a good quality wedding band, but we didn't spend much on my engagement ring. The one he bought was two diamonds and a sapphire, but he always wanted to replace it with something more valuable. He did that for my 40th birthday after spotting a beautiful diamond ring in the window of Stanley Hunt.

**Jess**   So you got your upgrade.

**Norma**   I did. And then for my 89th birthday, you lot all clubbed together to get me something very special indeed.

**Jess**   The family all chipped in to help Nan buy a new diamond and sapphire ring, which she wears on her right hand.

**Norma**   The stones are a lovely reminder of my original engagement ring, of Michael and of our wedding day. I also have a pendant that my mum bought me for my 21st birthday, which has a picture of my dad in it. And Betty bought me a beautiful tree of life necklace about a year before she died which means a lot to me.

## CHAPTER ELEVEN

She said, 'I want to buy you something to keep, Norma, because I'm not leaving you anything in my will – that's got to go to the young ones.'

It's in Welsh gold, the same as the royal family have all their wedding rings made with. I haven't got enough space around my neck to wear all my necklaces at the same time, so I alternate.

**Jess** I bought you one too, a little sapphire pendant.

**Norma** Yes, but it doesn't show up, love.

**Jess** OK, I admit it's tiny, but sapphires are expensive, Nan!

**Norma** I'm just joking. It's beautiful. All my jewellery means something to me. Michael bought me a lovely gold bracelet from Links for our 15th wedding anniversary in 1977. It's very loose on me now so I can't wear it, sadly.

**Jess** You've always liked sapphires. Actually, my favourite colour on you for clothes is royal blue. You look great in blue.

**Norma** I don't take kindly to a pale colour. I certainly don't like white next to my face, it can finish me off.

**Jess** You've got a good eye for what suits you. I know you've always enjoyed clothes and you still love a shopping spree.

**Norma** I really do. Betty and I used to go to Sheffield on a Saturday – it was a shilling for a return ticket – and we'd have a walk round C&A and Cole's. Cole's was a huge store and you always came out with something if you'd been in there.

**Jess** These days you're head-to-toe in M&S and Edinburgh Woollen Mill.

**Norma** And Damart. I like a flick through the Damart catalogue and then phoning to place my order.

## FASHION AND BEAUTY

Jess    We often get asked where your clothes are from – you're a right style icon, Nan. A fashion influencer.

Norma    Are you kidding me on, Jess?

Jess    No, it's true! Although I wouldn't wear your clothes myself.

Norma    What's wrong with them?

Jess    Call me crazy, I'm just not a 27inch skirt and open-toed sandal kind of girl! I can't resist ASOS, Zara and H&M, mainly for loungewear. I've got a co-ord obsession which is out of control.

Norma    I reckon we'll need to set you up on Vinted soon.

Jess    How do you know about Vinted?!

Norma    I know lots of things, Jessica.

Jess    You are full of surprises. But I do have too many clothes for my wardrobe … I tend to spend more in the winter because that's my favourite fashion season. You can look so smart in a decent coat and a nice scarf.

Norma    It doesn't take much to look spruced up.

Jess    Ah, thanks Nan!

Norma    I wasn't talking about you.

Jess    Brilliant.

Norma    I'm only joking. I do admire your dedication to looking your best, I like to do that too. I tend to wear a top with a skirt now, but in the past it was always dresses. A little belt around the middle, a few buttons, a bit of a collar and an A-line skirt. Nothing too fussy.

We'd have our dresses for every day and those saved for best. If it was an ordinary run-of-the-mill day, you did not put on a 'for best' dress.

## CHAPTER ELEVEN

**Jess**   Did you ever go in for the mini skirt during the sixties?

**Norma**   No, I had to let that pass me by, Jess. I couldn't wear them because, well …

**Jess**   … You didn't have the legs for a mini skirt?

**Norma**   Not really. That was best left to others to carry off – it was all a bit way out for me if I'm honest, showing all that leg. Sometimes you see the young girls today out and about and I think they must be absolutely freezing cold. They'll catch their death.

**Jess**   I love how we can look at photos from the past and pinpoint the decade by the clothes people were wearing. I think my favourite is probably the sixties.

**Norma**   I preferred the Elvis Presley era just before that when the men wore their hair in quiffs and had shoes with those big thick soles. All the men carried a comb in their pocket so they kept their hairdos immaculate. And how I loved watching them jive. The girls all had very full skirts, which were perfect for the dancing. Do you know, I'd give my right arm to have a dance with Anton du Beke from *Strictly*.

**Jess**   You can't even stand up straight now, so I think that's off the cards.

**Norma**   A girl can dream, Jessica. I used to go to night school to learn ballroom back in the day. And I have to tell you, the lad who always picked me to dance with him went on to win medals.

**Jess**   You must have been quite good if he wanted you as his partner.

**Norma**   I think I was, actually. My sisters and I all loved dancing, but all three of us married men who wouldn't go within a mile of a dancefloor.

## FASHION AND BEAUTY

**Jess**  Do you miss dancing?

**Norma**  I do but do you know what I miss most of all? Heels. I'd love to put on a beautiful shoe and some nice silk tights just one more time. I used to wear heels every day but my feet are paying the price now. I've got the family feet. Everyone had them except Betty.

**Jess**  You've got size six feet – complete with bunions – that are as wide as they are long. Basically, you've got everything you wouldn't want in a foot. But Betty had dainty little feet.

**Norma**  Oh, she did! Size four and a half, just like a dancer. Me, Joan, my mum and all the aunties ended up with the same unfortunate feet. Auntie Con used to buy a pair of shoes, cut a hole in them at the top where her bunion went and then slide a piece of fabric of the same colour on the inside, which I thought was quite clever.

**Jess**  So her bunion poked through the hole? That was nifty.

**Norma**  I loved shoes and had a pair in every colour, but I wore what I called 'cripplers' and had to push my feet into them against their will. It was always a Winklepicker style, the ones with the very pointed toe. Put it this way, when your mum got married, by the time I got to the reception my toes were bleeding.

**Jess**  My mum always says 'no pain, no gain' when it comes to heels.

**Norma**  That's not done her very much good, has it?

**Jess**  Heels all day, every day, while standing in a salon was only ever going to have one outcome.

**Norma**  Her feet have gone the same way as mine.

**Jess**  I live in trainers now. I think my skyscraper heel days are long gone.

# CHAPTER ELEVEN

**Norma**     It got to the point where I couldn't get any of mine on any more. I had to admit defeat some years ago and ended up giving all my shoes away to friends.

**Jess**     And now all you can wear is an open-toed sandal.

**Norma**     And my toes have changed shape. They all overlap, like they're holding hands.

**Jess**     Your feet are the bane of my life.

**Norma**     Oh now, Jessica! Aren't you cruel?

**Jess**     I keep your toenails trimmed, which is an absolute delight for me. I have such a lovely experience with those trotters.

**Norma**     What is it they say about sarcasm, Jessica?

**Jess**     I don't know if it's an age thing, but your toenails are so thick they're like an elephant's tusk. I cut them and they fly across the room! I practically need garden shears to get through them.

**Norma**     Your grandad once offered me his pliers from the garage ...

**Jess**     Thankfully I haven't inherited the family feet. I've escaped it.

**Norma**     Don't get cocky, love. There's plenty time yet.

**Jess**     You're dying for me to get those feet.

**Norma**     Plenty time ...

## INTERLUDE
# Our favourite days out together

### Clumber Park, Nottinghamshire

Norma    One of the most beautiful parks in the whole country, in my opinion. I would love to be able to walk around the lake as I used to.

Jess    We can still drive in and pull up and walk around a little bit. It's so pretty and peaceful.

Norma    When you stop my wheelchair at the bluebell patch, it's a little piece of heaven.

### Morrisons Café

Norma    I love our outings here. It's more for the memories because your grandad and I always stopped for lunch after we'd done our shop.

Jess    It can be a bit hit and miss for the food, but being in that store feels like home. And it shows that days out don't have to be anything fancy, elaborate or something that breaks the bank.

Norma    The important thing is getting out of the house and going somewhere comfortable.

Jess    It's real life in there, isn't it? That's what we love.

# INTERLUDE

### Fish and chips in the car

**Jess**  We don't do anything too adventurous these days, but it doesn't matter. The simplest of things makes us happiest and a fish and chip lunch after a stroll around the shops is one of the best afternoons we could possibly have.

**Norma**  It doesn't get much better than that for me.

**Jess**  We normally eat them in the car and always get lots of comments asking why we do that. There's no real reason other than that we like to eat them while they're hot! Even when Nan was more mobile we did that.

**Norma**  It's what I did with your grandad, too. If we had a sausage roll, we'd eat them outside the car because they flaked too easily. Oh, those sausage rolls from Curtis of Lincoln were the best.

### A country drive

**Jess**  We're lucky to live in a part of the world where there is a lot of beautiful countryside. Sometimes we just get in the car and go for a gentle drive.

**Norma**  It's lovely when the sun's out and the fields are looking so lush and fresh. Very life-affirming.

**Jess**  Until I get us lost in the middle of nowhere and have to phone Jake in a panic.

**Norma**  You're very good at that. When you've got yourself in a muddle with the map or the directions, I try not to say anything.

**Jess**  You don't try very hard!

OUR FAVOURITE DAYS OUT TOGETHER

## Marshall's Yard

**Norma**  Marshall's Yard is a shopping centre in Gainsborough and it's lovely for a wander round. They have a B&M, a Marks & Spencer Simply Food, Superdrug, everything you could need.

**Jess**  And a Stanley Hunt.

**Norma**  Where your grandad bought me that diamond ring.

**Jess**  We were asked to turn on the Christmas lights there in 2024, which was such an honour. There were thousands of people there; we couldn't get over the turnout.

**Norma**  We had to have security, there were so many people. The place was mobbed. When I got on the stage and looked out at that sea of faces, children with eyes like saucers … It was a lovely feeling although it was a freezing cold evening. I had a hot water bottle on my knees.

**Jess**  We get invited to lots of swanky places and the vast majority of them we have to turn down. But when I asked Nan if she wanted to turn on the lights at Marshall's Yard, it was an instant yes.

**Norma**  It's a place that holds a lot of meaning and memories for me.

**Jess**  Did it used to be a factory, Nan?

**Norma**  Yes, a very big one. The Britannia Iron Works. They used to have an open day, which your grandad was a big fan of.

**Jess**  It's just the right size for you to go around in the wheelchair without being too tired.

**Norma**  It's not overwhelming at all. They've done it out perfectly and we do like it. We get stopped there by followers more than anywhere else.

**INTERLUDE**

## Sunday roast

Jess   The whole family likes to go out for a Sunday roast.

Norma   That's why it's one of my favourite things to do. Everyone gets together, which is more important than the food.

Jess   The food is still important though! Our number one choice of place closed down recently so we're on the hunt for a new spot.

Norma   But even if we go out and have a bad meal, we still have a nice time being together.

Jess   And then you trot off home with your handbag full of beef.

CHAPTER TWELVE

# Ageing and Caring

**Norma**  Do you know what I've never understood about getting older? Why some people – ladies in particular – don't like to reveal their age. They get all coy about it and end up treating it as if it's classified information.

**Jess**  Or even fib about it by knocking a few years off, Hollywood style.

**Norma**  I remember as a child being told it was rude to ask a lady her age. It truly baffles me because age is just a fact of life and shouldn't be something you're ashamed of. People knowing how old I am doesn't bother me one iota. In fact, more than that, I'm proud of how old I am. Getting to 91 is nothing to be sniffed at and I feel very blessed to have reached that milestone.

**Jess**  Watching how you've embraced every stage of your life has been inspirational for me. Even when your physical health has held you back, you've powered through.

**Norma**  We know lots of people – your grandad being one – who have had their lives cut short, so I see getting older as a privilege. It does come at a cost, though. The longer you live, the tougher it gets. When I'm sitting down, I feel about 30 years old. Standing up? About a hundred. I feel frustrated when I have to ask someone else to do things for me.

**Jess**  When I was younger, you used to tell me there was no such word as 'can't' …

## CHAPTER TWELVE

**Norma**  Well, there is now! I know I'm slow and I get so angry with myself, but we tend to laugh about it rather than stay cross, don't we? Jake tells me, 'If you go any faster, Norma, you'll get a speeding ticket.' I enjoy that, finding the funny side.

**Jess**  Your sense of humour has definitely ramped up as you've got older. You've always been quick-witted and funny, but in the past ten years or so it's been on another level. It might be partly a coping mechanism for losing some of your independence, but we really do have a laugh.

**Norma**  If we didn't have that, we might as well give up.

**Jess**  The 'fortunate' thing about Nan's ageing is that it's been more of a gentle decline over the ten to 12 years rather than a sudden switch. We've all had the gift of time to adapt and find new ways of doing things. The first little setbacks I noticed were when she was in her late seventies and started to struggle with small tasks like putting the bins out and bringing her shopping in.

**Norma**  I've gone from one stage to another quite gradually, but I can't pretend that things aren't getting progressively worse, especially when it comes to my mobility. I've also had a couple of operations on my hands in the last few years, one for carpal tunnel syndrome and another for a condition called trigger finger, which affects the tendons.

**Jess**  It meant Nan's fingers were stuck, splayed on her palm so her hand looked like a little fortune cookie. They've done as much as they can with both operations.

**Norma**  It's improved things mildly and means I can write – I'm just about able to do the crossword although it's barely readable and sometimes the words are in the wrong boxes. But I intend to keep doing whatever I can for as long as humanly possible.

**Jess**  Nan is very determined, always has been. She'll summon up

## AGEING AND CARING

everything she has in her to go through to the kitchen and make herself a cup of tea, pour a bowl of cereal and put a load in the washing machine. I actively encourage her to do this and only step in if I can see she's struggling. She wants to maintain a level of independence, so I don't interfere with that.

**Norma** Sometimes my shoulders hurt from the strength I use to press down on my frame and there are plenty of things I can't reach or do for myself. I'm also shrinking! I can't stand up straight so although I used to be five foot two, now I'm four foot 11 inches. But I will do my best.

**Jess** I'll help by making sure that whatever she needs is to hand and easily accessible on the kitchen counter. For example, we've got an old jam jar that I'll put the cutlery in rather than keeping it in a drawer that she'd have to faff about trying to open. Or if I've got an appointment and am going to miss her morning coffee, I'll leave everything out ready so all she has to do is flick the kettle on and add the hot water.

The longer she can carry on doing these things independently, the better for her overall wellbeing. Even if that means she leaves the kitchen like an absolute bombsite that I then have to clean up …

**Norma** I run out of energy by the time it comes to the clearing away.

**Jess** Hmm, what a coincidence. We keep the house to a decent standard but gone are the days of worrying about the aesthetic.

**Norma** A few years ago I wouldn't have liked having the tiered side table that I keep next to my chair in the living room. It's not very pretty, but it has everything I need within easy reach – my diary, my pills, my makeup.

**Jess** You're great at focusing on what you can do and being

# CHAPTER TWELVE

|   |   |
|---|---|
|   | grateful for the things you've still got. You've always had a 'glass half full' perspective. |
| Norma | I think that comes from my childhood and seeing my family and the people around us making the best of what we had. Life is what you make it and I always remember that it must be far worse for those whose minds are affected. Not to mention heartbreaking for the relatives who have to watch that happen. Dementia is the cruellest of diseases.<br><br>I keep my brain ticking over with the crosswords and wordsearches I love. I enjoy a good telly quiz show – *Eggheads* was my favourite when it was on. I like *Countdown* and anything with David Attenborough. |
| Jess | You're one of the cleverest people I know, full of knowledge. There are pros and cons to everything and we're so grateful that you're switched on mentally. Your memory is better than mine! And one of the benefits of having lived for so long is all the life experience you can share with the likes of me, my brother and everyone else in the family. I can come and get some brilliant advice from you, even if I do have to pick up all the cutlery you've dropped on the floor. It's a trade-off. |
| Norma | I might be limited in what I can do now, but I take a lot of pleasure in seeing you lot live your lives. I love it when you call round here before you head out for the evening, Jess, and I get to see you all dressed up. One day you might even take me with you. |
| Jess | I don't think the bright lights are ready for you, Nan! |
| Norma | You lot help keep me young. |
| Jess | One of the questions we're asked most of all is exactly how our set-up works. |
| Norma | It's quite simple, really. You give out the orders and I do as I'm told. |

| | |
|---|---|
| Jess | Sigh. My life would be a breeze if that was true, Nan. |
| Norma | I think I'm a good 'customer' most of the time. |
| Jess | If a little stubborn. |
| Norma | Pot, kettle, black. |
| Jess | People also ask all the time if we live together. |
| Norma | Good lord, no. |
| Jess | I've explained how I was able to give up my job as a social worker to care for Nan full time, but one thing I do want to make absolutely clear is that she has never asked me to do this. |
| | When she started to struggle, I knew that I wanted to be the one to help her. I wanted to be the one who stepped in. |
| Norma | I've gone over it many, many times, checking that you're happy with this arrangement that we have. |
| Jess | I know it's not my responsibility to look after you. Nobody's children or grandchildren should feel pressured to provide care or be forced into roles they never expected or wanted. |
| | I do it because I want to do it. You gave me the best childhood and I want to give back a little bit of what you did for me. It doesn't feel like a job or a chore. It's just a lovely thing and I'm full of gratitude that I'm able to do it. And when somebody is as appreciative and caring and loving as you are, how could I ever think anything else? You are an absolute dream to look after. |
| Norma | It's not just the care you give me, it's the company too. You're all go a lot of the time and there's always a job to be getting on with, but I love it when we get half an hour to sit down and have a chat. |

## CHAPTER TWELVE

Jess    Me too. And those chats are so special because I don't have to worry about the time or getting back to work. Nothing is rushed.

Norma    The other afternoon we sat and watched a nature programme on the telly, which we both enjoyed. I feel lucky to have that companionship.

Jess    Up until recently our days began with a phone call from Nan to me. She'd ring and say, 'I'm just swinging my legs out of bed' so then I'd time my arrival at her house for 45 minutes later. Since January 2025 though, things have slowed down a fair bit.

Norma    I was ever so poorly over Christmas 2024, wasn't I. And you and your mum came and gave me so much help. I couldn't have coped without you both.

Jess    You used to be adamant that you wanted to get yourself up and washed and dressed in the morning, but sometimes it was taking you two to three hours to get downstairs!

Norma    Looking back at that, I can't really believe I wouldn't accept the extra help. We've got a little routine now, haven't we, love?

Jess    I'm here first thing every morning now to help her up and get her ready for the day. I wash the areas you can't reach, don't I? The 'BTM' as we call it.

Norma    It's a polite term for bottom.

Jess    It's a bit better than saying 'wash your arse', isn't it?

Norma    Jessica, really.

Jess    It is interesting when you think about it that when I was younger, you'd tell me to wash my face first, the armpits, the down below and then the BTM. And now I'm helping you with yours.

## AGEING AND CARING

**Norma**  The shower frightens me to death. I call the bathroom the torture chamber.

**Jess**  I know you don't like it. I've helped you into the shower when your whole body has been shaking with fear.

**Norma**  I'm not at ease until we get back to our 'Safe Zone', which is when I'm out of the shower and sitting on the closed lid of the loo.

**Jess**  It's never long before you're downstairs having your breakfast now. You're usually there by nine.

**Norma**  It was teatime before I pulled myself round before sometimes, wasn't it? I'd stopped reading my newspaper because I was so tired, but it was a long time before I realised that it had become such a struggle to do things myself. I feel so much stronger in my legs now that we've got this routine. But I still feel worried about being a burden to you, Jess.

**Jess**  You're not a burden, Nan. I'm so pleased that you've accepted the help and that you're enjoying your paper again.

Once Nan is downstairs and settled in her chair eating breakfast and reading the newspaper, I'll potter about, bringing all the dirty washing down, sprucing up the bathroom and making the bed, plumping up the pillows just how she likes them. Some days you're feeling great and we film some content together. And other days are trickier, aren't they?

**Norma**  I do occasionally struggle with pain and discomfort. It's just part of getting older.

**Jess**  We'd never show any of that, but I do want people to know that despite how it seems, and how much we all put into making sure Nan's happy and comfortable, not every day is easy.

## CHAPTER TWELVE

The only day I'm ever not here is a Monday. My mum helps out as often as she can throughout the week, but Monday is her day off so she takes over the care on that day, although I often still pop in because I miss Nan. Otherwise I'm in and out all day, usually visiting at least three or four times, listening to your demands.

Norma   We're out of toffees at the minute, Jessica.

Jess   Yes, I know, boss.

And then I see her up to bed, getting her all tucked up and then locking her in until morning. Bedtime is my favourite part of the day because Nan always says, 'thank you', we have a kiss and a cuddle and then we say 'love you.' And I feel so grateful that I'm able to do this for her.

Norma   We should be sick of the sight of each other, shouldn't we?

Jess   Me and Mum never go away at the same time so that means there's always one of us to cover the other. We did have one day together where we went to London for a little trip, but we made sure my brother Cadan was off work so he could take over. Although bless him, he's not that much use, is he?

Norma   He doesn't listen. It might be his age, I suppose. I'll ask him to get me something from the kitchen and he'll disappear and come back a few minutes later saying, 'What did you want again, Nan?'

Jess   Cadan helps out with some of the shopping and those kind of jobs but we'd never expect him to do Nan's personal care. Because I do the bulk of it, if I go away on holiday, we sort out extra cover. We have Nan's cleaner Kay and also Mandy, who we've mentioned before, on hand to step in. It's a neat little system we've got going and it's all with Nan's best interests at heart.

Norma   Apart from when your mum washes my hair.

## AGEING AND CARING

Jess    My mum can be a little heavy-handed.

Norma    A little?! I have to hang on to that sink like grim death.

Jess    There have been aspects of the care you took a bit of time getting used to, haven't there? You found some of the intimate care a bit difficult at first. But again, we find the humour.

Norma    Like Alice and Maude.

Jess    Ah yes, your names for your boobs. I'll be helping you get dressed and you'll say, 'Watch out, you're hurting Alice!'

Norma    Those nicknames go back years. It's what my sisters and I used to call them but I have no idea who started it or where 'Alice' and 'Maude' came from.

Jess    Bladder jokes are a running theme as well. Incontinence is something that happens to a lot of people with age and sometimes the heavens will open and there's not a damn thing we can do about it. Nan has loose skin at the tops of her thighs which sticks together and we have to peel them apart.

Norma    I call that bit of skin the 'Bridge Over Troubled Water'. I haven't got to be precious about all this. I'd imagine even the late Queen Elizabeth had people helping her towards the end.

Jess    Exactly. And it doesn't faze me at all; I've seen it all before and I just get stuck in. Sometimes I have to put cream on delicate areas and I don't bat an eyelid. We've always been quite comfortable with being naked around each other.

Norma    When you were little, you were having a bath with your mum and you asked her, 'When I grow into a lady, will my boobs be pretty like yours or triangles like Nan's?'

Jess    I clearly had a way with words.

Norma    Just as well I don't take offence easily, isn't it?

## CHAPTER TWELVE

**Jess**  We do feel very fortunate with our situation compared to others. Without social media, I'd have to be out at work all day and then I wouldn't be able to do this with you. I'm really grateful that I can take care of you, and know how tough it is for carers out there. Many people have been in touch with us to talk about the challenges. The system is broken.

Carers' Allowance is shockingly low at around £80 per week. And to qualify for it, you have to work at least 35 hours a week as a carer. But you're not eligible for it at all if you earn over £125 per week from another job. People are being stretched to their limits and carer burnout is a real issue. I make sure to give back by picking a charity to make a donation to every month.

**Norma**  It's especially hard for the 'sandwich generation' you hear about in the news. That's where people – usually women – are providing care for ageing parents as well as their own children or grandchildren. And often trying to hold down jobs in between.

**Jess**  As a system it's been neglected for so long because when it's human beings with care needs, their families will always pick up the slack – so the government doesn't prioritise them. That's my theory, anyway.

**Norma**  There are so many struggling and not enough support. We've heard from people with disabled children saying how desperate they are for a break. The wellbeing of carers is just as important as that of the people who rely on them for care. Because if the carer's health fails …

**Jess**  … Exactly. Who picks up the pieces? One lady who reached out to us had been working full time while trying to care for her elderly parents. She was broken, exhausted. Eventually she quit her job and left her career behind because it was all too much. I've had people messaging me asking to be pointed in the right direction for support or to find out what help is available in their area. I do whatever research I can and share it with them.

I met one chap at a carers' event whose wife was dependent on him, 24/7, and he was telling me that even when he has support in, as soon as he leaves the room, she's calling for him in a panic. I get to go home and relax – I can't even begin to imagine how stressful it must be to have no escape.

If I was made Prime Minister tomorrow …

Norma   … Heaven help us.

Jess   … If I was made Prime Minister tomorrow, I'd raise the Carers' Allowance to at least the minimum wage because as it stands, it works out at about £2 an hour, which is diabolical.

I'd also change how professional carers are paid – a lot of companies will only pay the carer for the time spent providing care and don't include the travelling between houses. Things like that mean it's not a career that people want to pursue and yet it's one of the most important roles in our society.

Norma   Maybe these issues will be fixed by the time you need looking after.

Jess   I don't think it will be somehow. It'll be at the bottom of the list of priorities forever.

Norma   I do sometimes worry about what we would do if I was to need more help.

Jess   We'll always be honest about what's happening and if it ever got to the point that you needed 24-hour care, me and Mum have already agreed that we'd move in.

Norma   Oh Jessica, I think that's extreme.

# CHAPTER TWELVE

**Jess**    Would you rather have me and Mum move in and give you the care you needed or be in a nursing home where they're rushed off their feet? And that's before we've even considered the cost of getting somewhere half decent.

**Norma**    That sends a shiver down my spine.

**Jess**    Exactly. It's hard to plan these things because none of us know how the future is going to pan out. We might stay at this stage for the next few years and carry on fine as we are. But we're also realistic that there's a good chance things are going to get more challenging.

Jake knows that Nan is my priority and he knew that from the day he met me. He signed up for it, so he can't say I didn't warn him.

We try not to worry about it too much, but we know that we'll do whatever is needed to keep Nan happy and comfortable. I truly believe this arrangement has allowed her to live a longer and happier life.

**Norma**    It's kept me doing things for myself as well. I shouldn't think a carer would have the time to stand back and let me make my own breakfast and cup of tea because sometimes that can take me half an hour.

**Jess**    The carer would come in and do everything for you in a matter of minutes while you'd be sitting there wasting away in your chair. That's no shade on professional carers out there – they are run off their feet and have to work to a timetable. But you'd lose those skills. It's the same with getting out of the house and into the car – it is becoming difficult for you, but we make sure we do it. It's when you stop doing it that you lose it.

**Norma**    Use it or lose it. You're right.

**Jess**    I'll never be able to adequately express how this caring

|        |                                                                                                                                                                                           |
|--------|-------------------------------------------------------------------------------------------------------------------------------------------------------------------------------------------|
|        | arrangement has changed our lives and made this time in Nan's life so special.                                                                                                            |
| Norma  | Don't laugh, but I've felt younger.                                                                                                                                                       |
| Jess   | You don't look it. But as long as you feel it, that's the main thing.                                                                                                                     |
| Norma  | You little rotter! I just don't ever want to put people out.                                                                                                                              |
| Jess   | I know you sometimes feel like a burden. Which you're not, by the way. Ever. Apart from when you phone me up in a panic thinking there's a strange noise coming from your garden.          |
| Norma  | It sounded like someone was in the back, dragging round a piece of metal.                                                                                                                 |
| Jess   | This happened recently. It turned out to be the automatic air freshener spraying every nine minutes.                                                                                      |
| Norma  | Am I forgiven?                                                                                                                                                                            |
| Jess   | Just about. But you know you can call us any time you have a bit of a problem. People who rely solely on social care don't have that luxury.                                              |

Jess    I'm there to take you to any appointments, to go to the chemist to pick up prescriptions and make sure you've got enough shopping in. I've got the time to sit with you while you sort out your life admin, like ringing the bank, which you always find complicated.

Last week when you said spontaneously that you'd like to go shopping, that's exactly what we did and we loved it. Not many elderly people with care needs have freedom and choice like that. Having been a social worker responsible for putting care packages in place, I know people are never sure what time their carers are turning up or which ones it will be each day.

## CHAPTER TWELVE

**Norma**  I suppose it's impossible for them to have the same person going in every day, but when you're relying on people to provide your care, it would be more comforting to build up a relationship with them over time.

**Jess**  I look back and don't know how I managed to do everything around my old job. I used to have to take flexi time and then work late to compensate. It was and still is constantly on my mind: is Nan sorted?

I feel so sorry for a lot of your generation because it often feels like society is dismissive of you. Older people are too easily forgotten about.

**Norma**  Some people have a tendency to patronise and slip into this way of talking to us older folk as if we're babies.

**Jess**  Definitely. They completely underestimate your intelligence or just assume you're incapable of speaking for yourself. Either way, it's disrespectful and awful. I've seen it happen with doctors where whole conversations about you are addressed entirely to me.

**Norma**  I do pipe up sometimes, 'Er, just a minute, I'm still here, you know!'

A few years ago when I had that fall, the doctor came out and he asked all the questions to your mum rather than me. It was as if he thought I was a nincompoop.

**Jess**  Speaking of falls …

**Norma**  That is something I live in fear of.

**Jess**  You and me both. It's a sad fact that older people are prone to falling – slower reflexes, balance issues, visual impairments and medications can all play a part in that. And it's been a constant worry for us since you first fell in 2009. It was horrendous, you fell from the top of your stairs to the bottom.

## AGEING AND CARING

**Norma**  I don't know what happened. I had two beakers in my hand and it was all of a sudden. I wasn't able to get myself up again but I managed to pull the landline towards me so I could call your mum.

**Jess**  We all came charging round at full pelt, didn't we? It was a horrible moment, not knowing what state you were going to be in when we got there.

**Norma**  How I didn't break anything is a mystery. Maybe I was too well padded. I had nothing to show for it apart from a bruise on my leg.

**Jess**  You had one on your back, too.

**Norma**  Yes but no one could see that, so it was very disappointing all told.

**Jess**  Ever since then, Cadan has called you Steel Gran. He was only six at the time and he thought the lack of injury must mean you had superpowers.

**Norma**  I was in a lot of pain, though. You, your mum and Cadan all helped me up into my chair and I said I didn't think I'd be able to get out of it again, even to go to the toilet.

'Don't worry,' said Kate. 'If you can't get up, we'll go to Plan B.'

'What's Plan B?' I asked.

'I don't know yet,' she replied.

And then she produced a paper bag as if that was going to be the solution.

**Jess**  Mafia Kate to the rescue!

**Norma**  But it was eight weeks before I could leave the house again. I had a stairlift installed within a week, which meant I was safe going up and down between the two floors.

## CHAPTER TWELVE

**Jess** After that fall we had someone come out from social services who looked at everything in Nan's house and how it could be made safer by installing aids like grab rails. She was also given a red button, which she wears as a pendant around her neck and can press if she ever needs help. It connects to a call centre where someone then speaks to Nan via her lifeline unit, or 'The Box', as we call it.

If she's able to respond, she can ask them to call me or my mum and they have both our numbers on their system. If there's no response from her, they go straight to 999.

**Norma** It's the most wonderful service. It only costs a few pounds a week to be part of and we say it's like gold, don't we?

**Jess** It's absolutely priceless in terms of safety and peace of mind. Because there have been a few falls since that first one.

**Norma** I had a fall in the bathroom as well and I have to say, it was a bit embarrassing because I had no clothes on. The first thing you did once you came upstairs, Jess, was pick up a big towel.

**Jess** I had to get Cadan to help me lift you up and I knew you wouldn't want him to see your bits and bobs. So I spared you your dignity and put the towel over you first.

Actually, you weren't completely starkers because you still had your red button around your neck! Naked except for the red button.

**Norma** What an image.

**Jess** You had a fall in the kitchen that time where you just lost your balance.

**Norma** I had an egg on the side of my head before you could even say 'Jack Robinson'.

**Jess** Who's Jack Robinson?

**Norma** No idea.

| | |
|---|---|
| Jess | The doctor came out and checked you thoroughly and said either someone stayed with you for the next 48 hours or you had to go to hospital. I could see the panic in your eyes at the mere mention of hospital and so I moved in for the next two days to make sure you didn't go doolally. |
| Norma | Touch wood, I've been quite good at avoiding hospital stays. I'm not a fan of those places. Apart from when I was four and had scarlet fever and the bed rest I was put on for high blood pressure before giving birth, I've managed to dodge them, despite various ailments. |
| Jess | When you went in for the operation for the trigger finger and the doctor said you could leave as soon as you'd had a cup of tea and a toilet trip, I'd not seen you move so fast in years. |
| Norma | I gulped down a cup of tea, which tasted like dishwater, went to the loo and whoosh, I was on my merry way. The less time spent in hospital the better. |
| Jess | The doctors couldn't find anything that was causing Nan to fall. Her hearing aids were working, her sight was fine, there were no trip hazards in the house. They did an ECG to check her heart and that didn't come up with anything either. The only thing they could think of was dehydration. |
| Norma | That's why I have my juice with me all the time now and I make sure I'm constantly topping myself up. |
| Jess | You sure it's just juice in there and not something stronger? |
| Norma | I could do with something stronger, but no, I'm quite certain. |
| Jess | I do have to nag you to drink more fluids sometimes and I know it winds you up something chronic. But to be fair, you are on it most of the time. It's just a horrible feeling when you get that call from the red button people to say you've had a fall. We can't help but think of the worst-case scenario. |

## CHAPTER TWELVE

**Norma**  I've tried not to allow the falls to knock me back but one or two of them definitely did. The mental recovery can often be harder than the physical one, I think.

**Jess**  And certainly after that first fall we had to build up to going back out of the house and walking again. You used a walking stick for a while before switching to the four-wheeled walker and now the frame that you use all the time. I'm proud of you for digging deep and finding the courage to get back out there.

**Norma**  It wasn't always easy, but you've got to pull yourself together.

**Jess**  There are a lot of people who would use it as an excuse to give up and let other people do things for them.

**Norma**  Oops, you've found my secret …

**Jess**  As a family we've made a lot of changes to keep Nan safe. Jake's dad has built a step in the bathroom to help her get in the shower. I don't think she'd be able to get in without it. Jake has also fitted a rail by the side of the bed and that has made her so happy. Putting carpet down in the hall is something else we've done recently to help protect her in case of a fall.

**Norma**  These are the realities of getting old. But for those of us who reach a certain age, we've got to get used to it and take heart from the quality of life we still have. I'm slow, but I'm generally on the right track.

**Jess**  You're very accepting of the help and happy to use the aids provided to make your life easier. Your grabber, for instance.

**Norma**  I love my grabber; I wouldn't be without it.

**Jess**  A grabber is a tool that works like an extension of the arm and it means Nan can reach items she'd otherwise be unable to. The number of elderly people I met in my old job who

## AGEING AND CARING

refused to use one never failed to amaze me. Even if it would have significantly benefitted them.

**Norma**  My sister Betty was like that. She refused point blank to go round the supermarket in her wheelchair because she didn't want anyone to see her in it. And my other sister Joan wouldn't wear her hearing aids because she thought they'd make her look old. They were both too proud.

**Jess**  A bit of an awkward family, by the sounds of it.

**Norma**  It's daft. You miss out if you don't use these things. Getting my wheelchair was the best thing I ever did because it meant I could go to all the places I enjoyed. I just needed someone willing to push me.

**Jess**  Enter yours truly …

**Norma**  I understand why some people feel too proud or they might see it as like admitting defeat. But if you don't use them, you fall. A bit of bruised pride or serious injury – which is worse?

**Jess**  People really need to reframe how they view these aids. Some see them as things that limit their independence when the reality is that they do the opposite. They allow people to have freedom and control.

On top of that, when people don't accept the help and the equipment, they're not just disadvantaging themselves, it's affecting everyone around them as well. Basically, either use the aids or miss out on life. Nan has welcomed all of them with good grace.

**Norma**  I've had a long time to get used to the way things are and I know I can't change it. There is so much in the world to enjoy. You can still feel at one with nature while in a wheelchair and I'm so calm when I'm in beautiful places like Clumber Park with all the bluebells.

# CHAPTER TWELVE

There's a lovely quote from a poem by Dorothy Frances Gurney that says, 'One is nearer God's heart in a garden than anywhere else on Earth.' How lovely. I enjoy the peace, the tranquillity and the views, which I wouldn't experience at all without my chair.

Jess   I say all this, but I don't know whether or not I'll be accepting a wheelchair at 90.

Norma   Ninety? Oh, I'm not so sure you'll still be here, Jess.

Jess   Wow.

Norma   The equipment also allows me to stay here in my home. It horrifies me to think of being taken away and put into a nursing home. I can't stand the thought of it. You're in a different world when you go into one of those places.

A friend of mine who was in the latter stage of her life went into one and it just made me feel so sorry whenever I went to visit. Don't take this the wrong way because I know the staff do their best, but they can't see to everybody one-to-one all the time.

Jess   That said, there are some amazing care homes out there, staffed by people who are brilliant at their jobs. Some people thrive in that environment, don't they? Bingo at ten. Afternoon tea. You never know, if you moved into one, you might get yourself a little boyfriend.

Norma   I should be so lucky.

Jess   You definitely get more care here, though, than you would do if you were in a home. And we have seen people become institutionalised once they're in and that can cause them to go downhill.

Norma   Home is where your memories are and where your heart is.

## AGEING AND CARING

**Jess**    Where possible, home is the best place for everyone. And there's an element of Grandad in every room here, which is important to you.

**Norma**    I've been in this house since 1975. We moved out of Retford to this area when your mum was five months old in late 1968. Your grandad thought the house on Harewood Avenue where we'd lived since our wedding had reached its full potential and he wanted to be a little closer to where he worked at the power station.

I didn't want to leave. Retford was where my roots were. I remember saying to Betty, 'I'm not moving. Over my dead body.'

But your grandad talked me round and I do love it here. We bought a place where we stayed for six or seven years until we moved into this one.

**Jess**    Could you imagine yourself living anywhere else?

**Norma**    No, you'll not take me out of here now.

**Jess**    And we'll make sure this is where you stay. For all the aches and pains, it's where you are happiest.

**Norma**    Provided my sweet bowl is kept filled up.

INTERLUDE
# Just how Norma likes it …

### Cup of tea

**Jess**  Nan describes her cup of tea in the morning as 'nectar'. But it has to be made the Norma way.

**Norma**  I have four or five cups a day and it has to be Ringtons. Unless I was absolutely forced to, I wouldn't drink anything else.

**Jess**  That's a bit of a fib. You have had PG Tips in the past when you've run out of Ringtons and you managed just fine.

**Norma**  Put it this way, I wouldn't have any other brand on a regular basis. I don't like my tea black, but I do like what my mum used to call 'a good hot cup of tea'. So not a lot of milk.

**Jess**  You don't like it brewed for too long, though.

**Norma**  No, and I don't take sugar either. I have a coffee around 11am but tea is always my go-to.

**Jess**  You take sugar in your coffee, though. At home we use Nescafé cappuccino sachets, which you'll have with a teaspoon of sugar. But when we're out and you get those sachets of sugar, you have been known to have 18.

**Norma**  I think not.

**Jess**  That is the truth. But you deserve that sugar.

**Norma**  I take my tea in a mug but I do love it out of a china cup and saucer.

INTERLUDE

**Jess**   Ooh get you, Mrs Fancypants!

**Norma**   You see people walking round drinking tea out of beakers now. My mother would never have drunk tea out of a beaker. She would have gone spare.

## Biscuits

**Norma**   I don't know what's happened to biscuits lately. I used to love a Jacob's cream cracker with cheese, but they seem to be very thin and tough to bite into. For a while I preferred a good old digestive with a bit of cheese but I've been going off that as well.

**Jess**   I think your taste buds have changed.

**Norma**   My all-time favourites are a classic Rich Tea and the Ringtons ginger snaps. Good for dunking.

## Toast

**Norma**   You make the perfect toast for me, Jessica. You're very good at putting a decent chunk of butter on there – always Lurpak Spreadable.

**Jess**   Followed by Bonne Maman strawberry jam or their bitter orange marmalade. You like the toast not to be too well done. But not anaemic either.

**Norma**   No, I don't like it pale and you get it just right most of the time. On white bread. I know I should have brown because it's healthier, but I don't like it nearly as much.

**Jess**   Occasionally we'll mix it up with the bread but it's generally Warburtons Danish.

Norma  It's perfect for toasting. Breakfast is the only meal I finish these days. I'll have my bowl of All-Bran with quite a lot of sugar followed by my two slices of toast and I eat every last bit.

## Bed

Jess  Nan is very particular about how her bed is made.

Norma  I have two pillows to put under my head, but I also have a V-shaped one which helps keep me comfy – I can't lay flat without it because of my curved spine.

Jess  It's a pregnancy pillow. Is there something you're not telling us?

Norma  Well, I didn't want it to come out like this, Jessica …

Jess  Nan has layers of sheets and I know exactly which edge of the hem she likes to be at the top.

Norma  You know I'm not one to complain …

Jess  Eh up, here we go.

Norma  But you didn't manage it quite right yesterday, love.

Jess  There's normally something I've got wrong. The duvet goes on underneath the bedspread and above a sheet. That sheet goes all the way to the top of the pillows and is then turned back so that she can snuggle under it. She has little teddies on the bed as well.

Norma  Don't tell everyone that! I've got my chosen few.

Jess  She has to have the TV remote nearby, her book, her puzzles and a pen. All within reach.

Norma  Once I'm in my bed at night, I don't move until the morning.

## CHAPTER THIRTEEN
# Life Lessons

**Jess**     I've always believed that different generations can learn a lot from each other, but never more so than in the last few years I've spent with Nan.

**Norma**     I think you might be unusual, though, Jess. I wonder if many of the younger ones have the patience to deal with us lot. They're all too busy with dates and nightclubbing and leading the wild life.

**Jess**     And sometimes we wonder whether the older ones are open-minded enough to accept what we younger ones can offer. Because you're a bit stuck in your ways, you fossils, aren't you?

**Norma**     I beg your pardon, madam.

**Jess**     Jokes aside, Nan has been the best teacher I've ever had.

**Norma**     You've not always been the easiest of pupils.

**Jess**     Valid. But my appreciation for everything you've taught me has grown as I've got older. I'm not talking about times tables and spellings; it's more about the values and way of life. It's how to be grateful and respectful, making sure to show appreciation when someone does something kind or helpful and always to offer help to other people in need.

Not forgetting the golden nuggets of advice that are the 'rules' I now live by. Things like:

## CHAPTER THIRTEEN

- If you haven't got anything nice to say, don't say anything at all.

- Never let the sun go down on your anger.

- Listen to other people and then form your own opinions.

- Oh, and possibly one of the most important: Brussels sprouts always need to have had a frost otherwise they don't taste right.

**Norma** That's what my mum always said. She wouldn't even consider buying sprouts until there had been a frost. That's what made them crisper.

**Jess** You've also drummed into me the importance of being polite and having good manners. So, thank you very much for that.

**Norma** How very polite of you to say so! You have turned out with very good manners, I'll give you that.

**Jess** The ability to pause and reflect is one of the most valuable skills you've taught me because sometimes I can be quite outspoken.

**Norma** Mistress of the understatement. You certainly don't have a problem saying how you feel, that's for sure.

**Jess** Which means I'm often tempted to say things in the heat of the moment and Nan has always advised taking a step back to reflect.

**Norma** I'll tell you to sleep on it first. A good night's kip can help lower the temperature and a new day can bring a fresh and, dare I say it, more reasonable perspective.

**Jess** It's the best advice because it makes me think about the impact on the people around me and consider whether it's really worth saying after all. There was a time in my life where I was very reactive and I'd say exactly what I thought

|         | there and then. It's easy to be lured into doing that with text messaging and DMs – you can lash out immediately even if you're not with the person you're angry at. |
|---------|---|
| Norma   | You used to be very hasty at coming to a problem. You've simmered down a bit now and you think things through a lot more. |
| Jess    | As well as the emotional guidance, you've also given me lots of practical advice. You've taught me everything I know about cooking and baking. |
| Norma   | Don't blame me for that! |
| Jess    | I'm not that bad. |
| Norma   | We'll just pretend the cake you made the other day never happened. |
| Jess    | This might sound really silly, but you've also really helped me with basic life skills, like what to say when you get on a bus or make a phone call to the doctors or ask for directions. That might sound slightly weird, but a lot of my generation find those things quite daunting because there is so much social anxiety and we all spend far too much time online or communicating by text rather than in person. The number of times I've had a call to make and asked you first, 'What shall I say?' |
| Norma   | You get on quite well with that now, don't you? |
| Jess    | Totally. God knows where I'd be without you, Nan. |
| Norma   | I know where I'd be without you. |
| Jess    | Where's that? |
| Norma   | In a nursing home. |
| Jess    | Only if you start misbehaving. |

## CHAPTER THIRTEEN

Norma    You've taught me a lot too, Jess. You've opened my eyes to a lot of what is going on in the world and I take great pleasure from discussing it all with you. We exchange opinions and offer each other different outlooks.

Jess    You only see what you watch on the telly or read in your newspaper and you can sometimes blow things out of proportion. Especially if your newspaper has a certain agenda. I have the privilege of being able to go and do a bit more research online, accessing other sources, and can form a more rounded, balanced view of situations.

Norma    You're such a technical whizz and you've introduced me to lots of things that have made my mind boggle. If I ever need a new pair of shoes, you get your thingumabob out …

Jess    … My tablet.

Norma    That's it. And we'll have a look online and enjoy a good old whatsit.

Jess    A good scroll.

Norma    See, there's all these new words I can't keep up with. I know you try your best to educate me, but I can't get them to stick.

Jess    I've taught you a few.

Norma    You have but I can never remember them.

Jess    How about 'slay'?

Norma    I've forgotten what that means. I know about dragon slayers like St George, but it's nothing to do with that, is it?

Jess    No! It means amazing. If someone 'slays' something, they've done it really well.

Norma    I suppose that could make sense.

Jess    Here's another one: 'spill the tea'.

## LIFE LESSONS

**Norma**  I'm assuming that has nothing to do with having an accident with your brew?

**Jess**  You assume right. If someone has some gossip you want them to share, you tell them to spill the tea.

**Norma**  How peculiar. I have an awful job relating to these new words and phrases. It's almost like having to learn a new language.

**Jess**  And yet you correct me all the time on the way I speak.

**Norma**  Because sometimes your grammar leaves a lot to be desired, lady.

**Jess**  I'm not always sure about certain words. Like, I never know whether it's 'wrote' or 'written' so I'll say, 'I've wrote a note' ...

**Norma**  It's written, Jessica. I have written! Honestly, I just cringe.

**Jess**  Another one that bothers you is when I say 'you was' instead of 'you were'. You really don't like that, do you?

**Norma**  No, I don't. I'm not sure if they correct grammar in schools as much as they used to. When I was a girl, we had a real grounding in it because the two things they were mad on were times tables and speaking correctly.

**Jess**  Where we're from in Nottinghamshire, we say 'summat' and Nan will always look at me, bring out the old Norma Burton eye roll and say, 'something, Jessica'.

**Norma**  I'll have you speaking the Queen's English one day.

**Jess**  You might not have cracked it with my grammar, but I'm very good at budgeting and with my finances, thanks to you. You've always said if you haven't got it, you shouldn't spend it.

**Norma**  I think it all boils down to being aware of the state you're in

# CHAPTER THIRTEEN

and then not living beyond your means.

**Jess**  That's not always easy for people who feel they don't have a choice. But I've never been one to max out credit cards and get into debt. I'd be too scared.

**Norma**  No, you've always been very sensible with money. You've got your head screwed on the right way and you don't do anything silly.

**Jess**  Don't get me wrong, I love going on a shopping trip and treating myself now and again, but that isn't what makes me happy. My happiness levels don't depend on how healthy my bank balance is – some of the most contented times in my life have been when I've had the least amount of money.

**Norma**  I hope I've shown you where your money is best spent. Frivolities are nice for a treat, but you should always make sure you have enough for the essentials. Bearing in mind that there are certain items that you shouldn't ever skimp on.

**Jess**  You've always stressed the importance of having a decent pair of shoes with a well-made, solid sole.

**Norma**  And a good winter coat. You can't do that on the cheap.

**Jess**  Although that can sometimes backfire, can't it?

**Norma**  Oh dear. I know exactly the incident you're talking about. It was 1976, and your grandad and I had treated ourselves each to a sheepskin coat. They were suede and frightfully expensive – mine was £101 and your grandad's was £105, which was a huge amount of money back then.

They really were lovely coats and I felt awfully posh in mine, but the problem was they were far too heavy for us to wear. We couldn't move in them! It was like being in a straitjacket. Grandad would put his on to leave the house and then have to take it off again before he sat in the car. He'd manage about five yards in it in total. I don't think we wore them more than three times.

Jess  I can just picture the two of you!

Norma  Your grandad passed his on to someone else and I offered mine to your mum but she didn't want it.

Jess  Probably because it was so painful to wear!

Norma  I think we sold mine in the end.

Jess  You see, there's nothing I love more than hearing you tell these stories. I wish that more of the younger generation could see that you oldies can be really good craic! But I guess it's not very trendy to hang around with your grandparents, is it? It's not seen as cool.

Norma  Can older people be 'cool'?

Jess  Too right! Older people have lived a lifetime and will have so many memories and experiences to share. I never felt embarrassed because it was my nan picking me up from school; in fact I often preferred to hang out with you than kids my own age.

I find you completely fascinating – whenever you tell me a story, I want to know more and have hundreds of questions.

Norma  And I enjoy telling you my stories. I like having an audience and it helps keep the memories alive for me as well.

Jess  You bring all the family members back to life, the way you include colour and little details like the deliciousness of the Victoria plums your uncle Tom used to grow and how the juice would dribble down your chin. You're the only person who can tell me a lovely story like that. I think I'd add storytelling to the list of things you've taught me, and the importance of it.

## CHAPTER THIRTEEN

Norma    My mum would tell stories too, so I learned it from her.

Jess    You're still teaching me new things every day of the week.

Norma    As long as I'm here I'll be delighted to do just that. I do feel very lucky, you know. I look back on all of my life with great pleasure. It hasn't been madly romantic or extravagant, but it's been comfortable, warm and happy.

I don't think you can ask for much more than that.

INTERLUDE
# A word from Kate
*Jess's mum and Norma's daughter*

*I know I'm biased, but I reckon I've got the best mum in the world. She's kind, loving and sensible and the thing I always say about my childhood is that I was never unhappy.*

*We didn't have much money. Bonfire Night was always eating a hot dog while leaning over the garden fence watching someone else's fireworks. But I was happy, safe and loved.*

*My mum was always there. I remember once when I was about six, she went to a PTA meeting at my school, which meant she was gone between 6pm and 7pm. When she arrived home, I'd written her a note (which I think she still has to this day) saying, 'Please don't ever, ever leave me again!'*

*I was never frightened to go to her about anything that was worrying me because I knew I could trust her 100 per cent and that she would never judge. And whatever it was, she would help me deal with it and we'd sort it out. That's something I hope my own wonderful kids Jess and Cadan would say about me, too.*

*I have such fond memories of family holidays with Mum and Dad in the caravan when I was a little girl. We were like the Clampetts in this thing – every time my dad stood up, he'd hit his head on the gas mantle lamp and it usually rained for the whole week wherever we were. But none of that mattered.*

*My dad was a very unassuming man. I never knew what a responsible position he'd held in his job at the power station and how highly thought of he'd been there until he died because he would never have crowed about it.*

*He was a typical working father and husband, who very quietly went about his life providing for his family. He was also unbelievably*

## INTERLUDE

talented as a joiner – in another lifetime he would have made millions from those skills. But back then it was all about keeping a steady job and bringing in a wage. He and my mum were decent, hardworking people and always very happy as a couple, which gave me the stability and security to thrive.

Being the funny one wasn't my mum's role when I was younger. She was a mother and a wife, first and foremost – it was my dad that had the sarcastic sense of humour – but as she's got older, I've found her more and more hilarious. Of course, her eye rolls and one-liners are famous now. She might be struggling with her physical health, but she's razor sharp and hasn't lost any of her wit or intelligence.

When I see Jess and my mum together, it melts my heart. I absolutely love what they have done on social media, I'm so proud of them. The whole thing has rejuvenated my mum more than I can express in words and it's given us all so much pleasure. I know she loves being able to give back, using their platform to support causes like the local foodbank. Helping other people is my mum all over, always has been.

I'm happy to feature in some of the videos, but I'll leave Jess and my mum to take centre stage. Mind, the nickname Mafia Kate has stuck, and it makes me laugh. Just recently I helped a lady take her shopping to the car at Aldi and she looked at me and said, 'Wait till I tell my family I've met Mafia Kate!'

I thought that was lovely.

I'm hugely proud that so many have taken my family to their hearts. Hearing what they mean to people from those who stop us in the street or from the letters we receive is quite overwhelming. As is the fact that Mum is doing all of this in her nineties.

I often think, 'Wow, that's my mum.'

She has touched a lot of people's lives and my god, we are so lucky to have her.

# A Final Word

**Jess**   Well, that was an experience, wasn't it?

**Norma**   You don't say. It's quite something, writing a book. I feel like we've put the world to rights.

**Jess**   Haha! We could probably fill another three books with all your stories, Nan.

**Norma**   I was a bit nervous about doing this, I must admit. At first I thought, 'Who would want to read a book about little old me?'

**Jess**   I remember you saying that to me at the beginning. I had concerns as well but more because I knew it was a project that meant so much to both of us and I wanted to make sure we got it right. I also knew it was going to take up quite a bit of time and I'm hyper-aware of where we focus your energy these days. But not one part of writing this book has felt like anything other than a pleasure.

**Norma**   Not at all. I've loved doing this with you, Jess, and I'm proud of us. How special.

**Jess**   We've touched on some emotional topics and there have been quite a few tears while we've been writing. But we were prepared for that, weren't we?

**Norma**   I think that was to be expected, especially when it came to remembering your grandad.

**Jess**   Even though it's made us both a bit weepy at times, I'm so glad we went there and have shared what we have. It felt like

## A FINAL WORD

the right time to let people in, to show them our unbreakable bond, explain why we are so close and hopefully help some people too.

**Norma** I've adored having the chance to talk about Michael. My mum and her family, too. Oh Jess, we've had ever such a lot of fun writing it, haven't we? We've laughed and cried throughout – but mostly laughed.

**Jess** So much fun. And plenty of eye rolls.

**Norma** When I saw the girls from the exchange at our monthly lunch the other week, one of them said to me I seemed younger and happier. I think that's because of all the videos we make and writing this book. It all makes me full of beans!

**Jess** I've seen how much you've enjoyed it; it's shone through in your face every time another memory has sparked.

**Norma** Talking about the past has brought everything back and I've kept thinking of one thing and it has led on to another.

**Jess** What do you think Grandad would have made of you being an author?

**Norma** I've thought about this a lot and I imagine he would have loved it. He wouldn't have put that in so many words because he was a quiet type and that wasn't his style. But he would have been extremely proud.

**Jess** We said at the start that our main hope was to help people spark some of those connections or conversations in their own families and if we've done that, then that would be the biggest achievement.

**Norma** There might be some people who have had tricky times with their families and aren't quite sure how to move forward or show compassion. I hope we can do some good and help them heal, where possible.

## A FINAL WORD

**Jess**  And personally for our family, this book is something we will pass down the generations for years and years to come. Maybe one day my grandchildren will be reading this.

**Norma**  You'll have to have your own children first, Jess. Just saying ...

**Jess**  You can't help yourself, can you, Nan?

**Norma**  OK, I'll button it.

**Jess**  Well, that would be a first!

To you, our readers, we want to say a huge thank you for following our story. We wouldn't be here without you and we are grateful for every single day we get to do this. It's because of you that I'm able to devote my days to Nan and to care for her as I do. So from our family to yours, we send you love and appreciation. Thank you, everyone.

**Norma**  And God bless.

Now Jessica, go and get the kettle on, I need a cuppa.

# Dear Jess, dear Nan …

*To my darling Jess,*
 *When I became a mum, it was like I'd found my calling. I cherished every moment of those days and always thought it was impossible to love anyone as much as I loved my two children.*
 *But then I became a grandmother.*
 *From the moment I first snuggled you in my arms, Jess, being your nan has been the most joyous experience and helping to bring you up has been the honour of my life.*
 *Yes, even when you were demanding and hollering!*
 *You were alert from day one and always such a bright, determined little girl. So full of beans.*
 *Gosh, you kept us all on our toes. It was a full-time job just keeping you entertained – you were never the sort of child who would be happy to sit quietly.*
 *Your mum had been exactly the same and so luckily I'd already had a lot of practice.*
 *It was exhausting, I admit, but it also meant there was never a dull moment and you were ever such a sweet-looking little monkey with your hair in bunches and your fringe. I remember we were out for tea once and you shouted across the table, 'Grandad, why don't you have a fringe?' Of course, he was bald and that did make us laugh.*
 *We've had such lovely times together. I probably shouldn't confess to this, but when you were off school sick, I used to secretly enjoy it because it meant I had more time with you.*
 *The wonderful memories are endless. The days out to Creswell Crags, the bedtime cuddles reading Enid Blyton, the birthdays and the family Christmases. I would come round to your house every*

*Christmas Eve and watch you leave the mince pie, carrot and a glass of milk out for Santa and Rudolph.*

One memory that, more than 20 years on, still makes me proud and emotional in equal measure is when you, your mum and Cadan moved in with me after your grandad passed away.

You said, 'I'm going to stay with you so that you won't be lonely, Nan.'

You were only seven and yet you were already showing the care and compassion that remain part of your makeup. That's the kind of person you are and I know you will continue to be. You've always needed a lot of love but, my goodness me, you give out twice as much in return.

You know that I am a family person first and foremost. I have always been there for you whenever you've needed me and I've tried not to interfere.

With all of you, there have been times I've wanted to throw my arms in the air and say, 'For goodness' sake!', but I've never seen that as my job or my place. Instead, I hold my tongue and offer a listening ear and a shoulder to cry on.

I know you had a lot on your mind during your teens and much more to cope with than most. We were all so worried about you. I had many, many sleepless nights.

But what you went on to do – going to university and graduating with a First-Class honours degree – despite everything that was standing in your way, was remarkable. The day you graduated, I could have exploded with pride.

I'm so happy to see you settled and in love with Jake. He's a good lad. You've been good for him, too. A little word to the wise though: let him play golf, love. Don't whittle about it, let him have his time.

I've loved watching your relationship bloom as you've got to know each other and built a life together. The home you've made your own as a couple is so beautiful and it has been delightful to see the effort you put into making that little house look lovely. I know you take great pleasure being house-proud, which is why I get into trouble when I commit the heinous crime of dropping a sweet wrapper on the carpet.

## DEAR JESS, DEAR NAN ...

*Jess, I don't know what I would have done without you over the last few years. I feel very blessed to have your care and your company. Nothing is too much trouble for you and you think of everything. If I say I think I need some bread out of the freezer, you'll say, 'Oh, I've already done it.'*

*That's my mum's quality in you, being able to spot things that will help other people and doing them without hesitation.*

*You make me feel safe and comfortable and so very loved. We never run out of conversation and we laugh every single day. I have never had a lonely day because if you're not here you make sure that someone else is.*

*You're still my little monkey. That unmistakable gleam in your eye is never far away – these days it normally comes out just before we film one of our videos. What a clever young woman you are with this social media business. You've got this artistry about you, a wild imagination and a really creative streak, which I think comes from your grandad. I see a lot of him in you.*

*Thank you for being the most fabulous granddaughter I could have wished for. Thank you for being my best friend. I thank God every day for what I have.*

*Dare to dream, my darling. Continue to be kind and caring, never stop laughing and you will go far.*

*All my love,*
*Nan*

*Dear Nan,*

*Where on earth do I start? It's difficult to put into words just how much our relationship means to me and how it has shaped my whole life, but I'm going to try.*

*You are my warmth and my comfort. My constant, my safety. You have always been there to wipe away my tears and there is no one on this planet who gives better cuddles.*

*You listen without judgement and give advice without pressure and in doing so you have empowered me with the confidence to choose my own path and make my own decisions.*

*It's always been about doing what's right.*

*'You know what you need to do, Jess,' you'll say.*

*You and, before he passed, Grandad gave me the gift of childhood. Your home was my home (um, still is!) and it meant I always had a safe space to come back to no matter what was going on elsewhere.*

*Without that rock-solid support, I'm not sure I'd have had the strength to get through my exams and go on to university. The person I am today – my values, my morals and my self-belief – is because of you. You continue to be my number one inspiration.*

*Everybody deserves a nan like you. This might sound funny, but sometimes I wonder if nans like you are going to exist in the future. Your generation is the last one not to have a smartphone and there's something about that which makes you pure and wholesome.*

*That's not to say you're not switched on. You are completely with it and could give most people half your age a run for their money when it comes to intelligence and quick thinking.*

*But there is also an innocence to you that is increasingly rare in people now. There aren't many Norma Burtons left.*

*In a world of comparisons, where everyone is striving to be someone else or wanting the latest car, the show home or the luxury holiday, you are living proof that the best moments in life come from real people and relationships.*

*One of the traits I most admire in you is your refusal to let anything stop you. I think – I hope – that maybe I've inherited a bit* of that. When bad things happen, you keep going. You've made me understand that we can't control or change what's happening around us, but we can choose how we respond to it.

You accept that the ageing process is real and happening, but you dust yourself down and crack on. Even in the past when you've fallen and it's knocked your confidence, you won't be beaten.

'I've got to do it, Jess,' you say, 'otherwise I'll just sit – and that's no good.'

Nobody makes me laugh like you. You are so bloody funny, Nan! I often have to cut out bits of our videos because I'm doubled over laughing so much.

Your one-liners are the best. They often just randomly pop into my head and make me laugh all over again. That one where you said you had a body 'like a crinkle cut chip' still gets me.

I've said before that I'd love to pick you up and put you in my pocket and carry you around with me. I enjoy going on holiday, but I don't like leaving you behind. However, I know it's important and right that I go – if I let my heart win, I wouldn't ever leave you. You're my favourite person to spend time with.

Jake says there are a lot of things that I do that remind him of you, little mannerisms that I can only have picked up from you. For instance, when I'm travelling as a passenger in the car, I hold onto the seat belt, just like you. Or if I'm ever wearing glasses or sunglasses, I push them up on my face by touching the lens, which then gets covered in fingerprints. Remind you of anyone?!

Jake will say: 'That's Norma!'

I'm a home bird like you, too. I like being in my living room wearing my pyjamas and would much rather have a cosy evening in than a night on the town.

Unfortunately, I've also inherited your habit of burping but the less said about that the better, eh?

I'm so proud that I get to share how incredible you are with everyone. What a privilege. I always knew you were amazing, but when I started posting our videos and we were getting all these lovely comments about our relationship, it really brought it home to me *what an extraordinary woman you are.*

*You are loving beyond words, kind, caring, thoughtful. You've always been a do-er. When you were more mobile you'd come round and be straight in the kitchen: 'What can I cook for you? What can I clean? Do you have any ironing needing doing?' Always thinking of other people.*

*These last few years with you have been the most precious of my life. As long as I know you're OK, I'm happy. Sometimes that can be quite an overwhelming feeling, but I wouldn't have it any other way. I want to do this. I want to do this for you.*

*I can safely say that we know each other better than anyone. There are things I've told you that some of my best friends don't even know. And having the opportunity to sit and listen and learn all about your life and your stories is a complete joy. How lucky I am.*

*You once said to me, 'I want to be with your grandad, wherever he is. But I want to be with you more.' I know how much you miss him, but you also love your family and your little life here on this earth.*

*None of us knows how long we have left and so we have to make sure to treasure every day in a positive way and not waste time worrying about the what-ifs. I can't even begin to imagine life without you and so I think about what I've got here and now and we make the most of this time.*

*I hope that what you've instilled in me, I can one day bring to my own children. No matter what happens in the future, you have created a legacy that will continue on and I am so grateful for everything you have given me.*

*With love,*
*Jess*

# Afterword

Shortly after we finished writing this book, my dad, Dave Asquith, passed away. He was 61. His death was sudden and unexpected and has left a devastating void in my life.

Losing him has made the conversations I had with Nan about grief for the book incredibly pertinent – all the feelings she described around the death of my grandad, I'm now experiencing for my dad. At the moment, my grief is very raw and I'm still coming to terms with what has happened, but I'm thankful for the love and support of the people around me, and especially Jake, who has been my rock.I loved my dad so much. And I know he loved me too and that he was proud of me.

Dad, I want to say thank you for the good times and the happy memories. I will treasure them for the rest of my life.

You have influenced and inspired me in so many ways. I hope I continue to make you proud.

I just wish we'd had more time.

I love you, Dad, and I will miss you forever.

*Jess*

# Acknowledgements

**We would both like to thank:**

Every single one of our followers and supporters. Without you, none of this would be possible. We really are just two ordinary 'girls', who appreciate you and the support you've given us more than you will ever know. The time you've allowed us to spend together has been so special, and the opportunities you've given us are ones we could have only dreamed of. Thank you for supporting this book.

Those of you who know or follow us will be aware that we have had sponsorship relationships, or have been gifted products by, Amazon, Ancestry, Head & Shoulders, M&S Simply Food, Morrisons, Stanley Hunt and The Perfume Shop in the past. We mention these brands in this book because we are recollecting our genuine experiences, because working with the brand has been a key part of our journey, or because we are offering a legitimate recommendation.

Beth Neil, we knew from the moment we first spoke that you were the person to help us with this special project, and without you we could never have made it a reality. You were so accommodating to our needs, deftly handling Norma's short attention span and Jess's terrible grammar, and you approached sensitive topics with so much care and empathy. You made sure that this book not only captured our voices and story beautifully – but also that we had fun every single moment of writing it. It has truly been a pleasure. Thank you.

Penguin Random House, for giving us the opportunity of a lifetime, especially Abi Le Marquand-Brown for facilitating each step of the process with so much care and understanding. Abi, you have really gone above and beyond for us. You are such a lovely person. We will be forever grateful.

Thank you to our incredible team at Outreach Talent Group, especially Megan Hart for being so supportive and working tirelessly behind the scenes.

## ACKNOWLEDGEMENTS

Thank you to all of our wonderful family and friends who have supported us on this journey. We love and appreciate you so very much.

Our furry friends: Jamie, Bob, Holly, Dove and Joey for bringing our family so much comfort and love over the years.

And finally… it goes without saying we would like to acknowledge each other. But you're probably all sick of hearing us go on about our bond by now, so moving swiftly on …!

**Jess would like to thank:**

My Scotty (Jake). My soul mate and by far my biggest supporter from day one. No matter what crazy ideas I have, you're always right beside me cheering me on and believing in me even when I don't believe in myself.

From cooking tea when I'm due home late to reminding me over and over again when I've been deep in self-doubt that we can in fact do this, you've been a physical and emotional support for me throughout this whole process. And here we are. We did it!

You have shown me what true love really is. Without you, I'm not sure I would have the strength and confidence in my abilities that I have today. And you will never understand what the love and care you've shown to my nan since the day you met her means to me.

I'm so excited for our future together and I wouldn't want to do this crazy thing called life with anyone but you. Thank you, I love you.

My baby brother, Cadan. I love you unconditionally. Thank you for your support through some of my most difficult times and for always believing in me. I am so proud of the man you've grown into and of everything you continue to achieve. I will always be there to support you as your biggest cheerleader.

My mum. You're a little bit crazy, slightly unorganised, but extremely hard working. Thank you for making me laugh, for being the third musketeer alongside me and Nan and, most of all, for being you. You've passed so much down to me – your love of hair, make up, clothes and fake tan! – but it's a shame I didn't inherit your creativity. You're the most artistic person I know! Thank you for believing in me. I love you so much.

My therapist, Sharron. I truly think that finding a therapist who is so passionate about their work and takes so much pride in what they do has

## ACKNOWLEDGEMENTS

played a huge part in my journey. Your support has been life changing. Thank you from the bottom of my heart.

Helen at What To Take. Thank you for helping me to change my relationship with food, improve my lifestyle and become the healthiest and happiest version of myself. I will always be grateful.

**Norma would like to thank:**

My Katie. Thank you for being such a delightful little girl. Watching you grow has been one of my greatest pleasures in life. I am so unbelievably proud of you and how hard you have worked. You've faced so many difficulties with such strength. You are talented and gifted, just like your dad. It fills me with happiness to see bits of him shining through in you. You were here at my house one day recently and I looked at you and felt a sudden physical surge of love. I know you know what I mean because we have a special bond and I'm sure you feel it too.

Thank you for being there for me always. The last few months have especially been a comfort to me at this stage in my life.

I can only hope your future brings you happiness, love and contentment. I love you more than you could ever imagine, my lass, and only ever want what's best for you. But I have to finish by saying, please, please, get rid of that blooming hat!

My little lad, Cadan. You have brought me so much pleasure over the years and have grown into the most loving, kind, caring, thoughtful young man. I will never forget your blonde bouncy curls and what a happy little boy you were. I especially loved our sleepovers together; I will always treasure those moments and how they brought me so much comfort. I wish I could bottle up the love I have for you. It's so very strong and so very special.

I hope your future brings you nothing other than happiness, I hope you meet someone special who loves you the way you deserve to be loved, and that you follow your dreams of seeing different parts of the world. Through it all, Cadan, remember to be you. I am so proud of you. I could say more, but we'll leave it there. Knowing you, you've probably fallen asleep!

Jake, otherwise known as 'boss'. They don't make many men like you these days. You have slotted into this family so perfectly; thank you for

## ACKNOWLEDGEMENTS

always being there for me. Your presence in my home has, in a way, filled a gap that Michael left. I enjoy your company so very much. And you really do make me laugh, especially when you comment on my speediness!

As I've got older you have helped in so many different ways and made my life easier without hesitation. Whether it's fitting me a new grab rail because I'm struggling, or picking up the rubbish after one of our parcel opening sessions, you're always there.

I have loved watching you love my Jess so deeply and give her such a wonderful life. I have never seen her this happy and I will always be thankful to you for that. I hope your future together is filled with happiness, love and lots of 'little Jakeys'. Even if you deserve a medal for putting up with my granddaughter.

My dad, Thomas William. Thank you for giving me such a strong start. I know we didn't get long together; I can only hope you know what a wonderful and rich life I've had. I really do believe that a lot of it is down to you, for the values and morals you instilled into my family. Thank you for loving me, my mum and my sisters so much that it gave us the strength to continue on when you were no longer here.

My beautiful mum, Jessie. I will never be able to express how thankful I am to have known you, and to have had you as my mum. There isn't a day that goes by where I don't think about you or miss you. I cherish my memories of your fabulous cooking, your sweet smell of Cuticura talcum powder and your perfectly soft skin - but most of all, I cherish the love that radiated out of you, all through our home and all through us girls. Your strength after Dad was gone is something I have always admired. You single-handedly kept us going. I love you so much, Mum, forever and always.

And finally, my son, who has chosen to remain private throughout this process, which I respect. I love you very much.